PHILOSOPHERS
OF THE
SCOTTISH
ENLIGHTENMENT

PHILOSOPHERS
OF THE
SCOTTISH
ENLIGHTENMENT

EDITED BY V. HOPE

EDINBURGH
at the University Press

© V. Hope and the contributors 1984
EDINBURGH UNIVERSITY PRESS
22 George Square, Edinburgh

Set in Linotron Times Roman
by Wyvern Typesetting Limited, Bristol
and printed in Great Britain
by The Alden Press, Oxford

British Library Cataloguing
  in Publication Data
Hope, Vincent
Philosophers of the Scottish
  enlightenment.
1. Philosophy, Scottish – History
2. Enlightenment
3. Scotland – Intellectual life
I. Title
192   B1401
ISBN 0 85224 477 0

CONTENTS

ACKNOWLEDGEMENTS

Professor Jim Moore is grateful to the Institute for Advanced Studies in the Humanities at the University of Edinburgh, where the first essay in this series was written; it was originally presented to the Scottish Philosophy Seminar. He and Professor Michael Silverthorne are also grateful for the generous support given them by the Social Sciences and

Humanities Research Council of Canada.

Professor John Bricke thanks Tim George for the benefit of many conversations about volitions. His research was supported by a University of Kansas General Research Fund Grant.

Dr John Jenkins is grateful to Peter Lewis for helpfully discussing with him a number of the issues in his paper.

Professor Tom Campbell is indebted to Dr Knud Haakonssen and Dr Ross Cromston, both of the Australian National University, for their help on an early draft of his essay.

The editor thanks Professor D. D. Raphael and Dr M. A. Stewart for their kind advice and comment on many points of detail, as well as for their help with the project as a whole.

CONTRIBUTORS

PÁLL S. ÁRDAL
Charlton Professor of Philosophy, Queen's University,
Kingston, Ontario

JOHN BRICKE
Department of Philosophy, University of Kansas

TOM D. CAMPBELL
Department of Jurisprudence, University of Glasgow

MELVIN DALGARNO
Department of Moral Philosophy, University of Aberdeen

TIMOTHY DUGGAN
Department of Philosophy, Dartmouth College,
New Hampshire

KNUD HAAKONSSEN
History of Ideas Unit, The Australian National University

VINCENT HOPE
Department of Philosophy, University of Edinburgh

JOHN JENKINS
Department of Philosophy, University of Edinburgh

PETER JONES
Department of Philosophy, University of Edinburgh

RUDOLF LÜTHE
Philosophisches Institut, Aachen

NEIL MACCORMICK
Department of Jurisprudence, University of Edinburgh

JAMES MOORE
Department of Political Science, Concordia University,
Montreal

GEORGE MORICE
Department of Philosophy, University of Edinburgh

MICHAEL PAKALUK
Department of Philosophy, Harvard University

MICHAEL SILVERTHORNE
Department of Classics, McGill University

George Davie, 1968

PREFACE

IN HIS introduction to 'Old Mortality' the Wizard of the North narrates his youthful encounter in an Aberdeenshire churchyard with the man who gave his nickname to the novel. He was a stone-mason who wandered the country tending the gravestones of the Cameronians, a wild religious sect which turned against the king. In spite of his lack of sympathy with religious bigotry, Sir Walter immediately identified with the old man. He too realised the importance of forever clearing away the moss and the dirt which settle on our past. So does George Davie.

Historian of philosophy, social historian, he has generally been controversial in his conclusions and his methods, which are characteristically intuitive. He is always polemical, never stays long in one region or settles in any camp and is frequently shot at as a trespasser in forbidden fields. His Scottishness is his religion. The more he insists on it, the more he infuriates some, is admired by others, both Scot and non-Scot. In spite of all controversy, his study of his heritage has three sound motives, easily recognised as his and ours.

One is sheer curiosity about our ancestors: to discover whether they were different from us and if so, whether we can still sympathise with their outlook, applauding their achievements and commiserating with their failures.

Next, seeing their influence on ourselves, we can better understand our inherited character. The past provides us with some kind of identity which excuses our differences from others; we do things in a certain way because of our history. Moreover, intimately connected with historical remembrance is a sense, difficult to control, but impossible to escape, of the need to resist decay and corruption in traditional values. Some wonder if there is any such need, since standards and tastes must alter with the times. Whether there is or not, underlying that sense is awareness of continuity, each generation handing on a vision of the good. We realise how much we owe the dead with whom we feel in a strange, because one-sided, relationship. We look back at those who were then looking forward and with whom we imagine we share the satisfaction of maintaining the same outlook.

Apart from these two reasons, of simple curiosity and the search for cultural identity, a third is to see if the past can suggest fresh solutions for current problems, for the philosopher, as has often been observed, proceeds, not by solving his problems once and for all, but by making variations on and additions to the answers first written down by the Greeks.

Scottish philosophy has developed classical ideas in its own way and must be of special importance to historians of philosophy who are themselves Scottish. As such it has formed the main theme of Dr Davie's work. His studies have brought to life its personalities and their ideas and have shown their relevance to contemporary problems.

Furthermore, he is a Scottish academic who is proud of his educational heritage. At a time when the universities are being standardised, sometimes with the conscious belief that they should model themselves on an English pattern, he has fought to demonstrate the importance of the traditional Scottish general degree which takes philosophy to be essential, even central, to any university curriculum because it is the only way of demonstrating first principles or of understanding how the different intellectual disciplines are related to each other. In his view, as he makes clear in *The Democratic Intellect*, it should never be omitted from a university education and, in particular, should never be sacrificed to specialisation.

If Scotland's philosophy and universities are his principal interests, his broad canvas is the intellectual life of the country from the seventeenth century. Since that time religious factions have fought among themselves for social supremacy, and legal, educational and economic interests have sought adjustment in a politically ambiguous situation, where what was once a nation has now become a minor partner in a so-called union of parliaments. Dr Davie describes this, not dispassionately, but with the same relish for battles and skirmishes as Scott, directing his reader to the clash of personalities and values, always implying their present relevance.

At the height of this period of re-alignment, in the eighteenth century, the philosophers, led by Hutcheson and Hume, tried to rationalise the respective claims of religion, government and commercial society. Their theories vary, all, however, separating religion from public morals and placing government at the service of society. Some, like Hutcheson, Hume and Smith, moved towards ethical conventionalism and a kind of spiritual or intellectual utilitarianism. Others, like Reid, retained the older view that right and wrong are as objective as physical law. In his monograph for the Historical Association, *The Scottish Enlightenment*, Dr Davie has described their recommendation that 'the key to the problem of ethical standards in the commercial age is to recognise the complementariness of the respective standpoints of the vulgar and the learned' (p.18) or, generalising, that it is necessary to foster a spirit of mutual sympathy between the social classes. The creed which emerges regards the arts and the sciences as the public means of intellectual and moral refinement. If they seem wasteful and luxurious, they will nevertheless repay their debt because intellectual advance leads to moral and economic.

But with progress comes specialisation and a narrowing of vision of the individual and his class. This causes a diminished sense of cohesion. In his *Dow Lecture* of 1973 Dr Davie comments, ' . . . intensive specialisation produces the dangerous consequences of an intellectual atomisation of society' (p.6). The Scottish antidote, he says, is an 'all-round spiritual participation by means of educational democracy' (p.7). Only if the various sections of the community, and not just the intellectual, understand, however vaguely, that they are interdependent, will they voluntarily cooperate as they should. The university is the specific institution for the higher education of all social classes on the assumption that, provided they have the same opportunities, people will develop the same tastes and understanding.

Dr Davie insists that philosophy has a unique contribution to make in counteracting the social centrifuge. Its role is to see the unity-in-diversity of the different intellectual activities and their general place in human affairs. To do this it must understand how intellect is related to the other faculties, to the powers, sensibilities and purposes of human nature, the programme stated by Hume in his introduction to the *Treatise*. (The *Treatise* must be Dr Davie's favourite text, always within mental reach, and Hume his favourite author, though latterly he has been remarking that 'in some ways Smith was a greater philosopher'.) Having discovered the presuppositions of commonsense philosophy can help specialists to recognise their mundane empirical roots, countering the permanent threat of their self-importance and fanaticism. It is materially assisted if every specialist has had a philosophical education.

George Davie's own philosophical education began at Edinburgh under Kemp-Smith (another Dundonian) in the second year of his degree in classics. On graduating in 1935 he decided to do a further degree, this time in philosophy. Finishing in 1938 he was immediately appointed as Kemp-Smith's assistant. He was twenty-six. In 1941 he joined the armed forces. He followed his normal pattern of switching identity, going as a soldier to sea with the navy. After the war he lectured at the University of Belfast on moral and ancient philosophy. He returned to his old department in 1959, retiring in 1982.

In 1953 he was awarded a doctorate of literature, for a thesis on Scottish epistemology, and was then invited to prepare it for publication. His thought developed unexpectedly in a different direction and it became *The Democratic Intellect,* a pioneering study whose aim was to open up not just the history of the Scottish universities but the question of philosophy's place in the modern university. The book created enormous interest and, incidentally, stirred up controversy, some of it locally at a high administrative level, among mathematicians who feared that the author was seriously mistaken about the nature of their subject. Whatever the merits of their case, such disputes are bound to arise when the philosopher tries, as he must, to connect an abstract theory, its objects and methods, with everyday experience. However, this was but a minor element in a work of astonishing breadth and scholarship. Only now are academics catching up.

Dr Davie, ever generous with his knowledge of Scottish philosophy, was invited by Professor H.B. Acton to join him in starting a seminar on the subject (attended at some time or another by most of the present contributors). It became an annual event (sadly robbed of Harry Acton by his premature death). Dr Davie's remarkable acquaintance with historical sources was a weekly feast of suggestion and comment for postgraduates and visiting scholars, one of the more senior of whom remarked that after even private conversation with Dr Davie he immediately made notes for further research. Wherever one goes, it is more than likely that George Davie has been there before. For he is like Scott in his addiction to his country's past which has become so much a part of him that one feels he has breakfasted with Fletcher of Saltoun, dined with Hume and supped with Hamilton.

To this remarkable man the following essays are affectionately dedicated. Each owes him something and hopes to earn his pleasure and approval, repaying in some measure what cannot ever be fully repaid.

Edinburgh, May 1984   VH

JAMES MOORE AND
MICHAEL SILVERTHORNE

Natural Sociability and Natural Rights in the Moral Philosophy of Gerschom Carmichael

THE PROPOSAL that natural rights may be somehow grounded in assumptions concerning natural sociability is bound to appear paradoxical to many contemporary readers. For much recent work on the normative foundation of theories of natural rights has been inspired by the assumption that human beings are naturally egoistic.[1] And the same assumption informs the work of influential historical critics of natural rights theories, who have identified the source of what they deplore most in ideas of natural rights in the selfish conceptions of human nature found in early modern political philosophers.[2] Against this contemporary philosophical and historical background, it may be at least curious to find a discussion of the moral foundations of natural rights in which the diametrically opposite assumption is made about human nature; in which it is not supposed that human beings are naturally egoistic, but that they are naturally sociable; and where the manner in which natural rights are attributed to human beings turns on the meaning that is ascribed to natural sociability. This particular formulation of the theory of natural rights constituted the central problem of natural jurisprudence and moral philosophy (for the two became closely identified) in Scotland in the early eighteenth century.

The natural jurisprudence tradition became the basis of the moral philosophy curriculum in Scottish universities only in the 1690's, following the Glorious Revolution and the subsequent reform of the Scottish universities.[3] Scottish students of civil law had been familiar with the work of Grotius and of the Dutch commentators on Justinian (Vinnius and Voet) and with the work of other natural jurists through study in the sixteenth and seventeenth centuries at Dutch, Swiss, French and German universities.[4] But there appears to have been little awareness of the significance of the work of Grotius, Selden, Hobbes and Pufendorf in the teaching of moral and political philosophy in the seventeenth century.[5] Expressions of outright hostility to the work of natural jurists would seem to have been rare. And there is no reason to suppose that Principal Robert Baillie of Glasgow expressed a view that was typical or representative of professorial opinion when he said that he would 'gladly consent to the burning of many thousand volumes of unprofitable writers', citing specifically the works of Grotius and Selden, and throwing in for good measure the writing of 'that very ignorant atheist and fatuous heretic' Descartes.[6] But while Baillie's view was an extreme one, discussions of natural law and natural rights appear infrequently and only marginally in the moral philosophy dictated to Scottish students in the seventeenth century. When the dictates deviated from duties revealed in Scripture, they focused upon the virtues, expounded by Aristotle and later in the century by Henry More.[7] The turning point in Scottish moral philosophy occurred only after the Revolution of 1688 and the subsequent dismissal from Scottish universities of professors who refused to subscribe an oath of allegiance to the new King and Queen and a declaration of acceptance of the fundamental articles of the Church of Scotland. In these changed conditions, we find a new generation of professors who made the set text in moral philosophy not Aristotle or Henry More but Samuel Pufendorf's *De Officio Hominis et Civis*. The crucial figure in this development was a younger relative of the nobleman who conducted the purge of untrustworthy academics from the University of Glasgow. The nobleman was Lord John Carmichael, Earl of Hyndford; his younger relative was Gerschom Carmichael, who would become the first Professor of Moral Philosophy at the University of Glasgow in 1727.

Carmichael was appointed a regent or professor of philosophy at the University of Glasgow in 1694. Within two years of his appointment we are told in a document presented by him to a Visitation Committee charged with investigating methods of instruction at the University of Glasgow (1695–97) that complaints had been made against him on the remarkable grounds that he had been innovating in his teaching.[8] Carmichael acknowledged that he had in fact introduced his students to the work of Pufendorf; and that he had made Pufendorf's shorter work *On the Duty of Man and the Citizen* the set text from which he dictated. But in the same document it is also apparent from his detailed account of the correspondence of his own theses with the relevant chapters of Pufendorf's work that he was offering his students a radically revised version of Pufendorf's moral philosophy. One of the central points of revision may be succinctly stated. Pufendorf had reduced all moral obligations to one comprehensive duty posited by the law of nature:

that every man ought, so far as in him lies, to promote and preserve a peaceable sociableness with others.[9]

Carmichael set down instead three irreducible but complementary duties or laws of nature: that all men act in ways which signify their love and veneration of God; that each man cultivate his own happiness and in particular the faculties of his mind; and that each promote and preserve sociability.[10] In his Philosophical Theses, published in 1699, he explained his reasons for this revision.

The restorers of moral philosophy in the seventeenth century (he mentions Grotius, Pufendorf and Cumberland in this connection) had endeavoured to avoid the prolix style of their immediate predecessors who did not hesitate to outline a great number of duties of which they claimed to have direct knowledge. But in their attempt to achieve a more simple and comprehensive statement of moral duties the natural jurists of the seventeenth century went too far in their efforts to bring all moral precepts under the rubric of one simple proposition. Pufendorf's definition of the law of nature was an admirable attempt to find a single rule for moral life; but his formulation failed notably to account for the duty to worship God, the most important of all our duties. Cumberland's definition of the law of nature was more comprehensive: that everyone is bound to promote with all his might the common good of the whole system of rational agents, in which his own happiness is included. But even in Cumberland's very general formulation there was something incongruous in classifying God within the system of rational agents; much better to distinguish the obligation to worship God from the obligation to promote the common good of rational agents, and, better still, to distinguish within that global obligation the more specific duties to cultivate one's own mind and happiness and to promote and preserve sociable relations with others.[11]

Now Carmichael may have overstated his differences with Pufendorf in respect of the three distinct laws of nature; in Pufendorf's shorter work On the Duty of Man and the Citizen (on which Carmichael was prelecting), this tripartite division of the subject is set out very clearly (although it is not as clear in Pufendorf's work On the Law of Nature and Nations). But there is no doubt that under the rubric of these three duties Carmichael was able to introduce a very substantive reorientation of Pufendorf's natural jurisprudence, particularly with respect to the content of the third law of nature or the duty to promote and preserve sociable relations with others. Pufendorf had deduced the fundamental obligation to be sociable from the insecurity, needs and capacity for mischief of human beings when they are not united in society under the absolute government of a sovereign power. The manner in which Pufendorf proposed that men unite in society and under government, by mutual agreement or consent, was attractive to Carmichael and other supporters of the Revolution Settlement, since it excluded the claim (by followers of the king over the water) of hereditary right. But the substance of Pufendorf's theory of social and political obligation, that the duty of sociability recognises that sovereigns should enjoy absolute power over their subjects, was not easily reconciled with the rights of men and citizens as they were now secured for British subjects by the Glorious Revolution. It was this absolutist implication in Pufendorf's theory of natural sociability which Carmichael sought to revise by restating the obligation to be sociable in terms of a duty to respect the natural rights of others. In order to effect this reformulation of Pufendorf, Carmichael returned to the exposition of natural rights theories found in the work of Grotius.

Grotius had described the natural inclination of human beings to live in society as the source of all the rights of men. He described this sociable inclination as made up of three distinctive human characteristics: our common *reason*, which allows us to communicate our thoughts to one another in language, our *will* to enter into agreements or contracts or promises with other members of our species, and our *affections*, which prompt us to congregate in families, communities, nations and states.[12]

Grotius claimed no originality of authorship for these perhaps not very remarkable insights; he cited Aristotle, Cicero, Seneca, Tertullian, Lactantius, Augustine; and the French translator of the works of Grotius, Pufendorf and Cumberland (Jean Barbeyrac) added countless other names in his notes.[13] But Grotius (as we will see) was well aware that not everyone thought life in society was natural in all (and in some cases, in any) of these senses. His statement of the matter brought together, however, some very different traditions of speculation on the origins of life in society and the enjoyment of rights; and they appeared in Grotius' eyes to be of sufficient mutual force to justify his famous pronouncement:

> all we have now said would take place, though we should even grant, what without the greatest wickedness cannot be granted, that there is no God, or that he takes no care of human affairs.[14]

Grotius' notorious statement made at the outset of his compendious abridgement of the rights of individuals and of nations in peace and war opened the way for speculation on the particular kind of deity that might be invoked in support of the law of nature, and to some it left open the possibility explored by Pierre Bayle and other sceptical thinkers that a society of atheists was possible.

Pufendorf's response to this supposition that God might neither exist nor concern himself in human affairs is sometimes thought to have been equivocal and ambiguous; but his language seems plain enough:

> we cannot by any means subscribe to the conjecture which Grotius starts . . . . For, should any wretch be so horribly senseless as to maintain that wicked and absurd hypothesis . . . and so hold men to derive their being wholly from themselves, the edicts of reason could not rise so high as to pass into a condition of laws, inasmuch as all law supposes a superior power.[15]

He rejected Hobbes' characterisation of the natural condition of mankind on the grounds that Hobbes' laws of nature were not, strictly speaking, laws in the absence of a superior power who might legislate the obligation to keep covenants, seek peace, promote sociability and uphold all the other laws of nature. Hobbes had failed to recognise that the state of nature was already a state, a realm governed by moral standards of right and wrong imposed not by any human legislator but by a divine legislator:

> among the opinions, then, which it highly concerns all men to settle and embrace, the chief are those which relate to almighty God as the great creator and governor of the universe.[16]

Pufendorf's conception of the deity as a superior power who enforces the law of nature or sociability by the fear he inspires in inferior creatures provided a model of the kind of power which would be capable of maintaining peace in society. Pufendorf's natural jurisprudence offered accordingly, for the human forum, as he liked to call this world, a compendium of the rights of superiors and the duties of inferiors (established to be sure by an agreement or compact or promise made by the inferior to the superior), of the rights of parents and the duties of children, of the rights of husbands and the duties of wives, of masters and servants, of sovereigns and subjects. It was a possible view of the necessary conditions of sociable living and it found many adherents. But Pufendorf's theory of natural rights and duties also provoked substantive criticisms. His most famous critic, Leibniz, fastened on the insufficiency of Pufendorf's theology:

> it is not enough, that we be subject to God just as we would obey a tyrant; nor must He be only feared because of His greatness, but also loved because of His goodness . . . To this, lead the best principles of universal jurisprudence which collaborate also with wise theology and bring about true virtue.[17]

Leibniz's criticism made a deep impression on Gerschom Carmichael who had been revising Pufendorf's natural jurisprudence on just these lines from the time he had begun his prelections on the text.[18] In place of the fear of God as a punitive superior who enforces his will by the terror he inspires in his creatures, Carmichael conceived of the deity as 'the object of the most consummate beatitude that man can enjoy.' For man, he went on to say, can only achieve that happiness to which he aspires, by the most intense love and veneration of the deity:

> It is clear that man cannot experience it in the consciousness of his own finite abilities, or in the possession of things of less worth than himself or in the contemplation of abstract truths. He may find it only in an immediate vision of God which will last forever. . . .[19]

There may well be prima facie difficulties in Carmichael's moral epistemology. But it would appear that he was convinced by the Port Royal logic (or that version of it to which he subscribed) that there are certain ideas which are so compelling that we cannot refuse to give them our assent.[20] The longing for beatitude or lasting happiness appears to have been for him such an idea. But it was an idea which was also capable of expression in signs or signals which could be communicated directly and immediately to God by the love and veneration which our conduct signifies to Him, or indirectly and mediately by the respect we have for the aspirations of other human beings, who long to have this same beatitude or happiness. It was in these mediated or indirect signals to the deity that Carmichael located the normative foundation of his theory of natural rights.[21] It was not the fear of God or the fear of a sovereign power or of a superior will which inspired respect for the laws of nature and the rights of human beings. Natural rights and obligations were secured by the recognition that every human being seeks beatitude or lasting happiness, and that our strongest convictions and aspirations direct us to respect the rights of every man to seek happiness of this kind.

Now there can be no doubt that Carmichael's derivation of

natural rights was itself controversial; later theorists of the understanding were sceptical of the compelling force of the ideas he described and of his account of human passions and desires. But whatever difficulties the Cartesian and Scholastic dimensions of his thinking may present, his work must be recognized to be a highly significant reorientation of the natural jurisprudence tradition as expounded by Pufendorf. Carmichael's conviction that every man is motivated by his aspiration for beatitude to respect the rights of others allowed him to expound the laws of nature and specifically the natural duties of sociability in terms of a distinctive theory of natural rights. Since his perception of a natural right was based not upon an obligation to a superior so much as on the intuitively apprehended longings of the soul, his theory of natural rights underlined the absurdity of supposing that human rights must be surrendered or alienated or transferred to a superior power in order to enjoy the benefits of social life. He summed up his approach to the study of moral life in the following way:

> We conclude therefore that the right cultivation of social life consists in this: that each man so protect his own right as to have due regard for all the rights which belong to other men in accordance with the assumption of natural equality. Thus it follows that in order to define the duties which are incumbent on men with respect to other men, we cannot follow a better course than to weigh up carefully in due order the various rights, and the foundation on which each rests, which may belong to individuals, to groups of men or even to the human race as a whole. From these (rights) we early recognize the corresponding obligations which belong to men as individuals.[22]

He distinguished the natural rights which human beings may be thought to enjoy, in the manner of Pufendorf and Grotius, into perfect rights (or those rights in the absence of which no social life is possible) and imperfect rights (or those rights which embellish life in society, but are not indispensable to it). His concern (again, like Pufendorf and Grotius) was perfect natural rights, among which he included the rights to life, to integrity of the body, to modesty and reputation, and the liberty of acting as one pleases within the limits of the laws of nature.[23] But Grotius and Pufendorf had also introduced another distinction of rights into natural rights which are derived from the nature of things unaltered by any human act, and adventitious rights which depend upon some action on the part of men. The typical action which marked the advent of the latter was an exchange of promises or a contract or an agreement. And within the class of such rights they located the rights of property (real rights) and rights to particular benefits or services (personal rights) and the rights which are acquired by the different agreements which mark the advent of smaller societies or groups such as marriage or conjugal society, the relationship of master and servant or domestic society, and the relations of rulers and subjects or civil society. Carmichael took over the nomenclature of these various classes of rights and continued to call them the adventitious rights of individuals or the rights of members of adventitious states or societies.[24] But his account of the foundation of these rights was so different from the manner in which they were derived by Pufendorf that it is doubtful whether the term adventitious may be considered apposite. As Carmichael expounded the rights of individuals and members of societies, it becomes evident that such rights are understood by him to be natural rights. In this respect his theory of rights stood in closer approximation to the political thinking of John Locke, whose second treatise on civil government provided the main source of theoretical inspiration for Carmichael's account of specific adventitious rights.

Following Locke, Carmichael rejected Pufendorf's justification of the right to property in the agreement or consent of others; such agreement was not required for the recognition of a right of private ownership, the right to property derived from the law of nature which obliges each of us to cultivate his own happiness. The most obvious method of cultivation of happiness with respect to the external things of this world is to labour upon them or work them up in a way that makes them useful to us.[25] But he consistently urged that no man should so mistake the meaning of happiness as to attach undue importance to external things or confuse the transitory pleasures of riches and power with beatitude or lasting happiness.[26] And Carmichael also substantially amended Pufendorf's tripartite theory of the original contract (or the agreements to establish civil society, the form of government and the relationship of allegiance of subjects to government) in a manner he thought consistent with Locke's theory of consent. These aspects of Carmichael's debt to Locke's natural jurisprudence are discussed in more detail elsewhere.[27] But there is one subject in particular which may illustrate his fundamental revision of Pufendorf's account of natural sociability and natural rights; this was the issue of slavery.

Pufendorf had traced the origin of slavery not to natural inequality in human reason, as Aristotle had argued, but to economic necessity. He thought it probable that poor and therefore helpless persons would willingly surrender their natural rights to life and liberty to masters of households, in return for food, shelter and other necessities of life.

> And it is probable that in the beginning these offered themselves voluntarily, being compelled by want or a sense of their own incapacity; and that they bargained for a perpetual supply of food and other necessaries, and so assigned their services to the master permanently.[28]

Once the economic advantages of the institution of slavery had impressed themselves on mankind, it became customary (or part of the law of nations) to spare the lives of men captured in war, so that these men and their families could be enslaved for the benefit of the households of the conquering armies. Pufendorf's reasoning on the institution of slavery was largely acceptable to his French editor and translator, Jean Barbeyrac, who was disposed on other topics (the right to property, the original contract to establish civil or political society) to amend Pufendorf's presentation by his own peculiar use of the political ideas of Locke. But on the subject of slavery, Barbeyrac concurred with Pufendorf that slavery was indeed economically viable and justified according to the rights of conquest. He required only that the children of slaves should be permitted their liberty, if they declare their desire to leave the household when they have reached the age of discretion; otherwise it will be supposed, he thought, that they have tacitly consented to remain in the condition of slavery.[29]

Against this background, Carmichael's assertion of the rights of slaves is remarkably outspoken and uncompromising:

> Nothing can be further removed from the law of sociability than the contention of most nations that war provides the right to introduce slavery. It makes one wonder that the human race should so forget its dignity as to conspire, voluntarily, as it seems, to bring upon itself such extreme hardship, abuses and misery.[30]

He acknowledged that men guilty of atrocious offences, especially if these are committed in the prosecution of an unjust war, might be condemned to slavery; but, like Locke, he was insistent that punishment of this severity did not apply to the family of the condemned man who must be assumed to be innocent of involvement in wars of any kind unless the contrary is established by obvious signs. Again, in the spirit of Locke's discussion of the rights of conquest, Carmichael argues that the conqueror, even in a just war, has no right to the land of the enemy; at most, the conqueror is entitled to reparation or repayment for devastation

caused unjustly by the aggressor.[31] But his discussion goes
beyond Locke's in his unequivocal denunciation of any notion
(such as Pufendorf's and Barbeyrac's) that slavery might be
justifiable on economic grounds:

> a man is never to be considered among the goods of his
> creditor whatever a man may owe another or a criminal may
> owe society. For men are not among the objects which God
> has allowed the human race to enjoy dominion over. Indeed
> it seems absurd, to paraphrase the words of Justinian,[32] that
> man should be classed among things, since all things were
> provided by nature for the sake of man.[33]

His final indictment of the institution of slavery is that it marks a
denigration of the dignity that is intuitively apprehended in
human nature; regrettably, the worst violators of the natural
rights of life and liberty were to be found in modern times and
among men who subscribed, at least professedly, to the Christian
religion:

> I have treated (this) matter . . . at some length, because I
> am convinced that this usurped right of ownership of slaves,
> as of cattle, as it obtained among the ancients is exercised
> today by men who profess to be Christians, to the great
> shame of that holy name, with greater tyranny perhaps than
> it was by the ancient pagans. It is not practised to be sure by
> Christians among themselves nor do we find it in Europe: we
> find it in other parts of the world. Its existence, to use the apt
> expression of Titius, is a sure sign of the death of
> sociability.[34]

Carmichael's approach to the question of slavery was one of
the many aspects of his moral philosophy that made a most
favourable impression on his successor, Francis Hutcheson. In *A
Short Introduction to Moral Philosophy*, Hutcheson tells us, in
the notes appended to that text:

> On this subject of slavery many just reasonings are to be
> found in Mr Locke's 2nd book on government; and Mr
> Carmichael's notes on Pufendorf, Book II, CX.[35]

Hutcheson's case against slavery, like Carmichael's and Locke's,
was qualified. He acknowledged that soldiers captured in a just
war may be assigned to a life of perpetual labour; but he insists
that 'one who has a just cause, yet should set just bounds to his
demands; nor can he demand anything from the conquered
except either under the name of punishment, reparation of damage done, or precaution against future injuries'.[36] Like Locke
and Carmichael, he denied that other citizens, not in arms, could
be assigned to perpetual labour or that slavery could ever be

extended rightfully to include women and children. As for the right of conquest, so much insisted upon by Grotius and Pufendorf, it afforded no better title to allegiance than the force used against innocent persons by highwaymen and brigands. 'Upon this subject', he observes again, 'see Locke on government, whose reasonings are well abridged in Mr Carmichael's notes on Pufendorf's smaller book'.[37]

Now Hutcheson's relation to Carmichael's moral philosophy is complicated by the fact that the distinctive elements in Hutcheson's works written in the 1720's – his derivation of the ideas of virtue and vice from a moral sense and his theory of the natural affections – have no parallel in Carmichael's work. Moreover, it is clear from the earliest statements of Hutcheson's ethical theory that he regarded the work of Pufendorf with great suspicion[38] and he was equally wary of writers on morals who 'fly to beatific vision so that one must be well advanc'd in a visionary temper to be profited by them.'[39] One finds the same reservation expressed concerning Pufendorf in particular in his inaugural lecture on the natural sociability of man, where an entirely different conception of sociability, based upon the natural or instinctive affections is expounded.[40] Some elements of this alternative theory of natural sociability appears in Hutcheson's account of natural rights in his posthumously published work *A System of Morals*. But it is of some significance for the history of moral philosophy and natural jurisprudence in Scotland in the eighteenth century that the work which was published repeatedly (in three editions in Latin and in four editions in English translation) was *A Short Introduction to Moral Philosophy*, based, as the Preface acknowledged candidly, on Carmichael's edition of Pufendorf. It was through the medium of Hutcheson's *Short Introduction*, as well as the continuing interest in Carmichael's own work on the part of natural jurists in Europe – later editions of his supplements, annotations and addenda to Pufendorf's work were published in Switzerland and Holland – that Carmichael's distinctive approach to natural rights remained an enduring contribution to natural jurisprudence in the eighteenth century and may still merit the attention of anyone interested in the theoretical foundations of natural rights.

1 See Machan, 1980, 1982.
2 See Strauss, 1951 and Macpherson, 1967.
3 Emerson, 1977.
4 Stein, 1963 and MacCormick, 1982b.
5 King, 1975.

6 Baillie, 1841, quoted King, 1982.
7 See King, 1975.
8 Glasgow University Archive no.43170.
9 Pufendorf, 1729, II.III.XV.137.
10 G.U.A. no.43170 and Pufendorf, 1724, Supplementum II.
11 Carmichael, 1699, pp.9–10.
12 Grotius, 1738, Preliminary Discourse, xvff.
13 Grotius, 1738.
14 Ibid., p.xix.
15 Pufendorf, 1729, II.III.XIX.
16 Ibid., II.III.IV.155.
17 Leibniz, 1972, p.71.
18 Carmichael, preface to Pufendorf, 1724.
19 Pufendorf, 1724, Supplementum I.v.iii.
20 Carmichael, 1722.
21 Pufendorf, 1724, Supplementum II.i–v, 53–6 and
   Appendix; Theses I–IX, 511–14.
22 Ibid., Supplementum II.xvii.62 and Appendix: Thesis
   XI, 514.
23 Ibid., I.IX.I.159.
24 Ibid., 159ff and Appendix: Theses XII–XXX, 515–19.
25 Ibid., I.XII.II. 215–16.
26 Ibid., I, Supplementum III.vi.98–9.
27 Moore (and Silverthorne), 1982.
28 Pufendorf, 1927, II.IV.I.101.
29 Pufendorf, 1820, II.VI.I.271.
30 Pufendorf, 1724, II.IV.IV.353.
31 Ibid.
32 Justinian, Institutes, II.I.37.
33 Pufendorf, 1724, II.IV.IV.354.
34 Ibid., II.IV.VI.320.
35 HUTCHESON, 1747, III.3.275n.
36 Ibid., 274–5.
37 Ibid., III.7.310n.
38 Hutcheson, 1750.
39 Hutcheson, 1724.
40 Hutcheson, 1730.

MELVIN T. DALGARNO

Reid's Natural Jurisprudence—
The Language of Rights and Duties

COMING AS it does from the leading philosopher of his day in the Scottish universities, Reid's account of systems of natural jurisprudence has considerable historical interest.[1] Further, in advancing the thesis that the language of rights can replace the language of duties, so that an account of human rights can cover all the duties we owe our fellow human beings, Reid's discussion has considerable philosophical interest. The first section of this paper considers some historical points; the second section is addressed to philosophical issues.

I

According to Reid, it is the direct intention of morals to teach the duty of men: of natural jurisprudence to teach the rights of men. He describes systems of the latter as a modern invention, and is lavish in his praise of the innovator, the 'immortal' Hugo Grotius whose *De Jure Belli ac Pacis* was published in Paris in 1625. Contemporary scholars might accuse Reid of ignoring intellectual antecedents of Grotius's theory of rights, but few would quarrel with Reid's judgment that it was Grotius who established the reputation for natural jurisprudence which led to the publication of numerous editions, annotated commentaries, rival systems, as well as the establishment of university chairs throughout Europe. Scotland was no exception.

William Scott, who lectured on Grotius in the University of Edinburgh, published in 1707 his *Hugo Grotii de jure belli ac pacis Librorum III. Compendium, Annotationibus et Commentariis Selectis, illustratum. In usum Studiosae Juventutis Academiae Edinensis.* The same year saw the introduction in Edinburgh of a Professorship of Public Law and the Law of Nature and Nations. At Glasgow, Gershom Carmichael (1672– 1729), whose successors in the Moral Philosophy Chair were Francis Hutcheson who had been his pupil, Adam Smith and Thomas Reid, taught Pufendorf's system.[2] His annotated edition and commentary on Pufendorf's *De Officio* was first published in

Glasgow in 1718: *S. Puffendorfii De Officio Hominis et Civis,
juxta legem naturalem Libri Duo. Editio nova, aucta Observationibus et Supplementis, Academicae Institutionis causa adjectis
a Gerschomo Carmichael philosophiae in Academia Glasguensi
professore.*[3] Carmichael acknowledged the debt of natural jurisprudence to Grotius: for almost fifty years no one had been able
to go beyond the boundaries of *De Jure Belli ac Pacis*, but a
major development had come in 1672 with Samuel Pufendorf's
De Jure Naturae et Gentium.

Aided as it was by the practice of Scottish students continuing
their studies in the universities of Holland where natural jurisprudence enjoyed great prestige, the work of Grotius and subsequent writers like Pufendorf had an impact on several areas of
Scottish intellectual life. It might be argued that the most significant impact was in Scots Law, but Reid's chapter which points to
the connection between natural jurisprudence and the Rights of
Man movement suggests the need to consider a rival thesis. At
any rate, the impact on Scots Law was certainly considerable.
Stair's remark that 'there are not wanting of late of the learnedest
lawyers, who have thought it both feasible and fit, that the law
should be formed into a rational discipline, and have much
regretted that it hath not been effectuated, yea scarce attempted
by any', picks out Grotius as a leading inspiration for his project
in *The Institutions of the Law of Scotland.*[4] And the influence is
confirmed in Stair's system of arrangement, as well as by cita-
tions and points of detail.

Scottish philosophers have been charged with paying insufficient attention to their own Institutional writers in law. There
may be some justice in this charge. It is ironic that Reid in his
account of natural jurisprudence should appear to credit the
Romans with methodising the law according to the divisions and
sub-divisions of men's rights.[5] A. H. Campbell describes this as a
plan the 'excogitation of which indicates a high degree of abstract
jurisprudential thinking'.[6] Stair knew that the credit for this did
not belong to the Romans:

> The Roman Law taketh up for its object Persons, Things,
> and Actions, and according to these, orders itself, but these
> are only the extrinsic object and matter, about which law
> and right are versant. But the proper object is the right
> itself, whether it concerns persons, things, or actions: and,
> according to the several rights and their natural order, the
> order of jurisprudence may be taken up.[7]

Caution directs against giving the credit for this excogitation to a
single thinker, but Campbell rightly stresses the extent to which

Stair has a special claim to a share of this credit with his penetrating grasp of the implications of this idea.

According to Reid, the enterprise of natural jurisprudence is to give a more detailed and systematic account than had previously been given of the duties we owe our fellow human beings. The key to this lies in employing the language of rights, developed in the study of law, so as to have the advantage of clearly marked distinctions and a battery of technical terms with meanings more precise than the terms in common language. Reid's account is simple and bold. The essence of the enterprise is, in his words, *arrangement* and *methodising*; this is what justifies calling natural jurisprudence a system and a science.[8]

This account is bound to strike the reader of Grotius or Pufendorf as highly selective. These writers are associated with the rational derivation of human rights and duties from the nature of things. This project will seem more ambitious to the modern reader than mere methodising. And Pufendorf's *De Officio* seems anomalous so far as Reid's thesis is concerned about rights providing the key to arrangement. Due to the availability of Carmichael's edition, and its use in the Universities of Glasgow and Edinburgh, this is likely to have been the most used work of natural jurisprudence in eighteenth-century Scotland. Its preparation by Pufendorf as a short compendium of the large *De Jure Naturae et Gentium* placed a premium on methodical arrangement. Yet the title does not belie the contents: the arrangement is in terms of duties. Indeed, the index of the 1927 'Classics of International Law' edition does not even contain an entry for *Rights*.

To the extent that Reid's account is interpretatively selective, this stems in large part from his concern with persuasive definition of the terms *system of morals* and *science of morals*. In the chapter which precedes his discussion of systems of natural jurisprudence, Reid poses the question:

> From what cause then has it happened, that we have many large and learned systems of Moral Philosophy, and systems of Natural Jurisprudence, or the Law of Nature and Nations; and that, in modern times, public professions have been instituted in most places of education for instructing youth in these branches of knowledge?[9]

He is anxious to justify these developments, but is determined to do so on grounds which will not suggest that knowledge of our moral duties is the product of philosophical investigation. The celebrated enquiries of Hutcheson, Hume and Adam Smith into the foundation of morals, and the violence of the controversy over reason or sentiment as the basis of ethical distinctions, were all too likely, in Reid's view, to confirm Hume's remark about the rabble out of doors judging 'from the noise and clamour, that all goes not well within'.[10] For Reid, the danger was not that the general public should conclude that there were controverted questions in *philosophy*, but that they should think all went not well with morality itself.

Accordingly, Reid insists on a sharp distinction between what he calls the science or system of *morals*, the methodising of human duties in a systematic arrangement, and the science of *philosophy*, accounting for the powers of the human mind by which we have our moral conceptions and distinguish right from wrong. The latter activity tended to go under the name of the Theory of Morals. For Reid, this was an improper description. Its effect and the practice of including such matter in every system of morals is, says Reid, that 'men may be led into this gross mistake, which I wish to obviate, That, in order to understand his duty, a man must needs be a philosopher and a metaphysician'.[11] For Reid, the so-called Theory of Morals is a branch of the science of the philosophy of the human mind, not a branch of the science of morals properly conceived. These are different sciences based on different principles.

It may be difficult for the modern reader to appreciate the regard Reid held for arrangement as the science of morals. This involves sharing a perspective from which it seemed that moral treatises had developed from collections of aphorisms, through various treatments of portions of the field, into ordered comprehensive surveys.[12] It also requires consideration of how Reid was both influenced by and an influence upon the concern for ordering subject-matters which was such a marked feature of Scottish intellectual life. But it is clear how Reid would be attracted by the work of Grotius and his followers where the weight of attention comes down heavily on what Reid calls the system of morals rather than the so-called Theory of Morals. For Reid, talk of the derivation of rights from nature is little more than a way of speaking. He thoroughly approves the tendency of writers of natural jurisprudence to treat knowledge of our duties as given.[13] This accords with his view that the Law of Nature is the law of *our* nature in the sense of what is dictated by our moral faculty.[14] Further, attention to Reid's terminology requires a revision of the charge that his account of *systems* of natural jurisprudence is unbalanced. Reid would say that in not considering philosophical questions about the grounds of the derivation from nature he was properly attending to his advertised

project. To the revised charge that he thereby distorts the enterprise of writers who produced 'systems' in a sense that is not his,
one would expect Reid to defend his account as being correct
with regard to the substantial achievement of the writers in
question.

Another question for the modern reader of Grotius and Pufendorf is whether the switch to the language of rights is as central a
feature of their work as Reid thought, and had been teaching his
students since at least 1765. This emphasis of Reid's has radical
implications since it presents the current of enthusiasm for dec-
larations of the Rights of Man and Citizen as a development with
imposing credentials in its seventeenth-century base. The claim
that the direct intention of natural jurisprudence is to teach the
rights of men, and Reid's concern to justify conceptual links that
allow translation from the language of duties to the language of
rights, have manifest ideological implications in the context of
the second half of the eighteenth century. With its publication in
1788, just prior to the French Revolution, the *Active Powers*
defends the translation which in a short space was to be de-
nounced by Bentham in *Anarchical Fallacies*. For Bentham, this
was the replacement of the language of plain strong sense by the
language of smooth nonsense which carried daggers with it.[15]

To jump to the conclusion that Reid's chapter in the *Active
Powers* supports any and every declaration of rights is quite as
rash as the conclusion that Bentham's *Anarchical Fallacies* con-
demns every such enterprise.[16] It is on the utility of *just* systems of
natural jurisprudence that Reid insists: systems which give correct affirmations of our rights.[17] Nonetheless, so far as the French
Declaration is concerned Reid and Bentham were clearly on
opposite sides.

While it is true that Reid's chapter does not contain any
explicit remarks about the project of asserting rights in docu-
ments intended to have political effect, he does welcome for its
political effects the publicity attracted by the ideas of the natural
jurisprudence school.[18] The importance Reid placed on individuals being aware of their rights is apparent from the account
of political freedom found in MS 2131/2/II/10. There, he insists
that a people may be free under the most absolute government,
provided 'they understand their Rights, and have the Power and
the Will to vindicate them when atrociously violated'. This idea is
repeated in a letter of 1791, where Reid goes on to comment on
the growing momentum of the Rights ideology in his own life-
time:

I have been very long persuaded, that a Nation, to be free,

needs only to know the Rights of Man. I have lived to see this Knowledge spread far beyond my most sanguine hopes, and produce glorious Effects. God grant it may spread more and more and that those who taste the Sweets of Liberty may not turn giddy but make a wise and sober Use of it.[19] Reid's readiness to act as a steward for a meeting in Glasgow on 14th July, 1791 of Friends to the French Revolution has to be understood against the background of deeply held philosophical convictions. When this episode led him to be criticised and attacked, Reid invited a correspondent to consider whether 'you think it more odd that an old deaf Dotard should be announced as a Steward of such a Meeting, or that it should give any Man such offence?'.[20] What is clear is that there are no grounds in Reid's philosophy for thinking his participation at all odd.

II

Reid claims that the substantive notion *a right,* as used in talking of the rights of men, is very different from, and more artificial than, the adjectival use of *right* which, applied to actions, signifies that they are 'agreeable to our duty'.[21] He argues that the substantive notion covers all that someone may lawfully do, possess and use, and all he may lawfully claim of others. Although the term has been part of ordinary language for a long time, this meaning is too artificial to be the birth of common language: 'it is a term of art, contrived by Civilians when the Civil Law became a profession'.[22]

Reid insists that we can be at no loss to perceive the duties corresponding to the several kinds of rights:

> What I have a right to do, it is the duty of all men not to hinder me from doing. What is my property or real right, no man ought to take from me; or to molest me in the use and enjoyment of it. And what I have a right to demand of any man, it is his duty to perform. Between the right, on the one hand, and the duty, on the other, there is not only a necessary connection, but, in reality, they are only different expressions of the same meaning; just as it is the same thing to say, I am your debtor, and to say, You are my creditor; or as it is the same thing to say, I am your father, and to say, You are my son.[23]

This is the correspondence between rights and duties on which the claim is grounded that a system of rights can replace a system of duties. Reid considers the objection that while every right implies a duty, not every duty implies a right. To counter this objection he appeals to *imperfect* rights which correspond to the duties of humanity, and *external* rights which correspond to duties grounded upon mistake or erroneous belief. These introductions enable a system of rights to cover the whole duty we owe to our fellows and prevent it being 'a lame substitute for a system of human duty'.[24]

Lying behind this account of correspondence is Reid's highly perspicacious view, set out in MS 2131/8/IV/1, that rights are figures of speech. Reid firmly rejects the view which had been advanced by Pufendorf as well as views which were to be asserted in the nineteenth and twentieth century. He denies that rights are *qualities* either of a person or thing; that they are real relations; that they are to be identified with mental phenomena. Instead, they are merely a 'short technical way of expressing what would require many words' if we were to choose the most direct and natural language. In the latter language we could use the term 'requirement' and describe a person's position in terms of what the legal system or morality requires and does not require of him; and in terms of what the legal system or morality requires and does not require of others with respect to him. The language of rights is used in relation to what is within and what is outside the bounds of these requirements. Thus, I have a right to do what I am not required to forbear and I have a right that others do not do to me what they are required to forbear. Another way of putting this would be to say that rights and duties are mapping words; they map 'the Bounds which I must observe respecting others, and the Bounds which others must observe respecting me'.[25] Law and morality draw lines in terms of requirements: rights and duties are words to map the position of parties with respect to those lines. Reid, as much as Bentham although without the extent of the latter's influence, is a demystifier of such putative entities as rights. He did not have to wait for the present century to receive the advice that the way to understand rights was to understand what was being said in the sentences in which the expression occurs.

Reid's account of rights corresponding to duties or requirements in law and morals covers two distinct relations. Given the premise that A has a duty to forbear assaulting B, one may follow Reid in affirming (i) B has a right that A should not assault him, and (ii) A has no right to assault B. The first correspondence is between the respective positions of two different parties; the second is between respective ways of describing the position of one and the same party. The presence of this duty on A correlates with the presence of the claim-right on behalf of B. If A had no such duty, B would have no such right. This correlation has its

logical ground in the equivalence in meaning between active and
passive verbal forms. That you ought not to assault me in the
passive formulation is that I ought not to be assaulted by you. On
Reid's account, the substantive expression *a right* can be used as
a term of art to mean what is said in the passive formulation. This
is how the extent of men's rights *against each other* can be taken
from the extent of their duties concerning each other. Claim-
rights which are ascribed on this logical basis I shall call *Reflex*
claim-rights.

Similarly, the extent of men's liberty-rights can be taken from
the extent of duties incumbent on themselves. What I have a duty
to do, I have no right to forbear; what I have a duty to forbear, I
have no right to do. What I have no duty to do, I have the right to
forbear; what I have no duty to forbear, I have the right to do.
The logical ground of these affirmations is again one of meaning:
a right in one party, when we talk of a right to do, or of a right to
forbear, is simply an expression of art for the absence of a duty of
the appropriate content incumbent on that same party.

A firm grasp of the logical basis for the ascription of
such liberty-rights is revealed in what Reid writes in MS 2131/7/VI
1/1C:

> My Right to do such an Action implies that I may do it
> without transgressing the Law or being obnoxious to cen-
> sure and the Right extends 1. To all actions that I am obliged
> to do, 2. To the forbearing all unlawful actions, but 3. Most
> properly to all actions that are indifferent, which I may do or
> omit without a trespass. We may call this the Right of
> Liberty.

Reid thus recognises that the duty to do *x* is compatible with
having the Right of Liberty to do *x*, and that a duty to forbear *x* is
compatible with the right to forbear *x*. Were this not the case, we
would find ourselves in a world of moral tragedy where it would
be a violation of duty to discharge a duty. It is the liberty-right *to
do x* which is excluded by the presence of the duty *not to do x*.
Here the liberty-right and the duty have what Hohfeld called
'opposite tenors'.[26]

But while a student of Hohfeld would find MS 2131/7/VII/1C
admirably clear in its grasp of the logic of ascribing liberty-rights,
he would firmly reject the account of the correspondence between liberty-rights and duties which Reid presents in the *Active
Powers* with the claim that it is the duty of all men not to hinder
me from doing what I have a right to do. If we stick to Reid's idea
of using the language of rights to map the position of parties on
the basis of what is and what is not required, this is not what we

should say. If 'I have a right to do x' is shorthand for the situation I am in of not being required in law or morals to forbear x, there are no grounds whatever for any assertion with regard to duties on others respecting my doing x. The relation between right and duty which Reid should have asserted is that my right to do x entails my having no duty to forbear x. Reid would be the ideal opponent in the boxing-ring if he were to adhere to his assertion about all men having the duty not to hinder me from doing what I have a right to do. The rules of boxing do not require me to refrain from punching him on the chin once the bell goes to start the bout. Thus I have what Reid calls the Right of Liberty to punch him on the chin. I would not be slow to advise Reid to lower his guard and set his chin up nicely. This is precisely what he is required to do if he is to maintain his mistaken doctrine in the *Active Powers*; otherwise he will hinder me from doing what I have a right to do.

When someone is in the position of having the liberty-right to do x, *and* the position of others is that they must not interfere with the exercise of that liberty-right, the party in question has *reflex* claim-rights against others in addition to his liberty-right. But as Hohfeld and Glanville Williams have shown, these are logically independent ascriptions.[27] The possession of the relevant claim-rights does not follow as a matter of logic from the possession of the liberty-right. After one has discovered that no rule of law or morals prohibits the person from doing x, the rules must again be consulted to discover whether or not the system contains prohibitions on others relative to forms of conduct which would have the effect of interfering with the person's doing x. Shooting me as I walk down the corridor on my way to give a lecture is an interference with my liberty-right to give the lecture which is legally prohibited in this country, albeit not under that description. But asking me the time is not, even though this may hinder me for a few moments.

Reid also tells us in the *Active Powers* that what I have a right to demand of any man, it is his duty to perform. From the context it is clear that he means: what I have a right that someone perform upon demand, it is his duty to perform when I so demand. This is a clearer way of expressing what follows from the requirement that someone perform what I demand. It may verge on the pedantic to complain of Reid's language, but talk of the right *to demand*, or as in MS 2131/7/VII/1a of the right *to expect*, as corresponding to another's duty, can be misleading. This language of rights to demand or expect could serve to map a person's position relative to the absence of any requirement on him not to do any demanding or expecting. So far as logic is concerned, Smith's duty to Jones to deliver a shipment of wheat does not entail a right in Jones to expect delivery of that shipment. This is the fallacy of changed terms since nothing about expecting appeared in the antecedent. The correlative is the right Jones has that Smith deliver the shipment. However, the root of the determination one finds in several quarters to place the correlative in a right to expect does not stem from any confusion of claim-rights and liberty-rights. It stems rather from the sort of thinking about entitlements which is reflected in the way that in several legal systems, unless and until a party intimates that he will default on his contractual duty, the other party to the contract will have legal protection against losses incurred by his acting in reliance on the contract being fulfilled. But once notice of default is served, the right-holder is required to minimise his losses.

Reid is perfectly correct about the need to use many words if we are to unpack the sort of assertions people make about their rights. The positions they claim to enjoy may be quite complex in terms of a variety of unrestricted options open to themselves and restrictions imposed on others. Thus, my 'right to make a will' is not merely a matter of my having no legal duty to refrain from making one, or even this combined with my having no legal duty to make one. There are also the ways in which I am restricted and unrestricted in my capacity to alter the legal position of others by my will. There are also duties on executors and court officials to consider, as well as duties on people generally not to coerce me into making a particular will. All this and more may be covered by my 'right to make a will'. When the term 'right' is used in a broad way to tag such a complex manifold of relations resulting from the presence and absence of requirements, it may be all very well to speak of *reflex* claim-rights 'corresponding' to 'the right to make a will'. But if we are to use a stricter language of rights which will supply the basic conceptions needed to map the position of parties relative to requirements present or absent on themselves and others, we need the conception of a *reflex* claim-right which is correlative to a duty on others and the conception of a liberty-right which means the absence of a duty of the appropriate tenor on the party who has the liberty-right. These conceptions are logically distinct in the sense that the possession of *reflex* claim-rights against others is not entailed by the possession of a liberty-right. It may well be attention to the broader use of rights language where it is used to tag a complex position which led to the confusion in the *Active Powers* of what follows from what. At any rate, it is MS 2131/7/VII/1c which contains the truth about what is entailed by what.

F. H. Bradley pronounced it barbarous to ascribe rights on the basis of being the object of requirements imposed on others: the dirt on the road would have a right to be swept up or let lie.[28] Reid, of course, could reply that the basis on which he ascribes rights is narrower than the basis Bradley attacks. For Reid, *reflex* claim-rights map the position of *persons* relative to requirements on others concerning them. Indeed, a further restriction is added in MS 2131/7/VII/1c:

> A man is never said to have a Right to anything he thinks hurtful to him, because a Right is always conceived to be something beneficial and not hurtful. We do not say that a Thief has a right to be hanged, because it is not supposed that any man would choose to be hanged.

Reid, then, subscribes to the so-called Beneficiary theory of rights which is usually associated with Bentham but which Reid would have associated with Hutcheson.

What requires emphasis is the important difference between the *reflex* claim-rights Reid ascribes on the basis of duties on others, which require them to act for the benefit of the right-holder, and the conception of a right which involves the right-holder having control over the duty of another. Although Reid is concerned in the *Active Powers* to give an historical account of the birth of the language of rights, he does not point to the difference between the original conception of a right which was developed in Roman Law and the term of art he employs.

The substantive *a right* was developed in Roman Law in relation to a special or particular situation which left its mark on the conception of correlative rights and duties which was evolved upon it. This was the situation of the creditor and debtor. The original focus in Roman Law was on the tie or bond between creditor and debtor rather than on the terminal positions in the relation. In this way, both the creditor and the debtor could be said to have an *obligatio*. But gradually, *obligatio* came to pick out the position of the debtor, and the creditor was said to have a *ius*. Figuratively, the relation was conceived as a chain or *vinculum juris*, where the debtor was manacled to one end of the chain while the creditor held the other freely in his hand. The latter could hold tight so as to bind the manacled party, dragging him to performance or a court action in the event of failure to repay. Alternatively, he could let his end of the chain fall, releasing the other from the bond.

The difference between the language of *vinculum juris* rights and obligations and the language of *reflex* rights and obligations emerges very clearly in arguments presented by Hobbes and J. S. Mill. The latter argues:

> If you may say that it is the moral duty of sovereigns to govern well, or else abdicate, you may say that subjects have a right to be well governed.[29]

Mill is quite correct about what we may say, but only in the limited sense of what may be said in the language of *reflex* rights and duties proposed by Reid. Hobbes accepts the premise from which Mill argues since he insists that it is the office or duty of the sovereign to procure 'the safety of the people' where safety is to be taken as including the 'contentments' as well as the bare preservation of life.[30] Now we may say interchangeably that the sovereign ought to govern his subjects well, or that subjects ought to be ruled well by their sovereign; this is precisely what we are saying if we follow Reid in using the language of *reflex* rights and duties for the respective positions of subjects and sovereign. But Hobbes does not use that language. He adheres to *vinculum juris* conceptions. The duty on sovereigns to govern well is not, for Hobbes, a duty *owed* to subjects. The institution of sovereignty creates no *vinculum juris* tie between sovereign and subjects in the matter of their being governed well. Therefore, Hobbes denies that subjects have any right against their sovereign and commends David as a clear-sighted thinker on this issue since, in repenting of his conduct with regard to Uriah, David confessed to God 'To thee only have I sinned'.[31] The respective positions of Mill and Hobbes, the one ascribing a right to subjects and the other refusing, are not in fact incompatible. It is simply that they are talking different languages. If what Reid describes as the *reflex* claim-right of subjects is violated, Hobbes will say that this is iniquity. He may even say that it is *injury* to God, since a *vinculum juris* bond between God and the sovereign may obtain. But Hobbes will deny that the subjects suffer *injury*. They merely suffer *damage*, since Hobbes requires the premise that a *vinculum juris* obligation be owed to subjects by the sovereign if there is to be the possibility of their suffering *injury* at his hands. Mill, of course, provides for no such premise.

It is abundantly clear that talk of rights is pregnant with confusion if the term is used by some for one conception, while others use it for a logically distinct conception. The extent of this confusion should not be underestimated. When, prior to discussing theories of rights, I asked a first-level Jurisprudence class in the University of Aberdeen whether they would say that they had a right not to be murdered, about 35 indicated that they would not say this while 30 indicated that they would. None, presumably, doubted that I had a duty not to murder them. It is evident that on the criteria for *vinculum juris* claim-rights, there is no such right not to be murdered. The duty under the criminal law not to murder is not of the *vinculum juris* kind. It is not owed to a correlative right-holder who has control over it. The figure of a chain created by an act of the parties, held freely in the hand of one of them, simply does not fit. I cannot be released by you from the duty not to murder you, and so you have no *vinculum juris* right not to be murdered by me. On the other hand, since the requirement not to commit murder offers protection to your interests, we need to go no further in establishing that you have the *reflex* claim-right not to be murdered.

There are some philosophers and writers on jurisprudence, attached to the so-called Will theory of rights which fits the paradigm of a *vinculum juris* right, who wish to outlaw the language of rights and duties advocated by Reid. Other writers, attached to the so-called Interest theory of rights, counter by attacking the Will theory. Neither group appears ready to admit that there are different conceptions embedded in different sorts of rights talk, or to recognise the merits of one conception in explicating certain areas of law and morals while insisting on the appropriateness of the other conception for other tasks. Since the language of *vinculum juris* rights and the language of *reflex* rights are both in actual use, what is needed is a firm grasp of the different logical bases for ascribing the different kinds of right, and of their respective entailments.

Sidgwick, for instance, regarded it as a mark of thoughtful persons that they would admit that the obligation of a promise is relative to the promisee.[32] To conceive promises as giving rise to this sort of obligation with a correlative right in the promisee, enables an explanation to be given of what disappears and what may remain if the promisee spontaneously releases the promiser from his promise. The specific *vinculum juris* obligation disappears, but the promiser may still believe that he ought to do what he promised. His judgment that he is under the latter obligation which is not of the *vinculum juris* sort, is perfectly compatible with the judgment that he is no longer subject to the *vinculum juris* obligation.

On the other hand, the language of rights which Reid advocates is apt for talk of human rights. One of the classical problems about natural or human rights was the question why they could not be alienated. The standard move was to look to the transaction whereby alienation could be attempted and find in it an absence of *causa* or consideration which rendered it null and void of effect. Hobbes makes this move in chapter XIV of *Leviathan*; Rousseau in Bk I, ch.4 of the *Social Contract*. The problem here is that outside particular legal systems it is difficult to obtain agreement about what constitutes 'reasonable cause', 'consideration', and 'irrationality'. While Hobbes and Rousseau take the same line, Rousseau employs it against Hobbes. Hobbes thought civil tranquillity a compelling consideration, 'the final cause, end, or design of men', for every man authorising a sovereign by giving up the right of governing himself. But for Rousseau the man who does this is 'out of his mind'. Where Hobbes sees a final cause, Rousseau sees the motivation of a madman.

But if we regard a human right not to be tortured or enslaved as a right in Reid's sense, and not as a *vinculum juris* right in the way classical theorists tended to do, we do not have to evaluate the rationality of attempted acts of alienation in order to pronounce on the inalienability of such human rights. On Reid's line, it is the fixed character of the human duty not to torture or enslave which makes the corresponding *reflex* claim-right inalienable. With regard to this sort of claim-right there is no presumption of alienability or waivability to rebut, and the grounds for its ascription focus attention where it ought to lie – on the grounds for holding it to be a requirement of morality that one human being should not torture or enslave another.

Reid believed that the criteria he adopted for the ascription of rights required him to admit a kind of right he called *external*. He had in mind the type of case where McGregor had stolen a horse which he had lent McKay, but McKay, like us, is unaware of the fact. Here we would judge McKay to have a duty to return the horse to McGregor. But since McGregor is not the true owner of the horse, he does not have a genuine right that it be returned to him. However, on Reid's version of the thesis about rights corresponding to duties, McGregor has to be ascribed the *reflex* claim-right, since this is the term of art which is shorthand for the moral requirement on McKay. In order to avoid admitting exceptions to the principle that rights correspond to duties, while signalling that McGregor's right is not authentic, Reid claims to follow writers of jurisprudence, who appeal to something like a fiction in law, in holding that McGregor has an *external* right. (Hutcheson used the term but meant by it a right which it would be morally unworthy of an agent to exercise or insist upon.[33] A legal right might be perfectly genuine and non-external in Reid's sense, yet external in Hutcheson's.) Such an ascription is, however, unnecessary.

First, we need to distinguish what we would judge from what is truly the case. What we would erroneously judge in our ignorance of fact, is that McKay has a duty to return the horse to McGregor and that McGregor has a *genuine* right that McKay do so. What is truly the case is that McKay does not have this duty and that McGregor has no such right. The case simply does not offer a counter-example to the thesis that there is a corresponding right to every duty. The reason Reid thought it did, is that in his view the duty in question was not mistakenly attributed to McKay. This is where a second distinction is required in order to clarify what is meant by 'the duty in question'. Morally, McKay has a duty to do what he honestly believes to be his duty. But the duty he mistakenly believes he has (which would correspond to a right in McGregor) is not a moral duty with regard to discharging that duty. The duty of borrowers to make restitution to true owners, is not the moral duty of doing what you conceive to be your duty. As an adequate description of this moral duty includes no reference to McGregor, there are no grounds for ascribing a corresponding right in McGregor whether genuine or external. The form in which Reid presents his discussion of *external* rights, in both the *Active Powers* and in his lectures, indicates a degree of disquiet on his part about the notion. This disquiet appears to have been justified; but Reid can omit *external* rights without threat to the thesis that duties carry necessary implications on the side of rights. Given his erroneous beliefs, McKay's moral duty means that in conscience he has no moral Right of Liberty not to return the horse to McGregor.

What may be a residual problem is the account Reid is to give of McKay's moral duty. If, as I suggest, it is not to be treated as a requirement with respect to McGregor, is it to be treated as a duty to self? And if it is, what follows about corresponding rights? Reid might well have subsumed it under the duty of Self Government which was his label for self-regarding duties. MS 2131/7/VII/1b reveals that Reid regarded such duties as an exception to the thesis that for every duty there is a corresponding right. But Reid sets these aside, since he believes that by introducing *external* and *imperfect* rights he can block the only objections to the thesis that a complete delineation of men's rights can provide a perfect delineation of the duties we have to our fellow creatures. Reid could defend the restriction to his correspondence thesis this introduces, by appealing to common language. Few are ready to follow Kant in talk of rights in themselves against themselves.

While Reid had no inclination to regard moral duties as *vincu-*

lum juris obligations, Kant was in the thrall of this idea. It may scarcely be credible that Kant should have assimilated the 'ought' of the categorical imperative to a *vinculum juris* obligation, but it is perfectly clear that he did. In the section of the *Metaphysic of Morals* entitled 'The Concept of Duty to Oneself Might Seem (at First Glance) to Contain a Contradiction', Kant poses the Hobbesian point about the *auctor obligationis* always being able to release the *subjectum obligationis*. It would seem, then, that in the case of putative duties to self Hobbes's dictum would apply: 'he that is bound to himself only, is not bound'.[34] But Kant's second glance did not discover that duties under the categorical imperative, with respect to self or others, required to be distinguished from *vinculum juris* obligations. Instead, his second glance discovered two persons in one to fit the requirements of the *vinculum juris* model: the noumenal self could be relied on to hold fast to the chain to which the phenomenal self was manacled.

Reid avoids Kant's problem because, for Reid, one is not the *auctor obligationis* by being the person with respect to whom someone else has a duty. This is equally true if the requirement is on oneself to treat oneself in a particular way. As Reid uses the concept of a right in relation to requirements, the person said to have a right is not the *auctor obligationis*.

But if the logical basis for the ascription of *reflex* claim-rights does not require a commitment to *external* rights, it does require a commitment to the rights which Reid called *imperfect*. Such rights must be admitted to the category of moral *reflex* claim-rights, although the division of *reflex* rights into the subcategories of *perfect* and *imperfect* is one which we might be well advised to drop as being of uncertain meaning. By *perfect* rights, Reid understands rights to one's life, limbs, liberty, and reputation; rights to humane treatment, or offices of expense from others when you are in distress, fall into the *imperfect* category. Neither kind of right, for Reid, is of the *vinculum juris* sort so far as the logic of ascription is concerned. But for many writers, perfect rights are defined in terms of perfect obligations which are duties owed to parties and not simply duties with respect to doing something to someone. J. S. Mill, for instance, identifies the sphere of justice as the sphere of perfect obligations with correlative rights. Mill identified imperfect obligations as obligations which had no correlative rights.[35] The terms *perfect* and *imperfect* were described by Mill as singularly ill-chosen. John Austin preferred the expressions *relative* and *absolute* duties which may have an even greater potential for confusion. A duty owed to a party with a correlative right was *relative*; a duty which was not owed in that way but was rather a duty *sans phrase* could be called *absolute* where that was a 'negative or privative expression'.[36] Reid's account cuts straight across the terminology of both Mill and Austin. For Reid, a duty which was absolute like the duty not to murder, gives others a right not to be murdered which falls for Reid in the perfect category. And the mark of an imperfect obligation is not, as for Mill, that no right corresponds to it; for Reid, imperfect obligations have their reflex in imperfect rights. If you ought to aid me in my distress, I ought to be aided by you. The moral requirement on you is equivalent to my *reflex* right that you aid me.

Reid had some difficulty in grounding a distinction between *perfect* and *imperfect* rights. One finds, for instance, this fragment on the back of MS 2131/7/VII/1a:

> Reasons for treating of the Imperfect Rights of Men in Jurisprudence. Wherein the difference of these properly consists. Not in this that the Perfect Rights are such whose observation is necessary to the being of Society. Nor 2. In this that the Perfect Rights may be vindicated by force. According to the first Perfect and imperfect Rights would differ in Degree not in kind.

Here, Reid intends to reject a doctrine of Pufendorf's which Mill endorsed in ch.5 of *Utilitarianism*; as well as Pufendorf's main doctrine on the topic, that perfect rights may be vindicated by force in the state of nature and by a court action in civil society.[37] In the *Active Powers*, the distinction is suggested that the different rights come from different sectors of morality: a perfect right corresponds to a claim of strict justice while imperfect rights correspond to the claims of charity and humanity. But this distinction is not developed, save for the observation that these respective claims shade into each other and Reid's refusal to endorse the distinction on the basis that imperfect rights cannot be enforced by human laws but must be left to the judgment and conscience of men. Certainly there is no suggestion in the *Active Powers* that imperfect rights are like external rights in not being genuine. There is a suggestion of this in MS 2131/7/VII/1b of around 1770, where imperfect and external rights are described as a 'shadow of Right'. And in MS 2131/7/VII/11 of around the same date, Reid marks the distinction in the following way:

> A Perfect Right is that which it is no favour to yield but an Injury to withhold. An Imperfect Right is that which it is a favour to bestow or at least no Injury to withhold.

This represents a considerable weakening of the position taken in the earlier lectures and in the later *Active Powers*, where imperfect rights are not described as 'shadows' but are held to be part of the requirements of Justice taken in the broad sense.

Reid's return to the stronger doctrine in his published account of systems of natural jurisprudence should be welcomed. Only the inhumane need fear the assertion that particular individuals can have rights corresponding to duties of humanity. The fact that we may not want to say that Oxfam has the right that we send them a donation, should not lead us to reject Reid's published account of rights. We must concentrate on the content of the relevant moral requirement. Do we have a moral duty to support *some* charitable causes? This requirement specifies no determinate party for the ascription of a corresponding right. But when the moral duty is concrete, as when someone who is starving asks my assistance, the duty is with respect to him and he has a corresponding right to my assistance. In discharging this duty of humanity I do not bestow a favour, I merely withhold an injury in a sense of that term which is different from that used by Hobbes but which is no less significant from the moral standpoint.

Reid's penetrating concern to clarify the logical basis of a way of talking about rights which was winning increasing acceptance in the eighteenth century and has become even more firmly established in this century, has not received the notice it deserves. This may scarcely be surprising since much that is of value is to be found in unpublished papers. It is, however, one reason among others to press for the publication of the Reid manuscripts.

1 Reid, 1895: A.P., V.III.; cf. Reid, 1765, 1767, 1770.
2 Moore, 1980.
3 See Hutcheson, 1747, pp.v–vi, in praise of Carmichael's commentary.
4 Stair, 1981, I.I.17, p.89.
5 Reid, 1895, 644; A.P., V.III.
6 Campbell, 1954, p. 11.
7 Stair, 1981, I.I.23, p.93.
8 Reid, 1895, 642; A.P., V.II.
9 *Ibid.*, 640; ibid.
10 Hume, 1978, p.xiv.
11 Reid, 1895, 643; A.P., V.II.
12 *Ibid.*, 642; ibid.
13 Reid, 1766.
14 Reid, 1765.
15 Bentham, 1843, II, 524.
16 Dalgarno, 1975.
17 Reid, 1895, 645; A.P., V.III.

18 *Ibid.*
19 Reid, 1791.
20 *Ibid*; see also Reid, 1796.
21 Reid, 1895, 643; A.P., V.III.
22 *Ibid*; *ibid.*
23 *Ibid*; *ibid.*
24 *Ibid.*, 644; *ibid.*
25 Reid, 1767, 142.
26 Hohfeld, 1919, p.39.
27 Williams, 1968.
28 Bradley, 1927, 187.
29 Mill, 1973, vol. XVIII, p.10.
30 Hobbes, 1946, ch.xxx, p.219; cf. Hobbes, 1949, ch.xiii, pp.142–3 and Hobbes, 1969, pt.II, ch.ix, p.179.
31 Hobbes, 1946, ch.xxi, p.139.
32 Sidgwick, 1907, p.305.
33 Selby-Bigge, 1897, I, p.162.
34 Hobbes, 1946, ch.xxvi, p.173.
35 Mill, 1967, p. 305.
36 Austin, 1861–3, Lect.xii.p.5.
37 Pufendorf, 1729, I.vii.7.

TIMOTHY DUGGAN

Thomas Reid on Memory, Prescience and Freedom

IN CHAPTER I, *Things Obvious and Certain With Regard to Memory,* of Essay III, *Of Memory,* of *Essays on the Intellectual Powers of Man,* 1785, Thomas Reid makes the following claims.[1] (1) 'It is by memory that we have an immediate knowledge of things past.' (2) 'Memory must have an object. Every man who remembers must remember something, and that which he remembers is called the object of his remembrance.' Remembrance is a present act of the mind of which we are conscious. The objects of that act are past things and may be, 'anything which we have seen, or heard, or known, or done, or suffered.' (3) 'Memory is always accompanied with the belief of that which we remember.' In infancy or in a disorder we may confound memory and imagination. We may think we remember that which we only imagine, 'but in mature years and in a sound state of mind, every man feels that he must believe what he distinctly remembers . . . This belief, which we have from distinct memory, we account real knowledge . . . The testimony of witnesses in causes of life and death depend upon it.' Later on Reid admits that 'Even in a sober and sound state of mind, the memory of a thing may be so very weak that we may be in doubt whether we only dreamed it or imagined it'.[2] But this, Reid insists, 'does not in the least weaken its credit, when it is perfectly distinct.' (4) 'The remembrance of a past event is necessarily accompanied with the conviction of our own existence at the time the event happened.' Reid takes it for granted that all of the above are facts which admit of no proof and which 'will appear obvious and certain to every man who takes the pains to reflect upon the operations of his own mind.'

In the following chapter, *Memory An Original Faculty,* Reid presents an ingenious argument concerning prescience or fore-knowledge, and the actions of a free agent. Before turning to that argument some preliminary observations are in order. In calling memory an *original* faculty Reid meant that we can give no account of its manner of operation. We know many past events by memory, but this is only to give a name to this power, 'how it gives this information . . . is inexplicable.[3] Reid says, 'The knowledge which I have of things past, by my memory, seems to be as unaccountable as an immediate [non-inferential] knowledge would be of things to come; and I can give no reason why I should have the one and not the other . . . I find in my mind a distinct conception, and a firm belief of a series of past events; but how this is produced I know not. I call it memory but this is only giving a name to it – it is not an account of its cause. I believe most firmly what I distinctly remember; but I can give no reason for this belief'.[4] Sir William Hamilton in a footnote to this passage says, 'But if, as Reid himself allows, memory depends upon certain enduring affections of the brain, determined by past cognition, it seems a strange assertion . . . that the possibility of a knowledge of the future is not more inconceivable than of a knowledge of the past.[5] But this, I believe, is to miss Reid's point. Hypotheses about brain 'affections' or traces do not, in the required sense, render our knowledge of things past accountable. *How* brain affections, supposing there are such things, give us information about the past, and *how* they give us conviction remain inexplicable. The case is the same with regard to sense perception. Impressions on the sense organs, affections of various nerves and of the brain are all involved in perceiving the external world. But it is folly to suppose that in saying this we have accounted for our perceptual knowledge. Reid says, 'We perceive material objects and their sensible qualities by our senses; but how they give us this information, and how they produce our belief in it, we know not'.[6] Reid is explicit on this point. He says, 'If the impression on the brain be [as it is] insufficient to account for the perception of objects that are present, it can as little account for the memory of those that are past'.[7] We are entirely ignorant concerning how brain impressions contribute to remembrance, 'it being impossible to discover how thought of any kind should be produced by an impression on the brain, or upon any part of the body'.[8] Reid provides this instructive comparison. 'If a philosopher should undertake to account for the force of gunpowder in the discharge of a musket, and then tell us gravely that the cause of this phenomenon is the drawing of the trigger, we should not be much wiser by this account. As little are we instructed in the cause of memory by being told that it is caused by a certain impression on the brain. For, supposing that impression on the brain were as necessary to memory as the drawing of the trigger is to the discharge of the musket, we are still as ignorant as we were how memory is produced'.⁹ Reid's point that our memory knowledge of things past is no less unaccountable than prescience would be is echoed by Richard Taylor. Taylor, after inviting the reader to imagine a race of men 'whose knowledge of the future is comparable to our knowledge of the past, but for whom the past is shrouded in darkness and mystery,' goes on to say '. . . our memories happen to extend only to things past which we have experienced. We have no comparable awareness of things future, which we are going to experience. But this . . . seems not the least bit necessary. It is difficult to see how we could have any awareness ahead of things we are not yet experiencing, but it is really no more difficult or mysterious than supposing that we should have an awareness afterwards of things we are no longer experiencing – and this sort of awareness we do in fact have – in memories'.¹⁰

Reid stresses the analogies between memory and prescience. It might, however, be thought that a point of disanalogy is that there are kinds of events which we may remember but which could not possibly be foreknown. I may remember falling off a ladder and suffering a regrettable accident. But could I know that I will suffer a similar accident, say, next Tuesday? Surely, if I know such a thing, would I not take steps to ensure that it did not occur, e.g., would I not refrain from climbing ladders on that day? But, of course, if I do refrain from climbing ladders next Tuesday then I could not have known what it is that supposedly led me to thus refrain. The supposition that this is a kind of event that could not be foreknown because if foreknown it would be prevented, is actually incoherent. A foreknown event will occur and thus will not be prevented. A more interesting kind of event which we might suppose could be remembered but could not possibly be foreknown are events which require a degree of deception or ignorance on the part of the agent. I may remember, perhaps with regret, inadvertently putting arsenic instead of sugar in my wife's coffee. I may remember being deceived by my broker and as a consequence making a disastrous investment. But, could I foreknow such things? We may be tempted to say no, but this would be a mistake. All that is required in these kinds of cases is that between now and the time of the occurrence of the foreknown thing I forget what I now know. There are many things, even important things, which I knew but have forgotten. Similarly there are many things, even important things, which I know now but will forget. So, the only condition required for prescience of events requiring for their occurrence ignorance, deception and similar states of mind is the perfectly familiar one of forgetfulness. This can always occur since there must be a temporal gap between my foreknowledge of an event and the event itself, just as there must be a temporal gap between my remembrance of an event and that event. I can know an event as it occurs, but neither memory nor prescience can be contemporaneous with their object.

One other point has to be made before turning to Reid's argument. The argument very largely depends on the analogy between memory and prescience or *foreknowledge*. Thus, 'remember' must be used in its veridical sense such that 's remembers P' entails 'P did occur' just as 's foreknows P' entails 'P will occur' – 's remembers P, but not–P' is contradictory just as 's foreknows P, but not–P' is contradictory. Unfortunately, however, Reid's use of 'remember' is not always consistent. Indeed, just a few paragraphs before presenting his argument on prescience and liberty Reid says, 'When I believe that I washed my hands and face this morning, there appears no necessity in the truth of this proposition. It might be or it might not be. A man may distinctly conceive it without believing it at all. How then do I come to believe it? I remember it distinctly. This is all I can say. This remembrance is an act of my mind. Is it impossible that this act should be, if the event had not happened? I confess I do not see any necessary connection between the one and the other'.[11] Reid seems to be allowing here that one could distinctly remember an event even though that event had not occurred, thus collapsing the distinction between remembering (veridically) and thinking mistakenly that one remembers. There is, however, another interpretation of this passage. Perhaps Reid was confusing 'Necessarily, if s remembers P, then P' with 'If s remembers P, then necessarily P.' Reid certainly rejected the latter proposition and this may have led him, at least in this passage, to reject the former. Whatever the merits of this interpretation, it should be noted that this passage as it stands seems to flatly contradict the first thing that Reid said was obvious and certain with regard to memory, namely, that memory must have an object and that its object must be a past thing which 'we have seen, or heard, or known, or done or suffered.' Thus if I remember having washed my hands this morning, the object of that act of the mind must be something I have done, namely, having washed my hands, though, of course, the proposition 'I washed my hands this morning' is contingently true, not necessarily true. There is another interpretation of this passage which would absolve Reid of the charge of contradiction. The act of remembering that I washed my hands and face this morning is at the same time an act of believing that I did so. Thus, when Reid asks, 'Is it impossible that *this act* should be, if the event had not happened?', the expression 'this act' could be thought of as referring to this act of belief, which is in fact an act of remembering as well. And, of course, there is no necessary connection between believing that I washed my hands and face this morning and the events in question. On this reading Reid is simply guilty of a confusion of description in referring to the act, leading the reader to suppose that in this passage he is using remembrance in a non-veridical sense. (I owe this suggestion to Dr Vincent Hope.) In any case, in the following argument, and in another to be discussed below, 'remember' is used in its veridical sense. Reid's argument in the *Essays on the Intellectual Powers of Man* is as follows.

After remarking on the 'subtle disputes' during the scholastic ages concerning divine prescience and human liberty, Reid continues: 'It is remarkable that these disputants have never apprehended that there is any difficulty in reconciling with liberty the knowledge of what is past, but only of what is future. It is prescience only and not memory, that is supposed to be hostile to liberty, and hardly reconcilable to it.

'Yet I believe the difficulty is perfectly equal in the one case and in the other. I admit, that we cannot account for prescience of the actions of a free agent. But I maintain that we can as little account for memory of the past actions of a free agent. If any man thinks he can prove that the actions of a free agent cannot be foreknown, he will find the same arguments of equal force to prove that the past actions of a free agent cannot be remembered. It is true that what is past did certainly exist. It is no less true that what is future will certainly exist. I know no reasoning from the constitution of the agent, or from his circumstances, that has not equal strength, whether it be applied to his past or to his future actions. The past was, but now is not. The future will be, but now is not. The present is equally connected or unconnected with both.

'The only reason why men have apprehended so great disparity in cases so perfectly like, I take to be this, that the faculty of memory in ourselves convinces us from fact, that it is not impossible that an intelligent being, even a finite being, should have certain knowledge of past actions of free agents, without tracing them from anything necessarily connected with them. But having no prescience in ourselves corresponding to our memory of what is past, we find great difficulty in admitting it to be possible even in the Supreme Being . . . We are so constituted as to have an intuitive knowledge of many things past; but we have no intuitive

knowledge of the future. We might perhaps have been so constituted as to have an intuitive knowledge of the future; but not of
the past; nor would this constitution have been more unaccountable than the present, though it might be much more
inconvenient'.[12] Reid adds that had this been the case we would
have no difficulty in admitting prescience, but the greatest difficulty in admitting that there could be such a thing as memory.

Hamilton in a footnote to this passage says, 'This is a marvel-
lous doctrine. The difficulty in the two cases [i.e., foreknowledge
of the actions of a free agent, and memory of the actions of a free
agent] is not the same. The *past* as past, whether it has been the
action of a free agent or not, is *now necessary*; and, though we
may be unable to understand how it can be remembered, the
supposition of its remembrance involves no contradiction. On
the contrary, the future action of a free agent is *ex hypothesi* not a
necessary event. But an event cannot be now certainly foreseen,
except that it is now certainly to be; and to say that what is
certainly to be is not *necessarily* to be, seems a contradiction.[13]
(But Hamilton, as we shall see, holds the view that *all* past events
are necessary.) Hamilton has completely missed Reid's subtle
point. We may have certain knowledge of the past actions of free
agents in memory. And, of course, if I remember that you did x,
then you certainly did x. But it does not follow at all that you
necessarily did x, or that your doing x was a necessary and not a
contingent event. If I remember that you did x, then it does not
follow that you *must* have done x; it's just that you *did* do x. If I
remember that you did x, then it does not follow that you *could
not* have refrained from doing x, only that you *did not* refrain
from doing x. And x may or may not have been a free action.
Similarly, with respect to prescience, if I foreknow that you will
do x, then you certainly will do x. But it does not follow that you
necessarily will do x or that your future doing of x will be a
necessary and not a contingent event. If I foreknow that you will
do x, then it doesn't follow that you *must* do x, only that you will
do x. If I foreknow that you will do x, then it doesn't follow that
you *cannot* refrain from doing x, only that you *will not* refrain
from doing x. And x may or may not be the action of a free agent.

In the *Essays on the Active Powers of Man* Reid anticipated
Hamilton's claim that if an event is foreknown then it certainly
will be, and what is certainly to be is necessarily to be, putting it
this way: 'It may be thought that as nothing can be known to be
future which is not certainly future; so, if it be certainly future, it
must be necessary'.[14] Reid's response which I shall quote in its
entirety is right on the mark. 'It must be granted that, as what-

ever was, certainly was, and whatever is, certainly is, so whatever shall be, certainly shall be. These are identical propositions and cannot be doubted by those who conceive them clearly.

'But I know no rule of reasoning by which it can be inferred, that, because an event *certainly shall be*, therefore its production *must be necessary*. The manner of its production, whether free or necessary, cannot be concluded from the time of its production, whether it be past, present, or future. That it shall be, no more implies that it shall be necessarily than that it shall be freely produced; for neither present, past, nor future, have any more connection with necessity than they have with freedom.

I grant, therefore, that, from events being foreseen, it may be justly concluded, that they are certainly future; but from their being certainly future, it does not follow that they are necessary'.[15]

There is no need for extensive comment on this passage. Reid is simply making the impeccable point that whatever is remembered is past, and whatever is past certainly is past, and that this leaves open the question of whether the event was necessary or the action of a free agent. Similarly, whatever is foreknown is future and whatever is future certainly will be future and this too leaves open the question of whether the event will be necessary or the action of a free agent. Assuredly, *Que sera, sera*. But no one would be so foolish as to want it otherwise. Hamilton has committed the elementary fallacy of moving from 'x is certainly to be' to 'x is necessarily to be'.

Hamilton's comment exhibits another curious error. He claims that past events, whether they were necessary or the contingent actions of a free agent are *now necessary*, and this is why they can be the objects of memory. In his voluminous notes appended to his edition of Reid's works Hamilton says, 'Reid has absurdly argued in favor of liberty from the analogy of memory. He says that on the doctrine of necessity everything that is past would be necessary. *And so it is*. Whatever has been in past time, is necessary; and so likewise, *everything that is, is necessary* by the very fact of being' (my emphasis).[16] This view has at least the following two unfortunate consequences. First, it seems to entail that the *mere* passage of time changes the modality of events. My being in London yesterday may have been a contingent event yesterday. We may suppose that my presence in London was up to me, something within my power. But today, simply given the passage of time, that very event has become necessary! In fact, Hamilton is explicitly committed to the efficacy of mere temporal passage. In a footnote he says, '*We have no memory of past contingents*. A past contingent is a contradiction. An event is only contingent as future; in becoming past, it *forthwith* becomes necessary – it cannot but be' (my emphasis).[17] Hamilton, no doubt, was influenced by the fact that we can't change the past. The past is irrevocably fixed, and there is nothing we can do now, or at any future time, to bring it about that what has happened, did not happen. Similarly, there is nothing we can do now or at any future time, to bring it about that what is now, is not the case. This, of course, is true. But it is equally true that there is nothing we can do now to bring it about that what is future will not be future. We can't change the past but we can't *change* the future either. Some things we do now may be causally sufficient for some aspects of the future being what they will be. But this certainly is not *changing* the future, for what might we suppose we are changing it from? It is also possible that Hamilton moved from the uninteresting truism 'Necessarily, if I was in London yesterday, I was in London yesterday' to the plain falsehood 'If I was in London yesterday, then I was necessarily in London yesterday.' And similarly, perhaps he moved from 'Necessarily, if I am in London now, then I am in London now' to 'If I am in London now, then I am necessarily in London now.' A second unfortunate consequence is that on Hamilton's view *nothing* that was or is, is contingent. Two pages after the passage quoted above Hamilton defines 'contingent' as 'That which *when it happens* is neither necessary nor impossible' (my emphasis).[18] (This would not be a bad definition if we take, as Hamilton does not, 'when it happens' to mean 'whenever it happens, past, present or future.') But how can an event when it happens, that is, *when it is*, be neither necessary nor impossible if, as Hamilton insists, everything that is, is necessary? Hamilton seems to be caught in a flat contradiction. It would appear that the only possible candidates for the label 'contingent' are forever un-actualised possibilities. But this, in addition to being a strange doctrine, does not square with his definition of 'contingent'.

Reid, not surprisingly, considers the objection that it would be impossible to foreknow an event if that event were not necessary in the sense that the future event will be the necessary consequence of what presently exists. And, since foreknowledge is restricted to events which are necessarily connected to what exists now there can be no foreknowledge of contingent things such as the actions of a free agent. Reid's response is that in both the prescience of future contingents, and the memory of past contingents, 'the object of knowledge is neither what presently exists nor has any necessary connection with what presently exists. Every argument brought to prove the impossibility of prescience, proves, with equal force, the impossibility of memory. If it be true that nothing can be known to arise from what does exist, but what necessarily arises from it, it must be equally true that nothing can be known to have gone before what does exist but what must necessarily have gone before it. If it be true that nothing future can be known unless its necessary cause exist at present, it must be equally true that nothing past can be known unless something consequent, with which it is necessarily connected, exist at present.[19] But we do know, by memory, past things, even though nothing that exists at present is the necessary consequence of those past things. Given that we do know, by remembering, past things which bear no necessary relations with the present, we should have no difficulty in *conceiving* foreknowledge of future things which have no necessary connection with the present. On Reid's view the two are equally inexplicable. It is worth recalling that on Reid's account, it is by memory that we have an *immediate,* that is, non-inferential, knowledge of things past – things which 'we have seen, or heard, or known, or done, or suffered.' Thus remembering is quite unlike inferring, or retrodicting what happened on the basis of present evidence. I may remember entering Great Britain in 1961 in which case my knowledge of that event is immediate. If, however, my knowledge of that event is based on, say, an entry in my passport, it would be inferential, and not a case of memory. Similarly prescience, if there were such a thing, would be equally immediate and non-inferential. Prescience is not prediction based on knowledge of presently existing causes. *A fortiori* it is not based on, nor would it require in any manner, knowledge of *necessary* causes existing at present. It may be true, as Richard Taylor says, that, 'no one can know *by inference*, that a certain event is going to happen, except on the basis of his knowledge of certain conditions sufficient to produce that event. If no such condition exists, then it obviously cannot be known by *inference* that the event in question is going to happen, and if it is known, then there must be such conditions'.[20] Reid, however, in holding that both memory and prescience are immediate and unaccountable, circumvents this point about inferential knowledge.

Reid has, I believe, successfully made the point that prescience of the actions of a free agent is possible and that arguments to the effect that such prescience is impossible tell with equal force against the possibility of memory of the actions of a free agent. A point, however, that Reid does not discuss is that with respect to some such actions, namely *our own* (deliberate) actions, foreknowledge would make deliberation about those actions impossible. This is so, it is argued, because knowing what we are going to decide to do is tantamount to having decided already, and having decided already precludes deliberation with respect to that very decision.

In 'Can The Will be Caused?' Carl Ginet in the course of arguing that the will cannot be caused employs the premise that 'It is conceptually impossible for a person to know what a decision of his is going to be before he makes it . . . For a person to claim that he knows what he will decide to do, hence, what he will at least try to do, and *then* to begin the process of making up his mind what he will do – trying to persuade himself one way or another by offering himself reasons for and against the various alternatives – would surely be a procedure of which we could make no sense'.[21] Richard Taylor cites Ginet and argues the related point that 'one cannot deliberate about what he is going to do, even though this may be something that is up to him, at the same time knowing what he is going to do.' Deliberation, Taylor argues, supposes ignorance: 'If he does already know what he is going to do, there is nothing there for him to decide, and hence nothing to deliberate about'.[22] If Ginet and Taylor were right then there would be a significant category of things which can perfectly well be remembered but which in principle cannot be foreknown, namely our own future deliberate decisions. The point would be that whereas I can remember my past decisions which were the outcome of prior deliberation, I cannot have prescience of my future decisions which will be the outcome of as yet to come deliberation. And this, if true, would weaken the analogy between memory and foreknowledge upon which Reid leans so heavily. It might be supposed that Reid could embrace the point, observing that just as we cannot deliberate about our remembered past actions including decision, so too we cannot deliberate about any future actions including decisions which we foresaw. But if he did this it would contradict his claim, 'Every man knows that it is in his power to deliberate about *any* part of his conduct'.[23] (Reid means *future* conduct.) And a decision which we will make, and which, according to Reid, we *might* have foreknown, is a part of our conduct. Moreover, if knowing that I shall decide to do x precludes deliberation which will result in the decision to do x, then that decision when it occurs will not be a deliberate one, i.e. one which results from weighing pros and cons. And while that decision may be a voluntary act, it could be argued that it would not be a fully free and responsible act. It would be like a spontaneous or 'snap' decision to set one's neighbour's house on fire which suddenly comes upon one as opposed to a deliberate or pre-meditated decision. (By deliberate I mean resulting from deliberation.) If one thinks of such decisions as not fully free then this goes against Reid's main thesis that foreknowledge of the actions of a free agent is possible.

Before responding to Ginet and Taylor something should be said about Reid's account of deliberation and fixed purpose, or resolution. Reid characterises volition, or an act of will, as 'The Determination of the mind [the decision] to do or not to do something which we conceive to be in our power'.[24] He notes that this is not intended to be a definition, for if it were it would suffer from the defect that 'determination of the mind' is synonymous with 'volition'. But he further notes, 'it ought to be observed, that the most simple acts of the mind do not admit of a logical definition'.[25] The way to get clear about such simple acts is to reflect carefully on what it is like to engage in them and on what we may or may not coherently say about them. An instance of the latter is Reid's observation, 'I may desire meat, or drink, or ease from pain: but to say that I will meat, or drink, or ease from pain, is not English'.[26] Reid makes the following observations about willing. 'Every act of will must have an object; and the person who wills must have some conception, more or less distinct, of what he wills'.[27] Thus, we can distinguish voluntary acts from things done instinctively, e.g. the sucking behaviour of a new born child, and from many of the things done from sheer force of habit. A voluntary act for Reid is an act that one wills to do, understanding what it is that one wills to do. (It is worth noting that Reid, unlike so many philosophers, distinguishes between voluntary acts and free acts. Free acts are a subset of voluntary acts. He says, 'By the *liberty* of a moral agent, I understand, a power over the determinations of his own will. If in any action he had power to will what he did, or not to will it, in that action he is free. But if, in every voluntary action, the determination of his will be the necessary consequence of something involuntary in the state of his mind, or of something in his external circumstances, he is not free; he has not what I call the liberty of a moral agent, but is subject to necessity'.[28] Reid gives as examples of voluntary but unfree actions: (1) The actions of a madman who acts with understanding and will but who lacks the power or ability to will to do what he wills to do. (2) The act of a man who, say, discloses military secrets, when presented with irresistible incentives like 'the rack or the dread of present death'.[29]) 'The immediate object of will must be some action of our own'[30] and this distinguishes will from desire and from command. I may desire the action of another, e.g., that you shut the door. I do not will these things. I may desire what is not an action at all, e.g. the happiness of another. Moreover, I may will what I do not desire, e.g. to swallow a nauseous medicine. The object of command is the action of another. Typically one desires that the thing one commands should take place, but not always. Reid mentions 'tyrants who have laid grievous commands upon their subjects, in order to reap penalty of their disobedience, or to furnish a pretense for their punishment'.[31] The object of our volition, Reid says, 'must be something which we believe to be in our power, and to depend upon our will'.[32] Reid notes that a rational person may desire to visit the planet Jupiter, but that one cannot will to do so unless one believes such a visit is within one's power. Finally, Reid observes that 'when we will to do a thing immediately, the volition is accompanied with an effort to execute that which we willed'.[33] It might be objected that many of the things we will to do require no effort at all, e.g. my blinking my eyes now. Reid's response is that if we are inclined to say this it is because either very small efforts are not thought of as efforts at all, or because we give no attention to small efforts. Whatever the merits of this response, Reid's main point, I think, is that there is no temporal gap between willing to do something immediately and intentionally doing or trying to do that thing. This distinguishes willing to do something immediately from resolving to do something in the future. But, as we shall see, for Reid, resolution is nonetheless a determination of the will.

Reid calls deliberation a 'voluntary operation of the mind' by which he means simply that it is something which we can do at will. He says, 'Every man knows that it is within his power to deliberate or not to deliberate about any part of his conduct; to deliberate for a shorter, or for a longer time, more carelessly, or more seriously . . . In all these points, he determines, he wills . . . The natural consequence of deliberation on any part of our conduct, is a determination how we shall act; and if it is not brought to this issue it is lost labour'.[34] Thus the natural consequence of deliberation is a decision to do, or to forbear doing something which we believe to be within our power. Though, of course, a decision to do or forbear need not be the result of deliberation. It might be the effect of 'passion or appetite, without any judgment interposed'.[35] I may decide to do or to forbear doing x *now*, or I may decide to do x at some time in the future. Reid calls a deliberate decision to do something in the future 'fixed purpose, or resolution' noting that 'a fixed purpose to do, sometime hence, something which we believe shall then be within our power, is strictly and properly a determination of will, no less than a determination to do it instantly'.[36] So much for Reid's views on willing, deliberating and resolving. I now turn back to the question of foreknowledge, deliberation and decision.

As luck would have it, J. W. Roxbee Cox in 'Can I Know Beforehand What I am Going to Decide'[37] has, I believe, refuted the Ginet–Taylor thesis. His strategy is to provide compelling examples of first person foreknown decisions and to put his finger on the error which led Ginet and Taylor astray. (Not only Ginet and Taylor. Stuart Hampshire and H. L. A. Hart in Hampshire, 1958, say, " 'He has not yet decided what he is going to do' entails 'He does not yet know what he will do' . . . If it is up to him to decide what he is going to do then he must still be uncertain what he will do until he has made a decision." Although this claim is boldly asserted, it is never argued for.) Most would agree that it is possible to foreknow what the decisions of others will be, such knowledge being facilitated by an acquaintance with the other and his circumstances. Roxbee Cox asks, 'Why then the sudden humility in the case of our own decisions? What special ignorance must we necessarily suffer from about ourselves?'.[38] There are at least two ways that I might know in advance what I shall decide to do. First, if I have always decided in a certain way in past situations of a certain kind, I may conclude that I will decide in the same way in the future. Roxbee Cox offers as an example of this sort of knowing: 'I have found that when I come up to the city from my home, and consider where to have my dinner, I always end up by going to a French restaurant. I have no doubt that this is what I shall decide to do when I am in town next week'.[39] Second, on the basis of the decisions of other people like me in certain situations, I may conclude that I will decide in the same way in a situation of the same kind. An example of this is, 'Everyone I know with young children ends up buying a television set. I haven't thought much about the pros and cons, but I'm sure I'll end up by deciding to get one'.[40] Surely the 'I' in these examples could be correct in his beliefs, and if so there appears to be no sufficient reason to deny that he knows what he will decide to do, and moreover, that his foreknown decision will be the result of forthcoming deliberation. Richard Taylor makes the point, also made by Reid, that '. . . one can deliberate whether to do a certain act only if he believes it is up to him whether to do it or not, or, that it is within his power equally to do it, and to forgo it'.[41] And this is correct. The 'I' in the above examples could say: It is up to me whether to select a French restaurant or not; whether to buy a television set or not. I know that after weighing the pros and cons I shall finally decide on the French restaurant; on the television purchase. Still, I haven't yet thought seriously about the matter, and I certainly have not made up my mind. It is within my power to forgo the French restaurant, to forgo buying the t.v., though I know I won't.

Roxbee Cox's examples show that knowledge of what I shall decide to do can be got otherwise than from the making of the decision, and that '. . . prior ignorance of the result is not necessary for making up ones mind'.[42] He argues that Ginet's mistake is in assimilating knowing what my decision will be *and* making the decision. He says '. . . we may know beforehand *what the decision will be*; after making the decision we have knowledge *what to do*. Only deciding can produce the decision, and our knowing what the decision will be still leaves the job of making it to be done'.[43] Richard Taylor, claiming that deliberation presupposes ignorance asserts, 'If [one] does already know what he is going to do, there is nothing there for him to decide, and hence nothing to deliberate about'.[44] If Roxbee Cox is right, as I think he is, Taylor is wrong in saying 'there is nothing there for him to decide', if 'nothing for him to decide' is to be understood as 'there is no decision to be made.' The aim of the procedure of deliberating is precisely to make a decision. In Reid's language 'The natural consequence of deliberation is a determination how we shall act,' i.e. a decision concerning what we shall do. In the kind of cases envisaged above this is just what has yet to be done, in spite of the knowing what shall be done.

Roxbee Cox's examples of ways in which I might know in advance what I shall decide to do are garden-variety instances of inferential knowledge. In the first case, the inference is from how I have acted in the past. In the second case, the inference is from how others similar to me have acted. Reid, of course, invites us to grant the possibility of a direct, non-inferential, prescience analogous to memory. If we accept inferential knowledge of what one shall decide to do, there seems to be no reason to deny the *possibility* of an unaccountable 'Reidian' foreknowledge of what one shall decide to do.

1 Reid, 1895, 339; I.P., III.I.
2 *Ibid.*, 362; I.P., IV.I.
3 *Ibid.*, 341; I.P., III.II.
4 *Ibid.*, 340; ibid.
5 *Ibid.*
6 *Ibid.*, 341; I.P., III.II.

7 *Ibid.*, 353; I.P., III.VII.
8 *Ibid.*, 354; ibid.
9 *Ibid.*
10 Taylor, 1963, p.69.
11 Reid, 1895, 341; I.P., III.II.
12 *Ibid.*, 341–2; I.P., III.II.
13 *Ibid.*, 342; I.P., III.II.
14 *Ibid.*, 629; A.P., IV.X.
15 *Ibid.*
16 *Ibid.*, 976.
17 *Ibid.*, 631.
18 *Ibid.*, 978.
19 *Ibid.*, 631; A.P., IV.X.
20 Berofsky, 1966, p.290.
21 Ginet, 1962.
22 Berofsky, 1966, 281–2.
23 Reid, 1895, 538: A.P., II.III.
24 *Ibid.*, 531: A.P., II.I.
25 *Ibid.*
26 *Ibid.*, 532: A.P., II.I.
27 *Ibid.*, 531: A.P., II.I.
28 *Ibid.*, 599: A.P., IV.I.
29 *Ibid.*, 614: A.P., IV.V. See Duggan, 1979, for a discussion of acts that are voluntary but unfree.
30 Reid, 1895, 532: A.P., II.I.
31 *Ibid.*
32 *Ibid.*
33 *Ibid.*
34 *Ibid.*, 538–9; A.P., II.III.
35 *Ibid.*, 539; A.P., II.III.
36 *Ibid.*
37 Roxbee Cox, 1963.
38 *Ibid.*, 88.
39 *Ibid.*, 89.
40 *Ibid.*
41 Berofsky, 1966, 285.
42 Roxbee Cox 1963, 91.
43 *Ibid.*, 92.
44 Berofsky, 1966, 282.

PÁLL S. ÁRDAL

Hume and Reid on Promise, Intention and Obligation

I

IN THE following examination of Hume's discussion of promises an attempt will be made to reveal the importance of an aspect of Thomas Reid's criticism of Hume's account. Although both Hume and Reid agreed that promises are acts, they differed with regard to the place to be given to language, convention, intention, statement of intention and obligation in the explanation of the nature of these acts. I believe the discussion will help to demonstrate the need to keep separate the two following questions: (1) What constitutes a promise? and (2) Why, if at all, ought a promise to be kept? Stated in his own words, Hume wants to show 'that the rule of morality, which enjoins the performance of promises, is not *natural* . . .' This he proceeds to establish by 'proving' (1) *'that a promise would not be intelligible before human conventions had established it'* and (2) *'that even if it were intelligible it would not be attended with any moral obligation'*.[1]

In looking at the way in which Hume attempts to 'prove' the first of these propositions we find that he uses the method of presuming what conditions would have to be fulfilled 'if promises be natural and intelligible'. His claim is that if promises are natural acts

> . . . there must be some act of the mind attending these words, *I promise*; and on this act of the mind must the obligation depend.[2]

The problem, as Hume sees it, is to explain how, in promising, one can place oneself under a moral obligation. This needs explanation, although, as we shall see later, Hume does not believe that the concept of a promise is such that, by promising, one necessarily places oneself under such an obligation.

The obligation to keep a particular promise is a new obligation, in that it arises from that promise. We now want to examine whether there is a natural act from which the obligation could follow. Hume takes it for granted that there is no such *physical* act. 'I promise' does not seem to state the occurrence of any bodily act like blinking or waving one's arms. He therefore confines himself to the question whether a promise is a natural *mental* act. This act is thought to have the power to impose upon the person an obligation under certain conditions. If I could intuit such a mental act in you without the use of language or any conventional system of symbols, I could know that you were binding yourself to the performance of an action by promising to do so. The expression 'I promise' or an equivalent expression constitutes no part of the promise but only indicates that a promise is taking place. It would seem that the expression would be used to state a fact, i.e. the fact that the speaker is promising. Hume asserts that, although we could intuit each other's thoughts, promises would be impossible without society and its conventions.

II

The candidates for the honour of being the act of promising are limited to three: (1) a resolution, (2) a desire, and (3) an act of will. The fact that Hume describes the three acts as exertions of the faculties of the soul has, I believe, no special significance, in spite of its slightly religious flavour. I take it that Hume simply wants to suggest that these three are the only plausible candidates. Since desires do not seem to be acts of the requisite kind, in that it makes no sense to talk of them as done, whereas promising is something we do, Hume could perhaps have confined his attention to resolutions and acts of will. As it turns out, both of these have a special part to play in his account. In including desires, Hume is clearly using 'natural acts of mind' widely. The main point he wants to stress is that promises are intelligible only in the light of certain conventions. Desiring to eat, resolving to eat and, of your own free will, placing a piece of meat in your mouth, are intelligible without presupposing any social conventions. Society is not at all necessary to their performance. On the other hand signing a cheque, casting a vote, cheating at a game, buying and selling are acts that are made possible by certain human conventions. Promises, Hume is suggesting, belong to this latter class.

Let us now consider Hume's reasons against identifying promises with any of his three natural acts of mind.

(1) One cannot equate promising with a resolution, Hume thinks, for the simple reason that a resolution does not alone impose an obligation upon the person to do what he resolves to do. The term 'alone' is important here for it clearly is the case

that people may consider it morally obligatory to hold steadfastly
to their resolutions. Of course, a man ought not to stick to all his
resolutions whatever they may be. If he has resolved to do
something wrong, he clearly ought not to do this. But the same
applies to promises. It seems we ought not to keep a promise if
we have promised to do something wrong. If I promise to murder
an innocent man and think better of it, it seems absurd to say that
I am morally obliged to keep my promise, although prudence
may dictate that I do. Hume is here examining a view he takes to
imply that the moral obligation to keep a promise follows from
an act of mind quite irrespective of human conventions and social
situations. He is thus justified in rejecting the suggestion that the
act of mind which constitutes a promise can be a resolution. This
is not to deny that there may be an intimate connection between
the concept of 'resolving' and the concept of 'promising'. For,
although a man may promise without resolving to do what he
promises to do, the promisee and others that know of the promise, have in many cases a right to conclude that the promiser
has resolved to do what he has promised to do. But a resolution is
not always needed on the part of the promiser, for he may
promise to do what he always does from habit. The promise may
be called for because the promisee does not know this. Hume is
thus wrong when he claims that promises express the mental act
of resolution, although the promisee has a right to believe that
when a man clearly makes a promise he *intends* to do what he
promises to do.

(2) To promise cannot be to desire to do what is promised. It
is, indeed, singularly unplausible to suggest that this is the case,
for the fact that I do not desire to do x may be, and often is, a
reason why I am required to promise to do x. A man promises his
wife not to have too much beer on the way home from work. If he
does not like beer and this is known to his wife, there is no point
in promising not to overindulge. A man may promise to do what
he does not desire to do and his aversion may, as Hume says, be
'declared and avowed'. He might only give in to his wife after a
long argument and the eventual promise may simply be due to
the fact that he has become fed up with her nagging. One wants
to say the husband may be obliged even though he may have
neither a desire nor an intention of doing what he promises to do.

(3) Is a promise 'the *willing* of that action, which we promise to
perform'?[3] The reason why this cannot be the case is as follows.
When we promise something, what we promise is always in the
future. If A wants B to do something now, he would not seek a
promise from him. To will to do something is by Hume taken to

have an effect on the present. It 'has an influence only on present actions'.⁴ From this it follows that 'to will' and 'to promise' must be different. (Ordinary promises are not of course always future acts. One may promise to refrain from doing something from the time of speaking.)

Hume defines will as *'the internal impression we feel and are conscious of, when we knowingly give rise to any new motion of our body, or new perception of our mind'*.⁵

In his discussion of liberty and necessity in Book II, Hume does not make it entirely clear how the impression which constitutes willing is influenced by motives, and he devotes two chapters to the influencing motives of the will. Here he clearly treats the will as a kind of cause or influence and, whatever one may think of this notion of will, one must agree that, given this view of the matter, Hume is entirely correct in rejecting the doctrine that 'to promise' can be equated with willing. If we treat 'willing' as a mental phenomenon, distinguished from 'resolving', which can refer to the future, then it seems not unreasonable to give it the interpretation Hume here presents us with, for one must remember that he is investigating whether a promise can be said to be a natural act of mind. He writes of willing as the impression of an act whereas 'to the vulgar' the act of knowingly giving rise to thoughts or changes in your body constitutes the act of willing. Here Hume talks with the vulgar and treats the will as a mental act that causes changes.

Hume concludes from the fact that none of the candidates considered can be said to produce the obligation which is attached to a promise that if a promise is a natural mental act 'it must necessarily be the *willing* of that *obligation*, which arises from the promise'.⁶ He invokes ordinary ways of speaking in support of this conclusion. We say 'we are bound by our own consent, and that the obligation arises from our mere will and pleasure'.⁷ The obligation arises when the promise is made so the will would not be presumed to have an effect in the future only. The objection against a promise being the willing of the future act thus does not hold against the view that a promise is the willing of *the obligation* to perform the future act.

III

The problem now facing us is whether an obligation can arise from a volition. H. A. Prichard, who certainly did not agree with Hume about the nature of moral obligation, denied that the will could create an obligation. In his 'The Obligation to Keep a Promise', he says:

In fact, the difference between doing something and promising to do it seems just to be that while in the one case we bring something into existence, in the other we bring into existence the obligation to bring it into existence. Yet an obligation seems a fact of a kind which it is impossible to create or bring into existence. There are, no doubt, certain facts which we do seem able to create. If, e.g., I make someone angry, I appear to bring into existence the fact that he is angry. But the fact that I am bound to do some action seems no more one of these than does the fact that the square of three is odd.[8]

Prichard may, I think, be criticised here for suggesting that (a) doing something is always bringing something into existence, and (b) when you promise you always promise to do something.

It may be the case that, whenever you do something, you always bring into existence the fact that you have done it. One may wonder what else has been brought into existence by the running of a mile in under four minutes. Prichard seems misled by the example he has in mind, i.e. making someone angry, when it seems proper to say that you have brought the man's anger into existence. Once a man has been made angry, it is a fact that he is angry. But this does not mean that the fact exists in addition to the emotion. The existence of the emotion entitles us to say that it is a fact that the person is angry. The running of a four-minute mile by B entitles one to say that it is a fact that he ran the four-minute mile. But in the one case, something other than the fact is brought into existence (i.e. anger) but in the other case this is not so.

As regards the question whether to promise is always to promise to do something, one must be careful to note that this is only true if 'to do something' is used in such a way as to make it proper to say that when you refrain from doing something you are in fact doing something. One may also promise to be in a certain place or to remain in a certain condition. It may be irrelevant how one achieves this. Prichard is most likely aware of this, but fails to make his meaning clear.

The reason why Prichard thinks an obligation cannot be created by an act of will is that, as an objectivist, he thinks that obligations are 'discovered'. The analogy he draws with mathematics is instructive. We may choose to promise and thus bind ourselves, but we cannot choose that the square of three be even. This, he would most likely say, we discover. But, on a view like his we can no more choose to change our moral obligations than we can choose to change the truths of mathematics. This, however, is precisely what seems to take place in promising and creates the problem for the objectivist.

Returning now to Hume, we find, not unexpectedly, a different kind of argument. The reason why an obligation cannot arise from a volition is, Hume tells us, that volitions cannot give rise to new feelings. The argument presupposes Hume's view on the nature of obligation:

> All morality depends upon our sentiments; and when any action or quality of the mind pleases us *after a certain manner*, we say it is virtuous; and when the neglect or non-performance of it displeases us *after a like manner*, we say that we lie under an obligation to perform it.[9]

Several points need to be made about this passage.

Hume italicises the expressions 'after a certain manner' and 'after a like manner'. This makes it clear that not every pleasure arising from the contemplation of a mental quality entitles us to attribute a virtue to the person possessed of it. To have the emotions that to Hume constitute 'judgments' of virtue or duty involves, one may conjecture, in both cases, overcoming the natural bias of our passions. It must be appreciated that an unbiased view of a quality of mind or character may lead to approval of a natural bias in favour of certain people. Thus we may find ourselves approving of those who have greater concern for their children than for total strangers. Here the presence of a natural inclination may be found pleasing and its absence displeasing when an objective viewpoint is adopted.

A virtuous man is praiseworthy and a man who fails to do his duties is worthy of blame. To do no more than your duty is not to merit praise. Here 'duty' is meant to refer to the minimum standard of behaviour *required* of a person. 'Duty' may also be made to refer to institutional or other conventional requirements. The duties of a university professor would be a case in point. 'This is no more than my duty' seems often to refer to the sense of the word 'duty' Hume has in mind. In that sense it may well be your duty sometimes not to do your institutional or conventional duty.

Hume writes in the first person. He seems in fact to be analysing the situation in which we should say that we lie under an obligation. This we do when the non-performance of an action displeases us in a certain manner. There is at least this much truth in Hume's contention that we do not say we are under an obligation to do something if the performance of the action pleases us, but we are not displeased at its non-performance. Although Hume specifically refers to the impossibility of changing your own sentiments, it seems to me that he need not be understood to be giving an account only of the circumstances in which the agent would say of himself that he was under an obligation. We can equally say of another person that what he did pleases us and that we think him truly virtuous; though we don't think it his duty, we should not have been displeased if he had not done the deed; his omission does not necessarily indicate a defect or a vice.

'To be displeased with x' is, of course, not normally equivalent with 'disapproving of x'. For I can disapprove of *anyone's* behaviour, but I can only be pleased with or displeased with my own performances or the performances of people connected with me in certain ways. It would not be odd for me to say that I was displeased with my daughter's behaviour, but I could not say I was displeased with the behaviour of Ronald Reagan. But note again that Hume italicises the expressions 'after a certain manner' and 'after a like manner'. The kind of displeasure involved in considering a man to fail in his duties may thus have, as an essential causal factor, the taking up of an interpersonal, objective point of view. The disapproval of a person who fails in his duties may thus be a kind of hatred, not altogether unlike the hatred that constitutes our disapproval of a vicious person. The comparison with 'judgments' of virtue Hume here specifically draws would suggest this interpretation, if my general interpretation of Hume's account of judgments of virtue is correct.[10]

Hume does not think we can arouse new sentiments at will. Since we say we have an obligation only when a special sentiment is aroused under certain circumstances, a new obligation cannot arise from the will. (Notice that Hume does not talk about the impossibility of affecting the feelings of well informed spectators.) Is it then, a purely contingent matter that one cannot will an obligation? Could people gain such power over their emotions as to be able to change them at will, and would this mean that Hume's argument against the possibility of willing an obligation fails? Prichard's reason for the same conclusion was different in that no change in the world could alter the situation. To suggest an obligation might be created immediately through man's will would to him involve a logical absurdity.

But it turns out we are wrong in thinking that, for Hume, it just happens to be the case that man is incapable of willing an obligation. He puts the question thus:

> The only question, then, is whether there is not a manifest absurdity in supposing this act of the mind, and such an absurdity as no man could fall into, whose ideas are not

confounded with prejudice and the fallacious use of language.[11]

He clearly implies that to talk of willing a new obligation is, in that it involves willing a 'new sentiment', to talk nonsense. It is to say something 'unintelligible'. Yet it must be said that Hume is not at all clear as to the kind of absurdity involved in this, for he later writes as if it were possible to 'feign' an act of mind we call 'willing an obligation'. If this is so, it seems it must be possible to understand what is involved in such an act, although it is beyond the powers of human beings to perform it.

There is, however, a further point that might help to explain why Hume thinks willing an obligation unintelligible. When we have made a promise we are supposedly from then on under an obligation to perform the action, although we ourselves may not happen to feel pained at the non-performance of it. We may not feel obligated. In such cases, what counts is whether the spectators of our actions would feel disapproval at the non-performance of our action. This determines whether *they* can say that we are under an obligation to perform it. We should thus have to be able to will a change in the feelings of others if our obligation were to follow from the promise. If to will a new obligation entails the causing of new sentiments in other people through our volition, one may perhaps consider this absurd. But is it conceptually absurd? (Experiments performed to test the plausibility of the claim that transference of thoughts occur through extra-sensory perception presuppose that such occurrences cannot be ruled out *a priori* as impossible, that they are not conceptually absurd.[12]) Perhaps to see it in this light presupposes the acceptance of Hume's definition of will. It, you may remember, is *specifically limited to knowingly giving rise to changes in one's* own mind and body. It should be added that since the promiser does not know the time or place or identity of those who may consider him to be obligated, it may be conceptually unintelligible to consider him to will the feelings that constitute their thinking that he has an obligation.

One might also want to make the point that what one wills on this account would be a possible future feeling, what other people would feel, were they to contemplate the matter. Since this feeling does not arise as I promise, whereas the obligation does, Hume's contention that the will can only make a change to the present would still make it impossible to will an obligation, given his account of obligation.

IV

But Hume does not think the case against the will creating obligations hinges upon his special views on obligation. He tries in a long footnote to show that even though we thought obligation consisted in relations, a view he attributes to certain *rationalist* opponents, an obligation still could not arise from a volition.

The supposition that the obligation to keep promises arises from a volition without any other change in the universe taking place, is inconsistent with morality consisting in relations, since without a change in objects no new relation could arise. On this view there could thus be no natural obligation to keep promises.

And, if the act of will is itself a new object and that therefore a new relation may result from it, we are no better off. Hume puts the point as follows:

> Should it be said that this act of the will, being in effect a new object, produces new relations and new duties; I would answer, that this is a pure sophism, which may be detected by a very moderate share of accuracy and exactness. To will a new obligation is to will a new relation of objects; and therefore, if this new relation of objects were formed by the volition itself, we should, in effect, will the volition which is plainly absurd and impossible. The will has here no object to which it could tend, but must return upon itself in *infinitum*.[13]

It is not easy to see what precisely this argument amounts to. The difficulty arises from the interpretation of the expression 'is formed by the volition itself'. I take this to mean that the volition is supposed to form one of the terms between which the relation, which is supposed to constitute the obligation, holds. This new relation is supposed to be at the same time what you will, since you will the obligation. But in any such case the same volition cannot be at the same time part of its own content. If then the obligation which arises is supposed to consist in the volition and something else, you always need to presuppose a volition which is the willing of the obligation which consists in turn in a volition in relation to some other object. You are hence forced into an infinite regress of volitions. If you, therefore, try in this way to account for the obligation to keep promises, you always need to presuppose another promise to account for the obligation to keep any promise you may choose.

V

We have been looking at Hume's attempt at proving the first of the propositions listed at the beginning of the chapter on promises. We have in fact found that an answer has been given to both. 'The will never creates new sentiments', therefore, no new obligations. But Hume adds an argument he has already made use of in the discussion of justice. There can be no natural virtues, nor any 'natural obligations' unless there is a motive in man that leads to their performance. Thus, it is our duty to look after our children, but we are also inclined to do this. But for this inclination there would be no obligation. The keeping of promises is different. Hume writes:

> But as there is naturally no inclination to observe promises, distinct from a sense of their obligation; it follows that fidelity is no natural virtue, and that promises have no force, antecedent to human conventions.[14]

The main point to stress is that promises cannot be understood except in terms of a human linguistic convention. He thinks one must make the development of the convention intelligible as resulting from known human motives in known human situations without begging the question by an appeal to a natural motive of obligation to keep them.

Hume observes that, in cases of the exchange of goods, delivery often has to be delayed when the deal is made. Similarly, it may be to our mutual benefit that I should help you with the harvest of your corn now, in return for a similar service from you later. We can understand how these things come about because the individuals concerned find these arrangements useful to themselves and to those whose interests concern them.

But this self-interested 'commerce of men' must, Hume thinks, be distinguished from the cases where I help a man because gratitude makes me want to return a service to him.

> In order, therefore, to distinguish those two different sorts of commerce, the interested and the disinterested, there is *a certain form of words* invented for the former, by which we bind ourselves to the performance of any action. This form of words constitutes what we call a *promise*, which is the sanction of the interested commerce of mankind.[15]

(Note that he here says the form of words constitutes the promise.)

If I think you will, out of the goodness of your heart, or through gratitude, help me when I need help, it would be pointless for me to try to get you to promise to do this. This is the sense in which the form of words used in promising is a way of distinguishing the interested from the disinterested 'commerce of men'.

Once the form of words used to make a promise has come to be generally accepted, a man is in fact risking his reputation as a trustworthy person if he fails to keep his promise. So long as he has something to gain from being thought trustworthy, he has a certain motive to keep his promises even before he is thought to have a moral duty to do so. This shows that one may, according to Hume, understand what a promise is without thinking of it as involving a *moral* as opposed to a purely prudential obligation. (For a modern version of this view see F. S. McNeilly, 1972. McNeilly has reached, by a different route, a view not unlike my own.) One may understand what a promise is without having a concept of moral obligation.

VI

Hume states the problem about the nature of promises as if it had to do with the function of the expression 'I promise'. This is misleading in more than one way. Thus, it is obvious that 'I will without fail', 'you can count on me', 'and that is a promise' following 'I shall do x' may perform exactly the same function. But more important than this is the fact that insisting on the necessity of using expressions of this kind obscures an important ambiguity in the concept of a promise. A person may undoubtedly often be held to have promised without the use of any of the above expressions, if he has said emphatically enough in the appropriate circumstances that he will do something, or that something will undoubtedly be the case. But in the absence of the use of any of these special expressions, that I have elsewhere called emphasising expressions,[16] there may be some doubt as to whether a promise is intended. The addressee may then say 'I want you to promise me', meaning thereby to request the speaker to use one of the emphasising expressions. The answer might be 'Surely you know me better than to *demand a promise* from me. I know perfectly well how important to you it is that I should do what I am telling you I am going to do.' In a case like this, the speaker might refuse to make a promise. Yet, if he does not do what he said he would do, the addressee can surely complain that a promise was broken to him, although, in a narrower sense of the term, there was no promise. In a case like this, the reason why the demand for a promise is rejected is that the 'promisee' had a right to take what was said as a promise without the use of 'I promise . . .' or some other emphasising expression. In refusing 'to promise' the promiser is suggesting that the statement already made counts as a promise. My reason for preferring to say this to saying that although *as good as a promise* no promise is made when the emphasising expression is avoided is that it flies in the face of ordinary usage. We frequently hold people to have promised although they did not say 'I promise' or use any other emphasising expression. There is thus a narrower and a wider sense of 'promise', the criterion for the applicability of the term in its wider sense being the appropriateness of saying after the event that a promise was made. In the narrower sense of the term, the use of an emphasising expression is a necessary condition for the making of a promise. We should bear in mind that Hume focuses on the narrower sense of 'promise' throughout his discussion of the question whether a promise is a natural mental act.

VII

Hume thinks he has shown how the convention of promises came to be established without making any reference to the fact that fidelity to promises is thought obligatory and a virtue. Thus, the motive of moral obligation to keep promises must be thought of as *added* to the natural motive of interest. The case is entirely comparable with that of respect for property, and the reason why fidelity to promises is considered a virtue is the general utility of the convention. '*Public interest, education, and the artifices of politicians* have the same effect in both cases'.[17] People are not always perspicuous enough to see the general utility of faithfulness to promises. Here education and the propaganda of politicians may help to keep them honest.

In a promise, the promisee has a right to assume that the promise expresses a resolution or intention in all normal cases. But since no obligation is in such cases attached naturally to resolutions, there seems to be a problem about a mere form of words making all the difference in the case.

> Here, therefore, we *feign* a new act of the mind, which we will call the *willing* an obligation; and on this we suppose the morality to depend.[18]

It may be said that it is a defect in a person's character to frequently change his resolutions. But notice that this is not the same fault as untrustworthiness with regard to any duties one has to others. Such a person may see no special virtue in consistency *as such*, stubbornly sticking to his resolutions. (I owe this point to a discussion with my colleague, A. M. Macleod.)

The 'feigning' Hume talks of has been called 'a remarkable bit of self-deception because Hume has already maintained that it does not make sense to talk of 'willing an obligation'.[19] I do not want to rule out the possibility that Hume is confused on this point. My interpretation would then have to be understood as an attempt to show how he *could have* defended himself against the charge that his account involves an impossible feat of self-deception. This act of will has been compared with the feigning that leads us to believe in the continued and independent existence of objects external to us and in our self-identity. But Hume does not compare the act of feigning that leads us to believe we can will an obligation with the fictions he mentions in his account of the external world and self-identity in Book I of the *Treatise*.

I think the answer to this problem is to be set out on the following lines. A distinction is implied between the philosopher and the vulgar, the general public. A philosopher will, indeed, understand what is involved in a promise. He will, in so far as he has mastered the true Humean view, know that there is no such natural act of mind as willing yourself to be under an obligation with the magical power of binding you to a promise. But in so far as this is understood, he will have no use for feigning anything at all. We don't have here any remarkable feat of self-deception on his part. But members of the general public, in so far as they are unable to see why 'a certain form of words' should bind them, will feign an act of volition in that they think that the obligation belongs to a promise because of the act of binding yourself to it. This is, in fact, a natural error to fall into if we remember that we can, of course, choose to make or not to make a promise. If we *choose* not to do so, we in effect choose to avoid the obligation. But, the public fail to realise that this does not mean that, if we make a promise, the *keeping* of the promise is obligatory only because we have willed it to be so. The obligatory nature of the promise is not created by the promiser's will.

If the preceding explanation is accepted, the fictitious act of 'willing an obligation' is not strictly analogous to the feigning involved in accounting for one's belief in continued independent existence of external objects and personal identity. In the case of these latter, the feigning is inevitable and *cannot* be dispelled by any philosophical analysis, whatever its result. But to believe in promises being obligatory because of an act of mind, is in no sense a 'natural belief', in the special sense given to that term by Kemp Smith, although believing that an act of mind engenders the obligation is quite natural.

The will which is supposed to lead to an obligation must be expressed by certain signs if it is to bind a man to a promise. The expression then comes to be thought of as 'the principal part of the promise'. A man is no less under an obligation though he does not intend to keep his promise, has not resolved to try to do so, and has, in fact, no intention of binding himself to it. He is not willing to place himself under an obligation. Here the form of words is taken to constitute the promise. But Hume thinks that although the form of words constitutes the promise on most occasions, there are exceptions: (a) If a person does not know the meaning of the phrase he uses, and does not intend to promise, he is not bound by 'I promise to x' or any equivalent expression; (b) Even if he does know the meaning, but talks in jest and makes it *obvious* that he is doing so, the words do not bind him. Thus, the promise is not identical with the occurrence of the verbal expressions that normally make promises. But note that, on Hume's account, the responsibility for ensuring that what is not meant as a promise is not taken as a promise may lie with the speaker. Of course, the context of the utterance makes it in many cases obvious that a promise-locution does not make a real binding promise. A conspicuous example is a 'promise' made by one actor to another within a play. But there are other contexts in which it is not nearly so obvious that a promise-locution is not seriously meant. If a person is joking, it is his responsibility to make it reasonably clear that he is joking. If not, what he says may make him responsible for failing to keep a promise, although one is, of course, not always blameworthy for failing to appreciate a quite unusual sense of humour in those to whom one addresses oneself.

Intending what you say as a promise is, of course, quite different from intending to do what you promise to do. The false promiser intends his words to be taken as promises. He may even think the promisee has a right to claim performance from him, although, in making the promise, he does not intend to honour that right.

A deceitful promise is made without the promiser's intention to keep it. A man must be taken to have promised although the promisee sees through his deceit. Although the promisee does not rely on the promise or expect it to be kept, the promisee *has succeeded in making a promise* to him albeit a false one. The promiser can be blamed or praised for making a false promise, though no one relied upon it or expected it to be kept. It is the point of the promise which is missing, when this point is to create reliance or favourable expectations in the promisee. But a promise does not cease to be a promise when it fails to achieve its purpose.

Hume's account seems to make it possible to explain why a certain kind of *force* should invalidate contracts. The concluding remarks of the chapter put the point well:

> If we consider aright of the matter, force is not essentially different from any other motive of hope or fear, which may induce us to engage our word, and lay ourselves under any obligation. A man, dangerously wounded, who promises a competent sum to a surgeon to cure him, would certainly be bound to performance; though the case be not so much different from that of one, who promises a sum to a robber, as to produce so great a difference in our sentiments of morality, if these sentiments were not built entirely on public interest and convenience.[20]

In the case of the robber, we have, indeed, a promise which is not considered binding. We should not nevertheless want to say that no promise was made to the robber. This is a case where it is justifiable to break a promise and to make a false promise. Here then, we see that to say that a promise consists in placing oneself under a prima facie obligation is quite unacceptable, since it would entail that a man who comes to see that he was wrong to promise to commit murder would have a conflict of duties. He does not. He has no duty in any sense to commit the murder. Of course, one may come to see what one has promised as immoral, while believing that the promisee was, through no fault of his own, unaware of this. The promise may in such a case still impose an obligation upon the promiser. But the obligation would be to explain to the promisee why one does not think one has an obligation to do the promised act and is consequently not doing it.

It is also important to note that there is a tremendous difference in the importance of promises. The obligatory nature of the promise varies with the relative importance of the promise and how solemnly it was given. Hume certainly believes this, as well as maintaining that one is not always morally obliged to keep all one's promises.

VIII

In rejecting the view that promises are mental acts, Hume, according to Reid, has failed to realise that there are social as well as solitary acts of mind. This distinction is not the same as the one between public and private acts, the doing of a sum on the blackboard and the doing of a sum in one's head. Social acts of mind are rather acts '. . . which necessarily imply social intercourse with some other intelligent being who bears a part in them'.[21] And Reid further specifies the way in which other human beings come into the picture. A social act is not just any act that involves some sort of co-operation, e.g., a team sport; or where more than one person is necessarily involved, e.g., making love; or the description of which necessarily mentions another person, like falling in love, or hating or thinking of another person. A social act of mind '. . . cannot exist without being expressed by words or signs, and known to the other person'.[22] The verbal or other symbolic expression is here essential, whereas in the case of solitary acts of mind, the verbal expression is merely 'accidental'. The three candidates for being a promise that Hume mentions, in considering whether promises are natural acts, are all solitary acts of mind. A resolution need not be expressed in language, nor need a desire or an act of will. These acts do not in any way involve communication in language whereas social acts of mind necessarily do. They are indeed speech acts and Reid gives the following examples: asking for information, testifying a fact, giving a command to a servant, making a promise and entering into a contract.

Reid says: 'What makes a promise is, that it be expressed to the other party with understanding, and with an intention to become bound, and that it be accepted by him'.[23]

It is not certain whether Reid is entirely fair in attributing to Hume the view that promises do not essentially involve a verbal expression. It depends upon whether one thinks that when Hume says that the verbal expression soon becomes the principal part of the promise, he is implying that at some stage he thinks it was no part of it at all, and that prior to the verbal expression there were promises consisting in solitary acts of mind. I am inclined to think that Reid completely misunderstands Hume in attributing this view to him, for Hume is excluding special cases, such as jokes when he says that 'the expression makes on most occasions the whole of the promise'.[24] I cannot claim to have shown Hume not to be confused on this point. He certainly expresses himself confusedly. Reid seems to have had a clearer grasp of promises as essentially speech acts, although he failed to appreciate their conventional nature. This does not, however, entail that a promise is a social act of mind in Reid's sense, since the will to become bound is not a necessary part of a promise for Hume. For Hume thinks the joker, who does not have the will to be bound may, in certain circumstances, be held to have promised, but Reid maintains that the expression, if it is not accompanied with understanding *and will to engage*, never makes a promise. The will to become engaged involves conferring a right upon the other party. Where Hume parts company with Reid is in his account of the relation between a person's will to become bound to do a promised deed and the right of the 'promisee' to complain that a promise was not kept when the deed is not done. Hume's position seems to be that, although the speaker does not intend to become bound, if, knowing the language, he uses an expression that normally would be taken as a promise, then he is binding himself to the performance of what he says he is going to do. (Hume cannot be absolved from the charge that he writes as if he conceives of promises as necessarily involving special forms of words such as, 'I promise . . .'. He thus confines himself to what I have called the narrower sense of 'promise', although he need not have done so. In the wider sense, no special form of word is needed in addition to a statement that you will do something or that something is the case, or will be the case.) There is, in addition to deliberately misleading use of language, a certain sloppiness due to insensitivity or apathy, for which people can be legitimately held responsible. One is often responsible for unintentional harm. 'But I forgot', 'I did not realise that this thing belonged to you' are not always valid excuses, though true. Similarly, 'I did not mean what I said as a promise' may be met by 'You should have realised that I had a right to take it as a promise'. If it is said that it is not a promise because it was not intended to be one, just as baptism was by some theologians supposed to fail if the priest withholds the proper intention, one forgets that promises essentially involve communication. How you mean what you say to be understood does not always co-incide with the significance of what you say. I believe the criteria for picking out promises are such that 'But you promised' may be true, although it is also true that the utterance referred to was not meant as a promise, whether honest or false. To think otherwise is to absolve a speaker from responsibility for respecting a vital right of the person to whom he addresses his words and others who may know what the speaker said he would do, and to whom his doing it may be important.

Reid, although he stresses that promises are speech acts, does not think they are conventional. The power to make promises is God's gift to man. The power of speech was not given to animals and they can consequently neither give testimony nor make promises. But does not the existence of language itself presuppose a promise? Michael H. Robins writes in arguing against Hume: 'A promise is intelligible prior to conventions, and is distinguished from intending, inasmuch as *what* is intended in promising is not exclusively a future act but the *obligation* to do it'.[25] It does seem odd to say that a man who makes a false promise is *intending* an obligation to do it, although he may be aware of such an obligation. But Robins goes on to argue that all rule-governed voluntary activities, like playing games or speaking a language, presuppose a promise to abide by the rules. But this way of thinking confuses tacit understanding with promising and, if no human interests are involved, it seems difficult to make it seem plausible that engaging in a rule-governed activity imposes upon you a *moral* obligation. Is it morally obligatory not to cheat at solitaire? I know that some people *feel guilty* about it, but it is not clear that such guilt feelings are reasonable.

Apparent counter-examples to the thesis that promises are conventional acts really support the view. Not only do words and head-shakings do duty for 'yes' or 'no', by a convention, but one can only make complete inactivity count as a promise by a special agreement. Consider a patient incapable of speech and all motions except a slight nod. We might say to him, 'If you promise not to try to move, remain completely still.' Here complete inactivity has been given conventional significance and the man's immobility thus counts as a promise. (The point I am making here I owe to a discussion with my colleague, Henry Laycock.) But, although allowing a man to believe you have made a promise may be immoral for the same reason as breaking a promise it cannot be thus described.

IX

In conclusion, I want to indicate why I think Hume got the emphasis right in stressing that the essence of a promise is more clearly tied to the 'guarantee' given to the promisee of a future act than the revealing of the present state of mind of the promiser, including his willing to become morally obliged. I am using the term 'guarantee' in an unusual sense. I mean it to refer to the assertion of complete certainty and it would thus cover emphatic threats, 'I promise to get you for this', and what I have elsewhere called salesman's promises, e.g., 'This washing machine will last ten years, I promise you'.

I used to think that promises are statements of intention that could be thought of as making an assertion both about the speaker's present intention and his future act. This view had the advantage of treating deceitful promises as straightforward lies. Although I am still not certain that this analysis is wrong, I now think that it may be misleading.

Consider the following:

(1) I believe that there is a God.

(1,) There is a God.

(2) I approve of capital punishment for murder.

(2,) Capital punishment for murder is morally justified.

(3) I intend to go to Toronto tomorrow.

(3,) I am going to Toronto tomorrow.

(1) and (2) and (3) all focus attention upon the state of mind of the speaker when understood in a certain way. There are occasions when the mental state of the speaker is of greater interest than the truth or falsity of his beliefs, the adequacy of his value judgments or the fact that the speaker intends to do something rather than what he intends. In each case also, the words may be used to make a hesitant commitment to a belief, a value or a future act. This hesitancy factor is particularly clear in the case of 'intend' although with the emphasis on the first person pronoun a similar use is often made of (1) and (2). Thus, '*I* approve of capital punishment' could be naturally followed by some such qualification as 'but of course I realise that those who disagree with me may be proved right'. And, '*I* believe there is a God, although I realise that none can be certain of his existence', would seem quite a natural statement. But no stress on the first person pronoun is usually needed to introduce a hesitancy factor into 'I intend to do x'. One may, of course, diminish its force by saying 'I fully intend to do x' or 'my intention to do x could not be stronger'. But I submit that a categorical statement of intention is most naturally made in English by asserting 'I am going to do x'. 'I will . . . ' can also be used, but is often less natural than the continuous present. Now, there may be a reason for this, for 'I am going to x' has in many of its uses both a reference to the present and the future act. This is so when *you are not already engaging in the activity*. The statement 'I am going to Toronto' made by me sitting in my study would naturally be taken to refer to a future act as well as to a present situation. It may either get the reply 'Do you really mean (intend) to go?' or 'When are you leaving?' On the other hand, when I am asked 'Where are you going?' when I am sitting in the train and I reply 'I am going to Toronto', it is tempting to say that I am here referring to what I am doing at that moment, although I am indicating my future destination. It indicates an intention at that moment as well as characterising the act that I am engaging in, sitting there allowing myself to be transported to Toronto. I am going to Toronto, although there is a crash and I am killed. If the train is diverted and never reaches Toronto, but ends up in Ottawa, I can say both 'I was going to Toronto' and 'I was not going to Toronto but to Ottawa, although I thought I was going

to Toronto'. In one use the focus is on the future act and the present intention in the other. It is clearly the first of these uses of 'I am going to x' which is typically used to make a promise. How does the intention get conveyed? We are clearly not focusing our attention on the intention *as opposed to the future act*, since in promising, one is *reassuring the promisee that the future act will be done or giving a 'guarantee' that it will be done.* This is why I consider it misleading to say that 'I am going to Toronto tomorrow' makes a statement about the speaker's present intention when it is used to make a promise. It clearly reveals it and is indeed a typical way in which one does reveal one's categorical intention. Similarly, 'There is a God' is a forceful and typical way of revealing to people that one does believe there is a God. Is there a stronger way, a more emphatic way of doing this? And does a man not clearly reveal his moral attitude to capital punishment by emphatically saying that it is morally justified? It would be pedantic in the extreme to claim that in these cases one has not *told* people that one believes in God, that one has a certain moral attitude, and that one has a certain intention. One has used a typical way of conveying the relevant information about one's subjective state. If it is pointed out that I am admitting that one is not stating that one has a subjective state, then I am prepared to accept the consequence that there are other ways language has of conveying information about states of affairs than making the statements that would describe the states of affairs. My reason for not wanting to say that in making the statements of intention that may constitute promises, one is *implying* that one has an intention to do the act is this: the form of words used in making a promise is the most emphatic way one conveys in English the information that one has an intention, as well as to assert that an act will be done. Indeed, when a man promises by saying that he is going to do x, one has a right to be more certain that he intends to do it than that he will do it, for something unforeseen may always prevent the future deed. It is decidedly odd to say of a man who repeatedly asserts 'There is a God' that he has *implied* that he believes there is a God. The link between the categorical assertion and the belief is somehow made to seem too weak. If you want to tell people what you unhesitatingly intend to do, you tell them what you are going to do. It seems to me unnecessary and, indeed, unnatural to say that in promising, one is taking responsibility for having an intention. One is by one's words made responsible for doing the deed. Even a false promise may be deliberately accepted by the promisee and kept by the promiser. The promisee may, for example, correctly trust that the promiser's basic decency will lead him to change his mind. In such a case, the promiser does not fail to honour the promisee's right and thus not live up to his responsibility. To say that the promiser is committing himself to having an intention seems equally unsatisfactory. He is, rather, committing himself to doing the promised deed and, in so doing, stating his intention. Just consider the utter artificiality of trying to find out whether a man is making a false promise by asking him: 'Are you taking responsibility for intending to do x?' or 'Are you committing yourself to the intention to do x?'

John R. Searle,[26] in making room for the possibility of insincere promises, writes as part of the account of the nature of a promise, '*S intends that the utterance of T will make him responsible for intending to do A*' (p. 62). Here s stands for speaker, T for the sentence used to make a promise and A for action promised. Normally, one would take a person who 'intends to make himself responsible for x' to be accepting the legitimacy of certain criticism in the absence of x. Although it is somewhat unnatural to think of a man who makes a false promise to be aiming at a responsibility he is generally hoping not to have to answer for, one may certainly make a false promise, knowing that doing so is wrong, and being prepared to accept criticism as legitimate. But Searle claims that a nihilist, who thinks promises ought never to be kept, can still make promises.[27] Why should he, in making promises, intend the promise-locution to make him responsible for having an intention to do what he promises to do. He no doubt is hoping, with at least most of those who make false promises, that the promisee will take him to be intending to do what he says he is going to do. Furthermore, he may in our eyes *make himself responsible* if he makes a promise, but is he not inconsistent if he *accepts as legitimate* criticism for making a false rather than a sincere promise, since he on Searle's account, considers the whole institution of promises evil?

It has emerged that when I say that promises are statements of intention, I do not want to assert that they are statements about the promiser's intention. Such statements never commit a speaker firmly enough to the action to constitute a promise. One cannot make a promise by strengthening one's statement about one's present intention, even if one includes in this statement the information that one now thinks one has a moral obligation to do what one says one is going to do. The reason is that the possibility is left open that one may change one's mind, even about the obligation, before the time of performance. On the other hand, the statements of intention I have taken to be necessary in the making of ordinary promises stress the *certainty* of the future act. Without this, a promise has not been made. But, how can one guarantee to do something in the future? One may after all drop dead at any time. True. Perhaps the lesson to be drawn from this is that one should be more careful in making promises and never promise to do more than try one's best, it being understood that one's best may not be good enough.

But are promises not always understood as promises only to do one's best or to do something *Deo volente* (if God allows)? I think not. Let us refer again to the example of my ending up in Ottawa through no fault of my own, when I had taken the train that always has gone to Toronto and should have enabled me to get there in good time to honour a promise to a friend to meet him for lunch. Being a decent chap, I phone my friend to explain to him *why I could not keep my promise.* He, realising that I did do my best, and being another decent chap, will of course not blame me, and almost certainly will not say that I *broke* my promise to him. But the reason for this is not that I kept my promise. I cannot say to my friend, 'I am phoning you to let you know that I kept my promise to you, for I did my best to get to Toronto although I ended up in Ottawa.' Nor can I say that I did not fail to keep my promise because God just happened not to be willing to allow me to get to Toronto. Only if God had been willing, could I be said to have failed to keep my promise. The fact of the matter is that I did promise to meet my friend in Toronto and my being there at a certain time is a necessary condition for it being true that I kept my promise or did what I promised. Of course, I could have made the more guarded promise of only trying to do my best. But this would have been a different promise and the crucial question would then have been *whether I did my best.*

If I am right in what I have been saying in this paper, one cannot stress too emphatically the importance of distinguishing clearly between the two questions: (1) What is a promise? (2) Under what conditions is it blameworthy not to do what one has promised to do?

Two editions of Hume's *Treatise* are cited consecutively, Hume, 1972 and 1978. Therefore 'Hume' is followed by two page references for the respective editions.

1 Hume, 245; 516.
2 *Ibid.*
3 *Ibid.*
4 *Ibid.*

5 Hume, 143; 399.
6 Hume, 245; 516.
7 *Ibid.*
8 Pritchard, 1957, 169.
9 Hume, 254–6; 517.
10 Árdal, 1966.
11 Hume, 245; 517.
12 See *The Treatise of Human Nature*, II.III.I.
13 Hume, 1972, 246n.
14 Hume, 247; 519.
15 Hume, 250; 521–2.
16 Árdal, 1968.
17 Hume, 251; 523.
18 *Ibid.*
19 Melden, 1956.
20 Hume, 253; 525.
21 Reid, 1895, 664; A.P., V.VI.
22 *Ibid.*
23 Reid, 1895, 669: A.P., V.VI.
24 Hume, 251; 523.
25 Robins, 1976, 332j cf. Anscombe, 1978.
26 Searle, 1969.
27 *Ibid.*, 188–9.

JOHN BRICKE

Hume's Volitions

I WISH TO explore some of the *many* things Hume says about volitions. I stress the word 'many' to counter an impression that he himself gives, an impression reinforced by those few of his commentators who have discussed the matter at all, that he has little to say about volitions. He remarks: 'by the *will*, I mean nothing but *the internal impression we feel and are conscious of, when we knowingly give rise to any new motion of our body, or new perception of our mind*'.[1] This impression, he then says, "tis impossible to define, and needless to describe any farther'.[2] Perhaps misled by the second remark most commentators have focused almost exclusively on the first. Those who have taken a broader view have noted only those passages in which Hume likens volitions to passions or in which he denies that a volition and its upshot are non-inductively related. On the commentators' showing, there is just not much to comment about. It is not surprising, then, to find Penelhum claiming that Hume's doctrine of volitions is 'fragmentary' and 'vestigial', that Hume denies volitions 'any theoretical significance whatever'.[3]

Now in fact Hume says a great deal about volitions. To be sure, what he says is scattered about his writings and is often incidental to his discussion of such other matters as causation, the passions, assessment, or practical reasoning. At no one place does he present a full-dress theory for our inspection; and even when one assembles what he does say into one place no *quite* finished theory emerges. There are matters on which he is silent, or on which he does not speak clearly. On at least one fundamental point he is clearly mistaken. What he says is nonetheless of exceptional interest: in part because of its direct contribution to sound theory; in part because it assists our framing of the philosophical questions that need to be asked. At a time when the long-suspect notion of volitions is undergoing rehabilitation, a close textual and critical study of Hume's neglected views would seem to be in order.

After some terminological preliminaries I shall examine

Hume's thesis that volitions are internal impressions, his account of the causal setting for volitions, his characterization of their objects and their effects, and what he says about the place of volitions in an analysis of action. At the end I shall consider his reasons for assigning volitions the theoretical significance that he clearly does assign to them.

Hume links volitions with actions, but in what sense of the term 'action'? At times Hume's 'action' is simply a substitute for an equally colourless 'event' or 'process' or 'operation'.[4] His contrast of 'actions of the mind' and 'actions of matter'[5] is just a contrast of mental and physical events. That between 'internal actions' and 'external actions'[6] *need* do no more in context than distinguish mental and specifically bodily events. As both etymology and Hume's actual practice suggest, however, the palmary sense of 'action', that to which the notion of volitions is directly pertinent, is that of 'voluntary action'.[7] 'Voluntary actions' are subject to the agent's will: they involve 'actions of the will'[8], 'operations of the will'[9], 'willing[s]'[10], 'act[s] of volition',[11] or 'volition[s].[12] No voluntary actions are free, i.e. undetermined, actions. 'It is not a just consequence', Hume writes, 'that what is voluntary is free'.[13] It is in his voluntary actions, however, that an agent displays his *'power of acting or not acting, according to the determinations of the will'*.[14]

Voluntary actions fall into two groups: those that occur 'when we knowingly give rise to any new motion of our body'; those that occur 'when we knowingly give rise to any . . . new perception of our mind'.[15] There are bodily actions, such as raising one's arm, and mental actions, such as rehearsing a proof in one's head. Instancing a mental action (or a sequence of them) Hume writes: 'by an act or command of our will, we raise up a new idea, fix the mind to the contemplation of it, turn it on all sides, and at last dismiss it for some other idea, when we think we have surveyed it with sufficient accuracy'.[16] We may, he says, 'voluntarily turn our thoughts to any object, and raise up its image in the fancy'.[17]

Voluntary actions are subject to the agent's will via his 'actions of the will', 'operations of the will', 'willings', 'acts of volition', 'volitions'. I take the quoted expressions to be equivalent in Hume's usage, and to be interchangeable with the seemingly more informative 'command[s] of the will'.[18] Apparently Hume is also prepared to substitute 'choice'.[19] Normally 'the will' designates a capacity or faculty of agents: the capacity to have or form volitions, thus to perform actions. (This is not to suggest that, in Hume's view, faculties are irreducible. On the vexed question of

Hume's views about mental dispositions see Bricke, 1980, 46–58.)[20] When 'the will' occurs in the passage with which we began, however, it must be taken as equivalent to 'a volition'.

Hume claims, in the two passages quoted at the start, that volitions are indefinable internal impressions. As impressions they are akin to sensations and passions, and to be contrasted with ideas or thoughts. As indefinable impressions they possess no internal articulation of a certain kind: they are 'simple act[s] of volition'.[21] Though indefinable, however, they take causal descriptions. In this they are 'like . . . pride and humility, love and hatred'[22] about which Hume had earlier written:

> 'tis impossible we can ever, by a multitude of words, give a just definition of them, or indeed of any of the passions. The utmost we can pretend to is a description of them, by an enumeration of such circumstances, as attend them.[23]

As we shall see, the causal story will require the introduction of some very interesting complexities.

Volitions are internal impressions: they are not projected onto the world as colours, shapes and smells are. They also have other perceptions among their causes, in this resembling passions and desires but differing from sensations. Hume likens them to the 'direct passions' (desire and aversion, grief and joy, hope and fear) in two respects: they are 'immediate effects of pain and pleasure'[24], and they are 'propense and averse motions of the mind'.[25] On the first point volitions and the direct passions differ from the 'indirect passions' (pride and humility, love and hatred, benevolence and anger): volitions and the direct passions are not, or do not essentially involve, matters of personal evaluation. On the second point volitions and direct passions differ from such 'pure emotions in the soul'[26] as pride and humility, for they have an intimate link to action.

Unlike thoughts, but like the passions, volitions do not have truth values. Because they are not capable of 'an agreement or disagreement either to *real* relations of ideas, or to *real* existence and matter of fact' it is 'impossible . . . they can be pronounced either true or false'.[27] Nevertheless they have links to thoughts, including in particular thoughts whose contents specify the so-called 'immediate object of volition'.[28] These links must not, however, be misunderstood. A volition is a 'distinct impression'[29] and thus is quite unlike the feeling that in part constitutes a belief or judgment. A feeling of the latter sort 'modif[ies] the conception' of what is believed; it is not 'only annex'd to it [the conception of what is believed], after the same manner that *will* and *desire* are annex'd to particular conceptions

of good and pleasure'.[30] A belief or judgment is a thought modified in a certain way; its modification is, of course, incapable of
independent existence. As distinct impressions Hume's volitions
are logically capable of occurring without the accompanying
thoughts of their objects. (For an examination of Hume's thesis
that belief is a matter of modification of a conception see Bricke,
1980, 112–23.)

Volitions are 'impression[s] we feel and are *conscious of*,
when we *knowingly* give rise to any new motion of our body, or
new perception of our mind' (my emphasis).[31] I shall take it that
Hume denies the possibility of volitions of which one is not
conscious.[32] The interpretation of 'knowingly' is best left until
later.

I have noted several respects in which Hume likens volitions to
passions. According to Penelhum, however, Hume takes volitions to *be*, not merely to be like (direct) passions; to be sure,[33]
Penelhum notes however, that Hume has some uneasiness about
this. He quotes Hume: 'The impressions, which arise from good
and evil most naturally, and with the least preparation are the
direct passions of desire and aversion, grief and joy, hope and
fear, along with volition'.[34] That the passage does not provide
unequivocal support for Penelhum's reading should be clear,
however, if one attends to the role of 'along with' in the shor-
tened form: 'The impressions with property P are the direct
passions, along with volition'. One must likewise attend to the
significantly parallel occurrences of 'into' when Hume writes:
'the propense and averse motions of the mind . . . are diver-
sified into volition, into desire and aversion, grief and joy, hope
and fear'.[35] A distinction is suggested when Hume 'wave[s] the
examination of the will and direct passions, as they appear in
animals'.[36] And, as Penelhum notes, Hume does say that 'the
WILL . . . properly speaking . . . [is] not comprehended
among the passions'.[37] But all is not plain sailing. Having written
of 'the *direct* passions, or the impressions, which arise immediately from good or evil, from pain or pleasure', Hume
proceeds to write that of 'all the immediate effects of pain and
pleasure, there is none more remarkable than the WILL'.[38] And
in a passage Penelhum does not cite Hume writes of a pleasure
that 'produces the direct passions, or the impressions of volition
and desire'.[39]

If Hume believes that volitions are not 'properly speaking'
passions, why the convolutions and worse in the collection of
passages just cited? Perhaps the strain is the product of a conviction that desires and volitions, despite deep differences, must

share a number of crucial properties. Not to note both sides of the coin would be, from Hume's perspective, to make a hash both of practical reasoning and of action. We shall see how this works out as we proceed. On the textual evidence, however, Hume is much less firm than is Locke in distinguishing volition from desire.[40]

Locke's volitions are 'thought[s] of the Mind';[41] Hume's, as we have seen, are distinct impressions. But as Aune has convincingly argued, there are three reasons to scrap this view of Hume's: in introspective terms, the purported distinct impressions seem to be fictions; they seem to be causally unnecessary adjuncts to voluntary movements; and it is difficult to see how their presence or absence can bear on the morally significant distinction between the voluntary and the involuntary.[42] It may well be that certain feelings or sensations are characteristic of voluntary action, at least in certain settings. Hume writes of a feeling of '*nisus*, or strong endeavour'.[43] But as Hume himself notes this feeling must not be identified with volition: it is only felt when we 'exert our force' in the face of resistance, whereas 'in common thinking and motion . . . the effect follows immediately upon the will, without any exertion or summoning up of force'.[44] *Such* feelings, it seems, are better viewed as *effects* of volitions, or of volitions in the face of difficulty.[45]

Little is gained if, mildly emending Hume's official doctrine, one takes volitions to be complexes comprising a Humean distinct impression and a thought (the thought, as Hume would say, of the volition's object). To preserve his deepest insights and at the same time meet Aune's objections Hume must revise his view in a much more drastic way. He must hold that volitions are themselves thoughts. And he must hold that insofar as feeling is essentially involved in volition it is involved in a manner analogous to that in which, on his own account, it is involved in belief. That is to say, he must construe volitions, as he construes judgments, as thoughts 'modified' in a certain way: in neither case does it help to introduce distinct impressions; in each case it is essential that the thoughts be modified in ways that make them more than mere thoughts.

Volition must, of course, be distinguishable from judgment or belief; otherwise utterly fundamental theses in Hume's philosophy of mind and of morals go by the boards. Here one might expect Hume to invoke phenomenologically available differences in the two modes of conception. A far more inviting approach is, however, suggested by his claim that volitions, just as certain passions, are 'propense and averse motions of the mind'.[46] Pursuing this Hume might say that the crucial difference is at least in part one of functional role. Volitions and desires are *conative* thoughts; beliefs are purely *cognitive* ones. Recall that in Hume's view volitions and desires do not take truth values, while beliefs do. His ostensible reason for the claim is that beliefs are, while volitions and desires are not, ideas or thoughts. This central claim can, however, be transposed into the interesting thesis that conative thoughts do not, while cognitive ones do, have truth values. Any thought, whether cognitive or conative, amounts to a representation of reality, but there are alternative modes of representation. To adapt an idea of John Searle's, there is a difference in 'direction of fit'[47]: cognitive thoughts purport to fit the world and thus take truth values; the point of conative thoughts is, roughly, that the world fit them. Cognitive thoughts are like the detective's list of the purchases he observed the suspect to make; conative thoughts are like the shopping list the suspect uses in making his purchases.[48]

The thesis that volitions are conative thoughts is quite obviously not Hume's. It is intended as an improvement on Hume, but one that in all essential respects derives from some or other thesis he defends. It has the added virtue of facilitating our investigation of the other strands in Hume's doctrine of volitions. No ineliminable distortion need be feared, for those other strands can, with a certain loss of brevity, be elaborated either in terms of the official view that volitions are distinct impressions accompanied by thoughts of their objects, or in terms of the mildly emended view mentioned and dismissed above.

Hume thinks of volitions as products of practical reasonings. He ends the second of the two sections of the *Treatise* that concern freedom and determinism by saying: 'having prov'd, that all actions of the will have particular causes, I proceed to explain what these causes are, and how they operate'.[49] He proceeds directly to the section 'Of the influencing motives of the will', a section containing the bare bones of his theory of practical reasoning. There he claims to prove '*first*, that reason alone can never be a motive to any action of the will; and *secondly*, that it can never oppose passion in the direction of the will'.[50] What, then, are the 'particular causes' of actions of the will, or of volitions? The 'two principal parts [of the mind] . . . which are requisite *in all its actions* . . . [are] the affections and understanding' (my italics).[51]

Within the framework of practical reasoning it is one's beliefs and desires, specifically, that result in one's volitions. As cognitive thoughts one's beliefs purport to represent the way the world is, what its causal properties are, and so on. It is only because these cognitive thoughts are beliefs, however, that they can be among 'the governing principles of all our actions'.[52] The 'passions' and 'affections' that operate in practical reasoning are, more narrowly, one's desires, whether these be the direct passions of desire and aversion, or such indirect passions as benevolence, anger or pity. Such 'pure emotions in the soul'[53] as pride and humility do not link up in the right way with action. The passions of love and hatred do so only via the desires (benevolence, anger) that they cause: they 'are not compleated within themselves, nor rest in that emotion, which they produce, but carry the mind to something farther'.[54] As the discussion of determinism makes plain, practical reasoning that leads to a volition is, relative to a set of background conditions, a causally sufficient condition for that volition.

The beliefs, desires and volition that constitute a bit of (completed) practical reasoning are related not only causally but also via their contents. Volitions are *conclusions* of practical reasonings. Hume addresses the intelligible interplay of belief, desire and volition when describing mechanics as 'the art of regulating the motions of bodies *to some design'd end or purpose'*,[55] when describing actions as 'perform'd with a certain design and intention'[56] or with 'knowledge and design',[57] when remarking that one 'will[s] the performance of certain actions as a means of obtaining any desir'd good'.[58] 'The WILL exerts itself', he says, 'when either the good or the absence of the evil may be attain'd by any action of the mind or body'.[59] The role of desire, that which makes a desire a conative thought, is to set possible goals for action, to represent actions or states of affairs as desirable in some or other respect, and thus to provide an impetus to action. (Here I silently introduce the notion that Humean desires are thoughts. This is, of course, literally false. Humean desires, just as Humean volitions, are impressions *accompanied* by thoughts. Hume's account is no more satisfactory in the one case than in the other. As with volitions, however, no ineliminable distortion is introduced if, for brevity's sake, one takes them as conative thoughts.)

Is it *only* volitions that serve as conclusions to practical reasonings? There is no evidence that Hume allows actions in this role; in any event to do so would import confusion. In some contexts, however, Hume has practical reasonings result in intentions. And, though he does not do so uniformly, he tends to distinguish intention or resolution from volition. (He appears to identify them at Hume, 1975, pp.66 and 88, but to distinguish them at p.100 when he writes of 'volitions and intentions'.) When distinguishing them he appeals to temporal considerations: resolution and intention pertain to the future; volition concerns the present. '[T]he will', he writes, 'has an influence only on present actions' and does not 'regard . . . some future time';[60] in the case of 'intentions and resolutions' there is a temporal 'distance from the final determination'.[61] There is thus room for the notion that one might attempt to 'fortify that resolution'.[62] Despite this difference, however, Hume stresses a common feature: each concerns the performance of a particular action. My intention concerns, for example, an 'action, which I am to perform a twelve-month hence'[63]; likewise my 'willing' pertains to my 'present actions'.[64] Apparently Hume holds that whether one's practical reasoning results in a volition or an intention depends on the time of appropriate action relative to the time of one's deliberation. He could simplify matters by treating volitions as a species of intentions, *viz*. the here-and-now ones. There are, however, no unequivocal indications that he is inclined to take this line.[65] Had he done so he might have undercut the familiar objection that it is inappropriate to introduce terms of art, such as 'volition' in a philosophical analysis of mental phenomena.

We are now in a better position to consider the relation of volition to desire. I suggested earlier that a certain strain detectable in what Hume says on the question whether volitions are passions may arise from a conviction that desires and volitions are both deeply akin and deeply different. I suggested, too, that Hume's views about practical reasoning and action require him to stress both the similarities and the differences. The similarities are readily apparent. Both volitions and desires have contents. In the context of practical reasoning their contents must intersect in suitable ways with one another, and with the requisite beliefs. (Here, of course, is the basic reason for treating volitions and desires as thoughts.) Neither volitions nor desires take truth values, for neither has the appropriate 'direction of fit'. Each has a conative link to conduct that belief does not have: to speak metaphorically, each moves the agent to action, or inclines him to move, and does not simply capacitate him for action by showing him that action is possible or how it is to be accomplished. Recall that both volition and desire are 'immediate effects of pain and pleasure'.[66] In Hume's view one desires to secure what one takes to be, or to be likely to produce, pleasure, and to avoid what one believes to be painful. In forming a volition one (normally) takes the steps judged necessary, here and now, to secure those objectives. If one thinks of desires as analogous to major premises in (Aristotelian) practical syllogisms, volitions, viewed as conclusions, must share with them that fundamental feature that sets them apart from beliefs.

Despite their likenesses, volition and desire have quite different functional locations in practical reasoning. When one reflects on this fact further differences suggest themselves, though these go largely unnoted by Hume. One can have competing desires at a given time with respect to some action; one can not form competing volitions at a time with respect to that action. One's desires can concern the future; one's volitions concern the here and now. One's desires can be unspecific, indeterminate (that the world be made safe for democracy); one's volitions must be much more specific, must be informed (with a qualification to be entered later) by fairly concrete notions of how one is to accomplish what one sets oneself to do. One can desire without believing the desire satisfiable; one can form volitions only concerning what one believes to be within one's power. (We shall see Hume's elaboration of this point below.) One can desire that something happen without believing that it will; to form the volition to do A, however, is to believe in A's occurring. A further deep difference will emerge at p.99 below. (Here I am influenced by Harman and by Davidson's discussions in *Essays on Actions and Events*. Neither Harman nor Davidson would, I take it, endorse volitions. I have omitted the qualifications needed to make each point *quite* right.)

Hume says a great deal about the effects of volitions. He also argues, quite elaborately, that causal links between volitions and their effects are to be discovered only inductively. He argues this while recognising that there is (the word is not his) an internal relation between a volition and certain of its effects.

That Hume views the connection between volitions and their effects as an inductive connection is plain. '[T]he will being here consider'd as a cause', he says, 'has no more a discoverable connexion with its effects, than any material cause has with its proper effect'.[67] In the *Abstract* he writes: 'When we consider our will or volition *a priori*, abstracting from experience, we should never be able to infer any effect from it'.[68] And in the first *Enquiry*: 'If we reason *a priori* . . . the wish of a man [may, for aught we know] control the planets in their orbits'.[69]

He offers three considerations in support of this thesis for the case of bodily actions. Psychophysical connections, thus connections between volitions and bodily events, are 'extraordinary' and obviously 'beyond our comprehension'.[70] It is surely an *a posteriori* question which organs of the body we can move voluntarily and whether all individuals are the same in this respect.[71] And it is an illusion to think one comprehends the connection between a volition and even a simple arm movement when one may be utterly ignorant about the complex physiological mechanisms that subserve that very connection.[72] The case of mental actions is no different: the 'empire of the will over our mind [is no] more intelligible' than is its empire over the body; the 'effect is there distinguishable from the cause, and cou'd not be foreseen without the experience of their constant conjunction'.[73] Again three supporting considerations are introduced. The manner in which a volition produces its mental effect 'is entirely beyond our comprehension'.[74] It is an *a posteriori* question what control we in general have over our minds: 'The command of the mind over itself is limited . . . and these limits are not known by reason, or any acquaintance with the nature of cause and effect, but only by experience and observation'.[75] Then, too, the scope of effective volition varies with circumstances, so can only be known inductively: 'We are more master of our thoughts in the morning than in the evening: Fasting, than after a full meal'.[76]

Elaborating his arguments for the case of bodily actions Hume writes:

> [T]he immediate object of power in voluntary motion, is not the member itself which is moved, but certain muscles, and nerves, and animal spirits, and, perhaps, something still more minute and more unknown, through which the motion is successively propagated, ere it reach the member itself whose motion is the immediate object of volition . . . Here the mind wills a certain event: Immediately another event, unknown to ourselves, and totally different from the one intended, is produced: This event produces another, equally unknown: Till at last, through a long succession, the desired event is produced.[77]

The passage reveals three fundamental elements in the view of volitions with which he is working. First, there is an internal connection between a volition and certain effects of special interest, in the sense of an internal connection between 'the immediate object of volition' and 'the desired event [that] is produced'. This connection does not obtain between the volition and certain other of its effects, including all its unknown physiological effects. The point, it seems, is that the content of a volition incorporates a specification of a certain event, which event is, for certain standard cases at any rate, in fact an effect of that volition. When one wills to raise one's arm one's volition makes reference to the movement of one's arm; it does not likewise make reference to those physiological events (also effects of the volition) that subserve the arm's moving. For brevity's sake we may call the effect a volition specifies in this way its *upshot*.

Why, in Hume's example, is the object of volition, an arm movement, not a physiological event? It is a matter of the agent's knowledge: the agent knows nothing of the physiological events in question but is assumed, I take it, to have the movement of his arm in mind. One can have as object of one's volitions, one can in the palmary sense *do*, only what one can and does represent as occurring. Thus it is that, when introducing volitions, Hume stresses our *knowingly* giving rise to new bodily movements or new perceptions. Insofar as one is not cognisant in this way of the effects of one's volitions one acts 'ignorantly and casually'[78]; such effects of volitions are 'involuntary and accidental'.[79]

A third element in Hume's view is that of basic actions, or of acting, to use a phrase of Harman's, 'in the normal simple way'.[80] '[N]ature', Hume writes, 'has taught us the use of our limbs, without giving us the knowledge of the muscles and nerves, by which they are actuated'.[81] In his example the agent moves his arm while knowing nothing about *how* he does it. The movement of his arm is 'the *immediate* object of volition' (my emphasis): it is not brought about by the bringing about of something else, where that something else is itself an object of volition. (Would knowing the physiology of arm movements enable one to have the relevant physiological events as immediate objects of volitions? As non-immediate objects of volitions? One can imagine how Hume might go here, but he says nothing directly to either question.)

By implication Hume must countenance non-immediate objects of volition. How are they to be characterised? Perhaps he thinks that the further ends with which one acts can be, or are, embedded in the contents of one's volitions, that one's volitions recapitulate, as it were, the salient elements in the practical reasonings that give rise to them. He does, after all, write of deeds 'perform'd with a certain design and intention'[82], or 'from a particular fore-thought and design'.[83] And he does, in the long passage quoted above, identify the event willed with 'the desired event'. He offers no explicit account of non-immediate objects of volition, however, and says nothing of the questions of individuation that their admission raises.

Another passage introduces yet other elements in Hume's

working view of volitions. He remarks that a 'man, suddenly struck with palsy in the leg or arm, or who had newly lost those members, frequently endeavours, at first to move them, and employ them in their usual offices'.[84] Such an individual forms volitions of the arm-moving or leg-moving kind; he is assumed 'to command such limbs'.[85] So one may form volitions that fail to have their normal effects, even in the case of basic bodily actions; volitions may fail to produce their normal upshots if the subserving mechanisms fail to work. In the cases Hume has in mind, however, the amputation is recent and the palsy sudden. Hume is apparently thinking of cases where the amputee or the palsied person fails, at the time for acting, to realise that the movement of a limb is not within his power. This suggests that were the amputee fully cognisant of the absence of his limb and the palsied person aware of the loss of control over his arm neither would be capable of forming the volitions that, without that knowledge, each forms. Believing oneself capable of acting in a certain way is a necessary condition for forming a volition so to act.

What bodily actions are within one's power is, of course, an empirical question. Some scattered remarks suggest a few obvious generalisations with respect to actions done in the normal simple way. Only movements of one's own body are subject to one's voluntary control in this way. Only some of one's parts or organs are subject to direct control: 'the will [has] an influence over the tongue and fingers, not over the heart or liver'.[86] Of course there are individuals who depart from the norm. Hume mentions paralytics and persons with palsy. There are also individuals capable of voluntary bodily movement outside the normal range: Indian fakirs, say, and people who can wiggle their ears. And what Hume says of mental actions holds of bodily actions as well: one's 'self-command is very different at different times'.[87] In the course of maturation and decline the scope of one's voluntary bodily control changes; and an individual usually capable of a certain bodily movement may, in unusual circumstances such as extreme fatigue, temporarily lose that ability. Given what we saw above of belief, these empirically ascertainable limitations must be mirrored (for true believers, at any rate) in the contents of one's volitions.

What, now, of the empirically ascertainable limits to volition for the case of mental actions? What limits are there to possible immediate objects of volition in their case? Presumably Hume would say of sensations roughly what he says of the passions or sentiments. The latter cannot be immediate objects of volition: they 'depend . . . not on the will, nor can be commanded at pleasure'[88]; they 'must be excited by nature, . . . and must arise from the particular situation, in which the mind is placed at any particular juncture'[89]; and ''tis certain we can naturally no more change our own sentiments, than the motions of the heavens'.[90] One has, of course, some measure of indirect control here; one can put oneself in circumstances that one believes will generate or eliminate, dampen or encourage, certain sentiments. Even so, 'our authority over our sentiments and passions is much weaker than that over our ideas'.[91] One hasn't the power, in the direct way here in question, to will to have, and thereby to have, the sentiments of fear, hope, grief, joy, love, hatred, and so on. The passions are not basic actions.

In the first *Enquiry* Hume asserts that we have some 'authority . . . over our ideas' although this 'authority is circumscribed within very narrow boundaries'.[92] He omits this qualification in the *Treatise*: 'The mind has the command over all its ideas, and can separate, unite, mix, and vary them, as it pleases'.[93] One may '*voluntarily* repeat any idea'.[94] And as we noticed much earlier, one has the capacity voluntarily to fix one's attention, to pursue a certain line of reflection, to abandon it. One has some measure of direct control over what one will imagine or think about. Imagining and thinking are possible immediate objects of volition, things that one can do in the normal simple way. Imagining and thinking can be – though they need not be – human actions in the palmary sense; they can, in the requisite way, be upshots of volition. One's beliefs, however, are not within one's direct control: 'belief consists merely in a certain feeling or sentiment; in something, that depends not on the will, but must arise from certain determinate causes and principles, of which we are not masters.[95] One must not be misled by a seeming implication of Hume's claim that 'actions are more voluntary than our judgments'[96]; Hume's position is that all actions are voluntary, while beliefs or judgments have no direct tie to volition whatever.

What of one's various mental dispositions, one's abilities, proclivities, traits of character, and the rest? One cannot – in the direct way in question – alter one's abilities or change one's character. Indeed, one's ability to exercise even indirect control over one's qualities of mind is severely limited. 'Moral virtues' such as 'constancy, fortitude, magnanimity' are 'equally involuntary and necessary, with the qualities of the judgment and imagination'.[97] Indeed, one 'might say the same in some degree, of the others [the other moral virtues]; it being almost impossible for the mind to change its character in any considerable article, or cure itself of a passionate or splenetic temper, when they are natural to it'.[98] How much indirect control one has is, of course, an empirical matter, but the following rough generalisation holds true: so-called natural abilities 'are almost invariable by any art or industry'; so-called moral qualities, 'or at least, the actions, that proceed from them, may be chang'd by the motives of rewards and punishments, praise and blame'.[99] Presumably, then, there is some scope for one's own efforts at altering one's proclivities. Hume's most interesting example along these lines concerns a strategy that in his view lies at the basis of civil government and society:

> Men are not able radically to cure, either in themselves or others, that narrowness of soul, which makes them prefer the present to the remote. They cannot change their natures. All they can do is to change their situation, and render the observance of justice the immediate interest of some particular persons, and its violation their more remote.[100]

What, finally, of volitions themselves? Can they be objects of volitions? When discussing promising Hume argues that to 'will the volition . . . is plainly absurd and impossible'.[101] As the context makes plain, however, what Hume objects to is the curious thesis that a volition might have *itself* both as object and upshot: 'The will has here no object to which it cou'd tend; but must return upon itself *in infinitum*'.[102] On the question whether a volition may take *another* volition as object and upshot, and thus whether volitions may themselves be items under one's control, he is, unfortunately, silent.

If Harman is right (and I think he is), intentions are self-referential. 'The intention to do A', he argues, 'is the intention that, because of that very intention, it is guaranteed that one will do A'.[103] A 'positive intention', he says, is 'a self-referential conception that something is going to happen as a result of that very conception'.[104] But as was suggested earlier, a Humean volition is indistinguishable from a here-and-now intention. So a Humean volition ought to be a self-referential conception that something is going to happen as a result of that very conception. Of course, Hume nowhere treats volitions in this way. It is important to be clear, however, that his remarks about the absurdity of a volition's having itself as object and upshot are quite irrelevant to the question of self-referentiality. The content of a self-referential volition makes reference to the volition itself, but the volition's upshot is a logically distinct action or event. (Incidentally, if volitions are in this way self-referential this is another deep respect in which they differ from desires.)

One assumes that the point of a doctrine of volitions is to elucidate the notion of action. So far, however, we have discovered nothing about how Hume's introduction of volitions is designed to serve this elucidatory task. Does Hume take volitions themselves to be actions? Does he construe the upshots of volitions as actions? Are the immediate objects of volitions to be understood as actions? Let us turn to these fundamental questions.

Perhaps Hume takes volitions to be actions, for he writes of 'actions of the will' and of 'act[s] of volition', as we saw much earlier. Perhaps he construes the upshots of volitions as actions; he writes of 'motives, volitions and actions'[105] and of 'passions, volitions, and actions'[106], thus perhaps suggesting that just as motives or passions prompt volitions, so volitions prompt actions. Penelhum appears to think that, in Hume, both volitions and their upshots are actions: 'volitions, or *acts* of will, . . . [are] the immediate causes of *action*' (my italics).[107] Árdal apparently agrees for the case of a volition's upshot: 'the relation between what we call a volition and the *action* is no more intelligible than any other *causal* succession'.[108] (my italics.) But there is room for misgiving. Perhaps Hume's use of the term 'action' is the colourless, general-purpose use detected earlier. And what of passages in which the language of action is eschewed (at least with respect to upshots)? '[T]he motions of our body . . . obey the will', Hume writes; and there is no intelligible connection between 'an act of volition, and a motion of the body'.[109] Then, again, it would be a mistake to hang a substantial claim on such turns of phrase; on a single page of the first *Enquiry* Hume writes both that an 'act of volition produces *motion* in our limbs' and that 'by the simple command of our will, *we* can *move* the organs of our body' (my italics).[110]

In the remark just quoted, and elsewhere[111], Hume likens volitions to commands. But to command is to act. Is this an indication that, in Hume's view, to form a volition is likewise to act?

On Hume's own account of things an ordinary speech act of issuing a command must involve both a volition and the uttering of the appropriate words. To what, then, is a volition to be likened? To the volition involved in commanding? To the complex that includes the volition involved in commanding? Clearly neither comparison will shed any light on the question whether volitions are actions. Is a volition to be likened to the uttering of words (the upshot) involved in the issuing of a command? But then it is no more clear what we are to say of volitions themselves than it is what we are to say of a volition's upshot. Perhaps both are actions. Then, again, perhaps neither is.

The point of the analogy is, I suggest, quite different. Since assertions are no less actions than commands are, it must be the differences between them that illuminate the nature of volition. Commands and assertions differ in their 'direction of fit': with commands the world is to fit the command; with assertions it is the other way around. In this respect volitions are like commands. Commands do not take truth values; assertions do. Once again volitions are like commands. In a word, the analogy is designed to point up the conative character of volition. This comes out plainly enough when, invoking a broader notion of command, Hume writes that we 'have command over our mind to a certain degree, but beyond *that* lose all empire over it'.[112] It comes out as well when he writes of the will 'governing our thought'[113] and of the will's 'authority'.[114]

Whatever the drift of the scrappy textual evidence, however, it is obvious that if Hume takes volitions, or their upshots, or both, as (intrinsically) actions he is left with nothing illuminating to say about the notion of action, or about the link between volition and action. On such an approach actions are primitive and unanalysable. Now Hume does, on occasion, have recourse to unanalysability; recall what he says both of the passions and of volitions. Within a Humean framework, however, analysis is, whenever possible, to be preferred. And so far as I can see there is nothing in his philosophy that blocks his adopting a reductionist theory of action, one that employs the notion of volition to elucidate that of action. So far as I can see, he could hold the reductionist view that actions are complexes whose characterisation requires an appropriate causal relation between a volition and a bodily movement (in the case of bodily actions) or a volition and a perception (in the case of mental actions). That is to say, he could insist that a volition-cum-upshot *constitutes* an action, and that neither the volition, nor the upshot, is itself an action. As an alternative he could claim that a volition *is* an action *provided that* it is related in the right way to some mental or bodily event. Indeed, he could maintain that bodily or mental upshots *are* actions *provided* they are caused by volitions in the appropriate way. The relative merits of these reductionist alternatives need not detain us. What would count as the appropriateness of the causal connection has been indicated, of course, in our earlier discussions of practical reasoning, of the internal relation between volition and upshot, and so on.

Hume apparently takes the *objects* of volitions to be actions, as when he writes of one's 'willing of these actions' or that one 'may will the performance of certain actions'.[115] This seems the natural thing to do. It also provides a suitable symmetry within the contents of the steps in practical reasoning that lead to volition. One may desire to perform action A, or believe that only by doing action A can one secure some objective. Why, then, say that the product of one's deliberations is not a volition that one do A but only a volition that some event E, not itself an action, take place? The view that volitions take actions as their objects is, it seems, readily fitted to a reductionist theory of action. On one version of such a theory, an agent's action A is analysable into the agent's forming a volition to A and that volition's causing, in the appropriate way, an event E (where E, in the circumstances, is a constituent of A). The agent moves his arm: his volition to move his arm causes his arm's movement (in the right way). Such an account must affect, of course, the rendering one gives of the internal relation between volition and upshot.

In his reflections on volitions Hume attempts to articulate and integrate the joint claims of common sense, science and morality.

From the side of common sense he thinks it obvious that there are volitions. One is immediately aware of them in one's every action; one is aware, by introspection, of their phenomenally distinctive character. There is little, I suggest, to this way of thinking. If there are volitions they are not phenomenologically prominent pushes and pulls but items whose characterisation is, philosophically, a demanding task. Nevertheless volitions, viewed as practical thoughts in the way intimated above, do provide some explication of our common ability to say, without inquiry or inference, what we are doing and why we are doing it. And viewed as practical thoughts they are not especially mysterious things: no materialist need reject them on behalf of his materialism; nor need they violate any laws of nature.

Hume's interest in the philosophical underpinnings of the behavioural sciences leads him to investigate the character of statistical explanation and the relationship between causal explanation and responsibility. It also leads him to sketch out a schema for empirical hypotheses about human action. (He also offers explanations that supposedly fit that schema.) From this perspective, I suggest, he is struck by the combination of causal and other properties of practical reasoning, and by the need to display the causal links between such reasoning and conduct. Settling on an action or course of action is something other than the mere movements or other mere events that result. On the other hand it is not to be confused with the beliefs and desires, or the transitions among beliefs and desires, that are at the back of those movements. From this perspective volitions have a clear-cut theoretical niche. Hume would say of them what Harman says of intentions: 'it seems quite obvious that actions cannot be explained in terms of beliefs and desires alone; these attitudes must be translated into intentions before one can act'.[116]

In this vein Humean volitions, austerely construed, provide an answer to Wittgenstein's famous question: 'what is left over if I subtract the fact that my arm goes up from the fact that I raise my arm?'.[117] Action minus upshot equals volition. That, surely, is one of the intended lessons in Hume's comments about sudden palsy and recent amputation. Given what he holds of the relation between volition and belief, however, Hume could easily say what Vesey says of such cases: 'So far as he, but not necessarily his arm, was concerned, he moved his arm'.[118]

Hume's working model for volitions provides an essential part of the structure in his account of assessment, of praising and blaming, of excusing and holding responsible. The question whether an action is voluntary has, in principle, a straight 'yes' or 'no' answer. Was the action, relative to a given description of it, both object and upshot of a volition? We are 'not blam'd', Hume says, for actions performed 'ignorantly and casually'[119], for what is 'involuntary and accidental'.[120] Such 'actions' are not ours at all; they do not originate in our beliefs and desires in the re-quisite way. *They* reveal nothing about *us*, about our goals or concerns, and so cannot bear in the most direct way on what is, at bottom, the assessment of persons. Assessment is responsive to discoveries about the scope of an agent's voluntary control, both direct and indirect, over what happens. This, as we have seen, Hume thinks to vary, within certain limits, from agent to agent, from situation to situation.

In these several ways Hume's doctrine of volitions bears on his moral psychology. It is not that Hume thinks only the voluntary is subject to assessment; he argues directly against this view. Rather, his doctrine of volitions assists him in giving a clear account of the voluntary and of its distinctive significance for questions of assessment, an account compatible with the claims of behavioural science and the deliverances of common sense.

References to Hume's *Treatise* are to Hume, 1978 and take the form 'T page number.' References to Hume's *Enquiries* are to Hume, 1975 and take the form 'E page number.'

References to Hume's *Abstract* are to Hume, 1938 and take the form 'A page number.'

1 T 399.
2 *Ibid.*
3 Penelhum, 1975, 113 and -17; see also Árdal, 1966, Aune, 1975 and Bennett, 1971.
4 Cf. T 399 with T 400.
5 T 400, -8, -17.
6 T 176, 465.
7 T 406, 609; E 66, 71, 88, 95.
8 T 405, 412, 413; E 67, 94.
9 E 93.
10 T 417.
11 T 415, 632; E 64.
12 T 407, 413, 415, 438, 574; E 69, 73, 88, 100.
13 T 609.
14 E 95.
15 T 399; cf. T 632, E 64, A 21.
16 E 67.
17 E 71.
18 E 67; cf. T 623, 629, E 48, 64, 65.
19 T 467; cf. T 416, 445, E 95.
20 T 439, 632.
21 E 69.
22 T 399.
23 T 277; cf. T 329.
24 T 399.
25 T 574.
26 T 367.
27 T 458; cf. T 415.
28 E 66.
29 T 625.
30 *Ibid.*
31 T 399.
32 See Bricke, 1980, 112–23.
33 Penelhum, 1975, 114.
34 T 438.
35 T 574.
36 T 448.
37 T 399.
38 *Ibid.*
39 T 439.
40 Locke, 1975, II, xxi, 30 and Locke, 1982, letters 2925 and 2979.
41 Locke, 1975, II, xxi, 4.
42 Aune, 1975, pp. 50–1.
43 E 67n.
44 *Ibid.*
45 See Bricke, 1974.
46 T 574.
47 Searle, 1979.
48 See Anscombe, 1963, p. 56.

49 T 412.
50 T 413.
51 T 493.
52 T 629.
53 T 367.
54 *Ibid.*
55 T 414.
56 T 475.
57 T 349.
58 T 417.
59 T 439.
60 T 516; cf. T 574.
61 T 536.
62 T 382.
63 T 586.
64 T 516.
65 Cf. Aune, 1975, Sellars, 1966 and Harman, 1975.
66 T 399.
67 T 632; cf. T 173.
68 A 23.
69 E 164; cf. E 65.
70 E 65.
71 *Ibid.*
72 E 66.
73 T 632.
74 E 68.
75 *Ibid.*, cf. T 632–3.
76 E 68.
77 E 66.
78 T 412.
79 T 350.
80 Harman, 1975, 443.
81 E 55.
82 T 475.
83 T 349.
84 E 66.
85 *Ibid.*
86 E 45.
87 E 68.
88 E 48.
89 *Ibid.*
90 T 517.
91 E 68.
92 *Ibid.*
93 T 623–4; cf. T 629, E 19.
94 T 140.
95 T 624; cf. E 48.
96 T 609.
97 T 608.
98 *Ibid.*
99 T 609.
100 T 537.
101 T 518n.

102 *Ibid.*
103 Harman, 1975, 441.
104 *Ibid.*, 448.
105 T 407; cf. E 91.
106 T 458; cf. T 464.
107 Penelhum, 1975, 113.
108 Árdal, 1966, 83.
109 T 632.
110 E 64.
111 E 48, 67.
112 T 632; cf. T 629, E 67n. 68.
113 A 21.
114 T 633, E 68.
115 T 417.
116 Harman, 1975, 441.
117 Wittgenstein, 1958, I, 621.
118 Vesey, 1964, 55.
119 T 412.
120 T 350.

JOHN J. JENKINS

Hume's Account of Sympathy – Some Difficulties

I SHALL NOT here be concerned with the place which the concept of sympathy occupies in Hume's philosophy but with his account of what happens psychologically when one person sympathises with another. This is stated most clearly in the section in the *Treatise* entitled 'Of the Love of Fame'. It is important to remember that, at this point, the point at which he introduces the concept, sympathy is the name given to a process of communication. It is essentially Hume's account of how a sentiment or emotion is, under certain conditions, transferred from one person to another. It is therefore not itself the name of a sentiment. Our temptation to think of it as such is a strong one because we now associate it with pity or compassion. But, for Hume, sympathy is the means by which pity and compassion, among other sentiments, may be communicated, and hence must be distinguished from them. He himself clearly implies as much.[1] It is, then, with this account of sympathy as a principle of communication that I shall be concerned.

His analysis of the process is basically as follows. External behaviour on the part of x produces an idea of the sentiment, of which it is an expression, on the part of Y, by virtue of Y's experience of a correlation between that kind of behaviour and that kind of sentiment in his own case. Thus far, it is a standard case of the argument by analogy for other minds (though it is doubtful whether Hume saw it in that light). This idea is then converted into an impression whose force and vivacity are such as to render it equal to the sentiment itself. That is, Y's idea of x's anger becomes Y's anger. Hume is emphatic about this last aspect. He does not mean that the anger in Y is a simulated anger: it is, in Hume's words, an 'original affection'. The conversion is effected by means of the impression of the self imparting some of its vivacity to the idea of x's sentiment.

There are a number of difficulties which I want to discuss in connection with this account, most of them internally related to Humean psychology, some of them of a more general character.

The first of these concerns the explanatory function which the impression of the self performs. It is not clear that Hume adequately explains why the impression of the self in particular should enliven the appropriate idea, since it is a part of the doctrine of impressions and ideas that all impressions have this tendency to impart their liveliness to associated ideas.[2] It is of course natural to answer on Hume's behalf that the impression of the self is stronger and more intense, as well as more constant, than other impressions, hence accounting for its superior influence, but it then poses a more general difficulty for the doctrine. If the impression is constantly present, constantly stronger in influence, how can Humean psychology allow for any *other* impression to enliven any other idea at all? This would appear to be feasible only if the impression of the self recedes in vivacity and constancy. From a purely matter of fact point of view we would probably accept that this occurs: we are not always vividly aware of ourselves. But it looks as though Hume cannot admit this and also claim that the reason why the impression of the self, as opposed to some other impression, imparts its vivacity is on account of its superior force, vivacity and constancy. If that impression is always 'intimately present with us', it is presumably a continuous obstacle to the more general process he wishes to speak about. For this reason, one might be tempted to speculate that when Hume restates the account of sympathy in Bk III, Part III, Section I, the omission of any reference to the offending impression is deliberate.

The second difficulty concerns Hume's right to speak about an impression of the self at all. He is criticised for doing so by J. A. Passmore,[3] by Jonathan Harrison[4] and by others. The problem is the obvious one, that it was apparently this impression of the self whose existence Hume had denied in the section on Personal Identity in Book I[5]; yet here he freely asserts it. One must say immediately that both Passmore and Harrison are a little less than charitable. The impression which Hume failed to discover in Book I was that of an underlying substance or ego. He does not deny that one might have an impression of the self which is given currency in terms of particular perceptions. Indeed, he himself, in the section on Pride and Humility, defines the self as a 'connected succession of perceptions'.[6] Therefore, once one recognises what the impression of the self amounts to for Hume, the inconsistency of which he is accused simply dissolves.

One related problem remains at this point. We have seen that, according to Hume, the impression of the self is always 'intimately present to us'[7], and we have seen that only by virtue of its constant liveliness is it possible for Hume to explain how it is always so readily available to impart its vivacity to an associated idea. But now, in order to serve the interests of his psychology, it seems as though Hume is asserting something which is empirically false. Is this impression of the self always in the centre of the picture in the sense that is required? Certainly it is true that, as reflective human beings, we are constantly doing or undergoing things, and in that sense we may, from our own point of view, be at the heart of the picture as a kind of agency. But clearly that is not the centrality of the self which Hume's doctrine requires. What that doctrine requires is the sort of highlighted consciousness of self which one might achieve in moments of meditation or introspection, self-examination or acute embarrassment. Sartre drew attention to an emphasised form of self-consciousness in the famous illustration of the engrossed key-hole peeper.

> Let us imagine that, moved by jealousy, curiosity, or vice I have just glued my ear to the door and looked through a keyhole. I am alone . . . I am a pure consciousness of things . . . there is no self to inhabit my consciousness . . . But all of a sudden I hear footsteps in the hall. Someone is looking at me. What does this mean? . . . It is (the) eruption of the self.[8]

There is, as one might put it, a full flush of self-consciousness in these circumstances. And one can easily think of other comparable situations. Now, no one supposes that this illuminated state could be a sustained or permanent one. Yet Hume's psychology at this point seems to require that it be so. How else can he explain how it is constantly available as a source of vivacity for the idea of some other person's sentiment? It is difficult to see how Hume can be rescued from this particular problem without his surrendering the claim that the impression of the self is constantly present. And if this claim were to be retracted it would, as we have seen, make it difficult for him to explain why that impression in particular should enliven an associated idea.

The third difficulty relates to Hume's quite casual assumption that sympathy explains not only the communication of emotions but also that of factual beliefs or opinions.[9] Intuitively, one might well find this unacceptable since beliefs, unlike sentiments or passions, are often seen as resulting from reflection and consideration; whereas, on Hume's account of the sympathetic mechanism, a belief which was sympathetically induced would be directly communicated. The thought of x's belief would be transformed into the belief itself.

In his book on Hume, P. S. Árdal acknowledges that the enlivening of the idea of a belief into belief itself may seem strange, but he thinks that reflection upon the matter will show the view to be perfectly natural.[10] In this connection, he invites us to consider the person who is constantly subjected to the widespread opinion that horsemeat is poisonous, and who consequently comes to believe this for himself. 'The thought of their belief that horsemeat is poisonous is repeatedly raised in his mind by their talk and by their actions . . . This recurrence of the thought in his mind may in time lead him to share the belief of others that horsemeat is, indeed, poisonous.'[11]

This illustration makes out a plausible case for the communication of belief, but the trouble with any example of this sort is that, while it may be susceptible to a Humean interpretation, invoking his account of sympathy, it does not obviously demand such an explanation; and unless it demands it, the illustration simply will not automatically show that the process has occurred, much less that it commonly occurs. It is not even clear from the illustration, as it stands, whether it really would be a case in which the *thought* of a belief that x is succeeded by a belief that x, quite apart from a sympathetic connection between the two states. It has the 'look' of a situation in which a man defers to a certain kind of social pressure, a man who 'crumbles' psychologically, not having evaluated the proposition for himself, and whose subsequent behaviour on the appropriate occasions becomes inhibited or is automatically channelled in a certain direction. We might well think that this does not amount to believing the proposition that horsemeat is poisonous. Much will depend upon what one takes to be the essence of belief. But there is at least a prima facie distinction between, on the one hand, believing a certain proposition and, on the other hand, simply being susceptible to associations which inhibit one's behaviour. It might be suggested, for example, that in Árdal's illustration, the effect of other people's opinions about the poisonous qualities of horsemeat is to inhibit the person in the relevant situations in such a way that, when he is offered horsemeat, he cannot help an aversion to it – not because he believes it is poisonous but because he cannot help associating it with things poisonous whenever the subject is raised or whenever the meat is put before him. Confronted by such behaviour, of course, one might say that, in some circumstances, that is just what we mean by belief, and that these are just the circumstances in which we would say it, as indeed Árdal seems to be doing. But this could be misleading if the agent denies believing the relevant proposition. The situation would not be unlike that in which a person is inclined to say 'I don't honestly believe that this house is haunted, but I can't help the creepy feelings and the gooseflesh which come over me whenever I enter it'. Or again, consider a statement of the form 'I cannot help thinking of x as a criminal because he so closely resembles y, whom I *know* to be a criminal'. It is not immediately obvious that a believing state is involved in this or the previous example. Nor, then, is it obvious that belief is involved in the case of the man who cannot bring himself to eat horsemeat. To insist that there is belief in these cases, regardless of the agent's affirmations and denials, would be to make the behavioural symptoms a sufficient condition of belief. It seems to me that this would be an extreme view. Ryle might be thought to come nearest to it, considering his general thesis in *The Concept of Mind*, but he nevertheless maintains (p.134) that belief is propositional and that 'to believe that the ice is dangerously thin is, among other things, to be unhesitant in telling oneself and others that it is thin . . .' He thus seems to concede that belief is not simply a matter of external behaviour involving no reference to the agent's avowals and denials. It is not to the point in this paper to go into the issue in great depth, but two main remarks are worth making. Firstly, if believing is taken to be a characteristically human phenomenon, divorced from an animal-like reaction to stimuli, it is difficult to see how a view which allows behaviour to be a sufficient condition, independent of agent assent, can do justice to this fact. Secondly, the view would seem to militate against certain distinctions which, ordinarily, we might wish to preserve. We might, for example, wish to characterise what the above situations have in common as cases of 'acting as if' (something were the case) and to distinguish them from believing. Yet someone who held that behaviour was a sufficient condition for belief may well have to deny the validity of such a distinction. J. Cook Wilson once delineated a state which he called 'being under the impression that'. H. A. Prichard unearthed a comparable state which he termed 'thinking without question', and H. H. Price, largely on the basis of Cook Wilson and Prichard, drew attention to a state which he called 'taking for granted'. All of these states were explicitly contrasted with believing. It is true that these writers subscribed to an episodic analysis of belief, the view that it necessarily consisted in a kind of mental activity, and this has significant consequences for the distinction they wish to make. It is also true that they endorse an over-rationalist analysis of the concept, such that Price, for example, could happily include in his analysis such mental components as entertaining p, having evidence for p, preferring p to q, and feeling confident in relation to p, thus allowing an easy contrast with possible states which approach or simulate belief but do not quite get there.

But a distinction between a state of believing and neighbouring states does not necessarily hang upon either a mental episode view or on an over-rationalist view of belief. There is a passage in Wittgenstein's *Investigations*[12], to which Peter Winch draws our attention in a recent article[13] and in which Wittgenstein appears to distinguish between a belief, on the one hand, and an attitude on the other. Wittgenstein holds that, while it is appropriate to say 'I believe that he is suffering', it is not appropriate to say 'I believe that he is not an automaton'. Wittgenstein's point seems to be that, where no question has arisen about a certain state of affairs, no information can be conveyed by a statement of belief concerning its existence. Thus, Wittgenstein wants to say, in my dealings with a person, my attitude towards him is 'an attitude towards a soul'. The emphasis is upon 'attitude'. It is not that 'I am of the opinion that he has a soul' or that 'I believe he is not an automaton'. It is rather that my regarding him as a soul involves a sort of 'taking for granted', a primitive acknowledgement of the fact that that is what he is. Partly, Winch wants to say, Wittgenstein sees this attitude as something for which I am not responsible: I do not deliberately choose to adopt it. It is in that sense something primitive and unreflective. Winch quotes, in illustration, a passage from Simone Weil in which she says: 'A person who crosses our path does not turn aside our steps in the same manner as a street sign, no one stands up or moves about, or sits down again in quite the same fashion when he is alone in a room as when he has a visitor'. Describing our behaviour in this sort of context as being deliberative, or as being the result of a *belief* that a person is present, simply misconstrues what is going on. In these circumstances, I find myself unconsciously acting in these ways.

Where does all this get us in relation to Hume? It reinforces the claim, made earlier, that belief is not necessarily what follows from the process of sympathetic communication as depicted in Árdal's type of example. Being exposed to the view that horsemeat is poisonous may certainly result in an attitude to horsemeat and the eating of it, something which one falls into undeliberatively, as Winch might put it; but there may well be something wrong about saying that the person concerned has formed the opinion that the meat is poisonous. And what must follow from this is that perhaps Hume is wrong in thinking that opinions can be sympathetically communicated in the same way as sentiments.

To return to an earlier point, even if we grant that a believing state succeeds the pressures of widespread opinion, as Árdal depicts it, it does not follow that it is the result of sympathetic communication. There are other, perfectly standard, ways in which belief comes about, and we should require reasons for discounting these before Árdal's conclusion can be comfortably drawn. For example, it is obvious that a man may be so impressed by the force or the vigour with which some other person holds a certain belief that he makes independent investigations, and comes to believe the proposition himself as a result. Or again, a person may recognise that those who hold a certain belief are the sort of people whose beliefs or opinions can be relied upon, and who endorses the belief as a consequence. And there are many whose beliefs are arrived at on a vaguely numerical basis; a consideration of the mere number of people who hold a certain view is sufficient to influence them. Admittedly, there is nothing particularly rational about the way in which such beliefs are arrived at, but at the very least one wants to say that they are 'considered' beliefs: they are not purely and simply the result of sympathetic communication, if only because they involve an intervening thought.

There is one passage in which Hume refers us to the phenomenon of what we would now call psychosomatic illness[14], as though by way of support for his view that sentiments or opinions can be transferred by means of sympathy. 'We may feel sickness and pain from the mere force of imagination', he says, 'and make a malady real by often thinking about it.' If this *is* being invoked as support for his general view, then clearly what Hume means is that we should find his view of the sympathetic mechanism acceptable in relation to opinions or sentiments because it involves no more and no less than is involved in psychosomatic illness, the occurrence of which we already accept as a fact. Psychosomatic illness, as he implies in the text, is an example of a lively idea being converted into an impression. There are two remarks I should want to make about this, on the assumption that it is a reinforcing argument on Hume's part. Firstly, we would obviously want to protest that psychosomatic pains of the sort to which he is referring demand a more complex explanation than Hume allows and that therefore they are not comparable with mere sympathetic communication. For him, they seem to involve no more than the act of 'staring' repeatedly at the idea of pain in some other person. Repetition has an enlivening effect upon the idea so as to convert it into an impression. But this is hardly a sufficient condition for psychosomatic complaints. At the very least we should probably want to say that there must be, in addition, some element of obsessive wishes, or obsessive fears. However, it must be said in fairness to Hume that this reflects upon the inadequacy rather than the inaccuracy of his psychology. After all, Hume himself had qualified his account of sympathy with the proviso that the phenomenon occurs more readily when blood ties, friendship, contiguity in place and time, etc. are involved, and it seems reasonable to infer that comparable provisos would have been made about psychosomatic maladies had he been concerned to give the matter more detailed attention.

But the second and more crucial comment is that, even if we were to allow that pains and illness may be sympathetically induced, there is no logical transition from this to the claim that opinions and beliefs may be so induced. It is presumably a fact that if a man is exposed often enough to the malady of another, he may come to display identical symptoms, at least granted certain other conditions, and we may want to agree that the psychological process involved does bear some resemblance to that which Hume calls sympathy. In a superficially comparable fashion, if a man is exposed constantly to the belief of another, he may acquire that belief for himself, as we saw in Árdal's example. What is important is that the occurrence of psychosomatic maladies will not *show* that such beliefs are sympathetically induced, as opposed to being the result of an intervening reflection of the sort mentioned earlier. This is because there is an important difference between the state of being ill, or displaying the symptoms of an illness, on the one hand, and the state of believing on the other. It is perhaps best put by saying that believing is something essentially propositional. Indeed, Hume himself often seems to hold this view. But is there anything propositional about being ill? Of course x being ill may be accompanied by x believing that he is ill, or again his believing himself ill may have been instrumental in inducing the illness. But then it is not x's *belief* concerning his illness that Hume is drawing our attention to at this point, but rather *his illness*. It is the process of 'making the malady real' that Hume points to – the *idea* of illness being transformed into a *sensation* of illness. In short, then, although there is a superficial resemblance between the way in which psychosomatic illness comes about and the way in which opinions are sometimes generated, nevertheless the clear difference between being ill and holding an opinion makes it quite implausible to use the occurrence of the former as an argument for the occurrence of the latter.

Now some further difficulties. The first concerns the 'object' of a sympathetically induced sentiment. As we have already seen, Hume appears to think that, provided I am closely enough related to x and can observe his external behaviour, this will be sufficient to enable me to share his anger, for example, if he happens to be angry. According to the official doctrine, the idea of x's anger is enlivened in my mind by the impression of myself, enlivened to such a degree that the mere idea of anger becomes anger itself. Those are the relevant facts in his initial analysis of sympathy. The potential objection is that, whether or not Hume's analysis is psychologically correct, it must surely be a precondition of its occurring that I know what x is angry *about*. It is precisely this that I may not know merely by observing the external symptoms of anger. The same point could be made about sorrow, grief, joy, jealousy, malice, and many other senti-ments. It is rather as though Hume has assumed that in perceiv-ing the behavioural symptoms of a person's anger (among other emotions) I simultaneously perceive the object at which the anger is directed. It is obvious that this is not necessarily the case. Where it is not the case, it is difficult to see how the idea of another person's anger can be converted into my real anger if there is nothing about which I can be angry.

There are two possible defences of Hume on this issue. One would be to say that, though I may not know what it is that x is angry about, nevertheless it can be said that his emotion has been communicated to me if I, in turn, simply vent my anger upon anything or anyone appropriately at hand. I would not then have to know the cause or the source of x's anger in order to be angry myself due to sympathy.

This is unacceptable on the face of it. Naturally it is possible for y to be angry upon seeing x angry and without knowing why x is angry; but this surely has to be a case in which there is an independent reason for y's anger. It seems unlikely that he can simply decide to become angry willy-nilly, and if he is ignorant of the source of x's anger then it seems as though his anger must have an independent cause. x's anger would have to constitute in itself a *reason* for y being angry. y, for example, might be an office sub-manager who feels his security or his promotion pros-pects threatened whenever his boss becomes angry, and so this becomes the reason for his own annoyance with his subordinates. He 'takes it out' on them, as we say.

The point of thus emphasising the independent cause or

reason is just this, that its presence seems to militate against an account in terms of a straightforward sympathetic communication (of anger in this case). Y's anger, in other words, is not simply, if at all, the process of enlivening the idea of x's anger, at least in those cases where, for Y, the source of x's anger remains unknown.

However, having said this, what must now be said is that Hume has an escape-route. One of the distinctive features of Hume's account of the human sentiments is that he sees the relation between an emotion and its object as contingent. That is to say, there is no necessary relation between, for example, anger and the object of anger, between love and the object of love, and between pride and the object of pride. That this is his view is obvious from the famous passage in Bk II, Part II, Section 6[15], and is further reflected in a later passage.[16] But it has the extraordinary result that pride, for example, can exist as pride and can be recognised for what it is independently of the idea of its object, the self. As Hume says in the earlier passage 'If nature had so pleased, love might have had the same effect as hatred, and hatred as love. I see no contradiction in supposing a desire of producing misery annex'd to love, and of happiness to hatred.' This view is, of course, in line with the general account of causality in Book I. No amount of inspection of an object or event, x, will tell us what effect it will produce. Similarly, no amount of inspection of a passion like pride or love will tell us what its object is or what behaviour it is likely to produce. This is something we have to learn inductively from a series of conjunctions, just as we do in the process of becoming acquainted with physical objects. This position therefore entails that we only discover that pride has the self for its object through experience of seeing these two things going together. The passion of pride – an independently existing passion – is invariably accompanied by the idea of the self; we notice this and make the usual inferences. We cannot discover this from an examination of the passion itself.

Where does all this lead us? The original objection to Hume was that it did not seem possible for x to be sympathetically infected by Y's anger if x does not know what it is that Y is angry about. It was said that Hume has an escape-route, and of course this is to be found in the notion of contingency which we have just discussed. On Hume's view of the passions, they are self-contained, internal occurrences, recognisable independently of the objects at which they are directed. Hence, in practice, what happens is that I observe the symptoms of anger or pride, for example; this provides me with a clue – inductively established – as to what passion is at work in the other individual; and then the sympathetic process can proceed as Hume depicts it. I do not need to know what it is that the other person is angry about, and I do not need to know what he is proud of. The passion is self-contained, and so my idea of it, in so far as I achieve it, is complete. It seems, then, that, in his own terms, Hume is able to answer this particular objection, but at the expense of a very strange psychology.

The other defence of Hume concerning the difficulty over passions and their objects is to say that sympathy simply cannot occur in those cases where the object or source of a passion in another person is not obvious to a spectator. This would be entirely satisfactory, avoiding the problem altogether. It is just that Hume never says this.

There is one final criticism of Hume on sympathy which I will now consider, and this is potentially a devastating one made by J. A. Passmore.[17] Passmore's comments can be paraphrased as follows. When I witness x expressing his anger, what I have an idea of is that of x being angry and not of anger as such. This being the case, since there is only a difference in degree between impressions and ideas, it follows that if this idea is enlivened it will lead not to my anger (as Hume claims) but simply to an impression or more vivid experience of x being angry. It could only lead to my actual anger if there were a change of content as between the impression and the idea, evidently a view which Hume cannot accept. If this is a valid comment, it must surely apply to all communication of sentiments and would therefore undermine the very mechanism of sympathy itself as Hume depicts it. It is not clear that Hume can be finally defended from the charge, but I shall speculate a little, partly about what is involved in Passmore's objection and partly about what Hume might have replied, consistent with the doctrine.

At the heart of Passmore's case is the claim that when we witness x being angry, what we have an idea of is just that, x being angry, and not, as Hume's position would seem to require, anger itself. One must say at the outset that there is an ambiguity involved in Passmore's claim, unresolved in his own text, which makes it difficult to assess its truth or falsity. This makes it correspondingly difficult to assess its impact upon Hume. It is not clear whether Passmore means that we do not as a matter of fact have an idea of anger when we see x express it, even though, in principle, we could have; or whether he means that it is psychologically impossible for us to have an idea of anger (or any other sentiment) *as such*. If he means the former, his case against Hume may not be a strong one, depending only on whether we can achieve a permissible interpretation of Hume. For, quite apart from disputing the factual claim involved, Hume might concede that we initially have an idea of x being angry but also maintain that, by definition where sympathy occurs, it gives rise to the idea of anger in itself – that is, unattributed anger. It is not possible, as far as I can see, to know exactly what Hume thought, but his language sometimes suggests that it is just a contingent fact that it is x's anger in particular which sparks off anger in me. Of course I begin by seeing x angry, Hume seems to be saying, but this leads me to have the idea of anger abstracted from x. And if Hume were to say this, the way would then be open for the idea of anger to be converted into the impression of anger in the spectator; that is, to be converted into the spectator's anger, without change of content.

However, if Passmore means that it is psychologically impossible to have an idea of anger (and other sentiments) pure and simple, the position for Hume is more serious, for this would in turn make it impossible for sympathy to occur. Let us then consider what reasons Passmore may have had for holding such a view. His most probable reasoning is that if we are invited to think about anger, or jealousy, or malice, etc., then we can only do so by virtue of thinking of x or y or z being angry, jealous, or malicious, and this will not fulfil Hume's requirements for the sympathetic process. This is because, as we saw, it would involve a change of content as between the impression and the idea. Passmore's charge would rely upon a behaviouristic account of the sentiments, an account which Hume, by and large, did not accept. Indeed, the essence of Passmore's objection would then be that, on Hume's account of the passions as discrete, isolatable, subjective sensations, it is simply impossible to have an idea of the sensation of anger, or jealousy, or pride. There are, he may be holding, no distinct sensations corresponding to these words, and thus there are no such ideas to be enlivened into impressions.

Whether Hume could dispute this or not it is not clear, but certainly it does not strictly follow from the claim that we cannot have an idea of a distinct sensation as such that we cannot therefore have a more general idea of the sentiment concerned. Even when interpreted behaviouristically, there can be an idea of anger in the abstract which is not necessarily tied to the idea of some person expressing anger. It would consist in thinking about those features of behaviour which we have come to associate with anger, or which we see as symptomatic of anger. Naturally, Hume's conception of a passion or sensation would have to be radically altered to accommodate such a view, but at least, by this means, his basic analysis of the sympathetic process would remain intelligible. For an idea of the sensation of anger or jealousy we would now substitute the idea of the symptoms of such moods; or, if the word 'symptom' is objectionable because of its dualistic implications, we would simply speak of the idea of angry or jealous behaviour. Sympathy would then involve the enlivening of such ideas into anger or jealousy in the spectator, and there would be no change of content.

Those, then, are some of the difficulties which seem to me to be involved in Hume's account of sympathy. It is possible to defend Hume from some of the objections levelled against him, as we have seen – though even this is difficult if one tries to do it in the precise terms of his own psychology – but certain problems remain. It is significant that when he wrote the *Enquiry Concerning the Principles of Morals*, he dispensed with the psychological story lying behind the operation of sympathy. In a footnote to Section v, Part II of that work he remarks: 'It is needless to push our researches so far as to ask, why we have humanity or a fellow-feeling with others. It is sufficient, that this is experienced to be a principle in human nature. We must stop somewhere in our examination of causes, and there are, in every science, some general principles, beyond which we cannot hope to find any principle more general. It is not probable, that these principles can be resolved into principles more simple and universal, whatever attempts may have been made to that purpose.' Is it possible that, in addition to the 'selfish hypothesis', he also had his own previous analysis in mind?

References to Hume's *Treatise* are to Hume, 1978 and take the form 'T page number' or 'T bk.pt.sect.'

1 T II.II.VII; 368–9.
2 T I.III.VIII; especially T 98.
3 Passmore, 1968, 126.
4 Harrison, 1976.
5 T I.IV.VI.
6 T 277.
7 T 317, 320, 354.
8 Sartre, 1957, III.1.iv, 259.
9 T 316, -19, 365, 427.
10 Ardal, 1966, 47.
11 *Ibid.*

12 Wittgenstein, 1958, II.IV.
13 Winch, 1980.
14 T 319.
15 T 368.
16 T 415.
17 Passmore, 1952, 129.

RUDOLF LÜTHE

Misunderstanding Hume: Remarks on German ways of Interpreting his Philosophy

PRAISE BY one of his peers may be fatal for any philosopher. This is true not only of praise that comes from incompetent and minor figures but also for praise that is formulated by respected and intelligent persons. Immanuel Kant was both respected and intelligent, but nevertheless I have to blame him for his re-action to Hume's philosophy because it must be regarded as the most important *historical* reason for the deplorable state of Humean scholarship in Germany. Of course there are other reasons as well. None of the elements which are traditionally attributed to Hume's thought has a genuine tradition in German philosophy. Moreover, his whole way of arguing, his strictly anti-speculative attitude may easily seem like a lack of philosophical depth (*Tiefe*) to those philosophers who think that Hegel was a great man. To some of them it may even seem a fault that Hume's philosophy is understandable. Philosophy of the Humean kind is sometimes considered 'thin' (dünn), thus provoking the idea that Hume's thought may be defined as 'thin philosophy by a thick philosopher'. Such an attitude on the part of German philosophers is neither restricted to Hegelians nor does it only apply to David Hume. Sometimes it even refers to British philosophy in general and is explained by a specific narrowness of the British mind. Nietzsche is an example of this astonishing view of Hobbes, Hume and Locke:

> What the English always lacked and still lack (. . .) is the genuine *power* of spirit, the genuine *depth* of the spiritual glance, in short: philosophy.[1]

Of course, nowadays nobody would repeat these sentences seriously, but still they point to an amazing pride among German philosophers in that philosophical tradition which is specifically German and strictly opposed to the British tradition of philosophy: the pride of German idealism. In a book published in Germany in 1981 one can read the following: 'We Germans are lucky, we have Hegel'.[2] I do not want to comment on this remark; I propose instead the following counter-formulation: 'The British are lucky; they have Hume'. Misunderstanding Hume is, of course, easy, especially for those people who have never even tried to read the original texts. It may be seductive to believe that Hume is a destructive philosopher – because destructive philosophy should not be read; such reading might prove ruinous to one's own philosophical innocence. But even reading Hume is not a secure way of avoiding misunderstanding his philosophy. The following remarks are intended to give a short 'phenomenology' of German misunderstandings of Hume's thought. I shall discuss three different images of Hume and try to show why all of them are wrong. The images discussed may be titled the anti-rationalist, the sceptic and the positivist.

1. Hamann and Jacobi: The anti-rationalist

Generally, English is not regarded as an extremely difficult language. But even philosophy written in English can only be understood correctly by people who have some knowledge of English.

One of the problems concerning terms used by Hume is the meaning of 'belief'. This being a central term its misunderstanding may prove fatal to any attempt to grasp the meaning of his philosophical argument.

The problem with the term 'belief' is that the most common German translation 'Glaube' has normally the meaning of religious belief or faith. Now, Sir Isaiah Berlin has described how the German Counter-Enlightenment misunderstood Hume's term 'belief' willingly, in order to make his criticisms of dogmatic rationalism a weapon against all rationalism and also against Hume's own philosophical intentions.[3] I do not want to repeat what Berlin said in his very instructive paper, but I think I should draw your attention to some of the features of this misunderstanding, because in a moderate version it is still alive today.

J. G. Hamann, the Magus of the North, and his less than second-rate disciple F. H. Jacobi belong amongst the first German readers of Hume's philosophy. Hamann read the *Treatise* in English and made Hume's philosophy an object of lifelong study. And as he was no dull person he knew quite well that Hume's position, although critical of the rationalistic idea that final proof is possible, did not include the idea that only revelation could give us truth. Hamann knew Hume's critical attitude towards religion in general and revelation in particular. But nevertheless he adored Hume for his argument that the basis of truth is *belief*. Why that? Hamann's own position was inspired by Pietism and his philosophy may be regarded as a religious opposition to enlightenment. But, we may ask, what can such a philosophy have to do with Hume's doctrine of belief? Let me quote Berlin: 'And indeed, it *has* nothing to do with Hume. But Hume, so it turned out, had, all unknowing, a good deal to do with it'.[4] Hume has to do with Hamann because this German 'magician' transformed the logical and psychological term 'belief', as used by Hume, into the distinctly religious term 'Glaube', thus identifying belief with 'faith' and 'revelation'. Hamann did not care much about the fact that 'belief' in Hume's sense is the result of experience, of the repetition and conjunction of impressions. The reason for this neglect is quite simple: Hamann was not interested in understanding Hume's meaning. He only wanted to use his philosophy as a weapon in his armoury against rationalism, especially against Descartes, Leibniz, and Spinoza.

In Hamann's narrow view, Hume's so-called scepticism was a destruction of rationalism which cleared the ground for an intrusion of religion. When logic and rationality cannot give us final proofs for our 'knowledge' about the world, then here is a *raison d'être* for religion: it takes the place left open by reason.

While this misunderstanding of Hume's doctrine is to be regarded as the result of what I would like to call a 'willing suspension of honesty' a second major misunderstanding might be due to the fact that some people, Hamann among them, do not understand irony. Hume's famous final passage in 'Of miracles' contains the sentence: 'And whoever is moved by *Faith* to assent to it (i.e. the belief in miracles) is conscious of a continued miracle in his own person (. . .)'.[5] Hamann takes this passage as a proof for his idea, that even Hume, the critic of religion and of all belief in wonders, cannot avoid looking at faith as a miracle of the spirit.

Although Hamann occasionally suspects that Hume might have said this scornfully or in jest, his predominant interpretation of the passage is governed by the idea that there the genuine power of faith is demonstrated by the fact that Hume presents himself as a witness for the truth that he wants to deny. Hume, in this view, is a 'Saul among the Prophets', witnessing the power of a truth that he does not even understand.

It is only consistent that Hamann does not understand what the *real* outcome of the *Dialogues* is. In his view this outcome is the (self-) destruction of Philo's scepticism and agnosticism. Hume's doctrine that both our own existence and the existence of all things outside of us must be '*believed*' is – in Hamann's view – an unintended proof of the miraculous nature of the world. Its existence is in itself a miracle because we cannot comprehend it rationally. If, therefore, Hume must believe in the existence of the egg that he eats, why, Hamann wonders, does he not believe in God? This is only a proof of his lack of philosophical consistency. Again Hamann does not care about the difference that eggs can be given in experience while God, as far as we know, is not accessible in the same way.

Being a true disciple of his master, Jacobi went on misunderstanding Hume. In his lengthy treatise 'David Hume on Belief, or Realism and Idealism. A Dialogue' the main feature of the anti-rationalist misunderstanding of Hume's philosophy figures already in the title: 'David Hume über den Glauben, oder Idealismus und Realismus. Ein Gespräch'. 'Glauben' – again this same mistaken translation of 'belief' – is presented as the only form of genuine knowledge. This does not, as yet, represent any progress in Hamann's and Jacobi's common attempt to misunderstand Hume. But Jacobi did manage to present some original contributions to this area of scholarship. Concentrating on the 'Dialogues' he discovered that Hume's *refutation* of the argument from design is itself well suited to prove the existence of God. Again Hume is presented as a witness *malgré soi* of the truth of Christian faith. The idea behind this original interpretation is even more peculiar than the arguments formulated by the Magus himself. It runs like this:

The argument from design rests on an analogy between the design in human production and that which is attributed to the productions of God. But God being unique, arguments resting on analogies cannot be applied to him and to his actions. Therefore – as Hume would have it – the argument from design fails to prove God's existence. Following a well-known strategy, Jacobi accepts this argument but only in order to extend it to the human mind. That also is unique and therefore cannot be comprehended by analogies. But I *know* of my own existence. Therefore there must be a peculiar power in my mind different from reason presenting the immediate knowledge of my own existence to my mind. Jacobi therefore invents a peculiar 'Gefühl der Existenz' (sometimes also called 'Wesenheitsgefühl'). And a being able to comprehend its own unique mind is of course also well-equipped enough to comprehend the unique God. In order to give his notion of 'Gefühl' more authority he quotes a passage from the *Treatise*, where Hume describes belief as something *felt* by the mind. Here, again following the example of his master's interpretation of Hume's philosophy, Jacobi misunderstands 'feeling' in Hume's sense as 'Gefühl', that is, as 'emotion'. While Hume only wanted to suggest that ideas in which we believe present themselves in a more lively fashion than other ideas, Jacobi takes him to say that belief is based on a special emotion (*Gefühl*) which, instead of being a part of our powers of experience, is a rival to them, giving us access to those areas of knowledge which experience cannot open to us.

2. Kant: The sceptic

Among those philosophers who misunderstood Hume's thought are not only Germans who died a long time ago but also British philosophers who lived in our century. In his famous *History of Western Philosophy* Bertrand Russell opens his chapter on Hume with the sentences:

> David Hume (1711–76) is one of the most important among philosophers, because he developed to its logical conclusion the empirical philosophy of Locke and Berkeley, and by making it self-consistent made it incredible. He represents, in a certain sense, a dead end: in his direction, it is impossible to go further. To refute him has been, ever since he wrote, a favourite pastime among metaphysicians. For my part, I find none of their refutations convincing; nevertheless, I cannot but hope that something less sceptical than Hume's system may be discoverable.

Hume is here regarded as a philosopher who managed to lead empiricism *ad absurdum* by consistently thinking it to its end, thus reaching a rigorously sceptical position. This view of Hume's philosophy comes quite close to what I regard as the most widespread of German attitudes towards his thought in our century. It may be described as 'Hume from a Kantian point of view' and runs like this: Hume is an important philosopher because he awakened Kant from his dogmatic slumber. But he managed to destroy dogmatism only by giving in to scepticism. Moreover, he never reached that level of philosophical reflection which is characteristic of transcendental philosophy, but remained an empiricist, down-to-earth scholar, afraid of genuine (speculative) philosophy. Therefore, his position has to be regarded as antiquated and obsolete. Its sceptical implications, however, are not only obsolete, but even dangerous because of their destructive powers. Therefore: you had better not read Hume, but Kant himself.

This attitude is indeed quite a fair summary of Kant's own most well-known remarks on Hume's philosophy, their main points being: (1) Hume was a sceptic (2) He only prepared what Kant himself brought to completion. Here I want to argue that both of these judgments are wrong and that therefore the conclusion that Hume's philosophy is antiquated and obsolete is also erroneous. My implication is, of course, that it is not dangerous but in fact fruitful to read Hume – even if one has already studied the philosophy of Kant.

There can be no doubt that Kant was deeply impressed by Hume's arguments against traditional metaphysics and against dogmatic rationalism. Scarcely any other philosopher is treated with such respect in Kant's writings. But nevertheless Kant's praise of Hume's thought was fatal to his reception in Germany, because it introduced him as a philosopher who only prepared what Kant himself brought to perfection, one who stated the problems that Kant solved. These attitudes, although far from enthusiasm, might not of themselves have sufficed to thwart the reception of Hume's philosophy in Germany even before it really started, had they not been accompanied by the well-known and apparently ineradicable misunderstanding of Hume as a sceptic. For dressing up Hume in the guise of a destructive thinker stopped any genuine interest in his arguments. Scepticism, although always alive, has always been regarded as self-destructive and so effectively dead. And why, one asked oneself, should Hume's scepticism be different? – But it was. And that is something overlooked not only by Hume's contemporaries who thought that such a destructive and anti-clerical thinker should not be made a professor in Glasgow or Edinburgh, not only by the so-called Common-Sense Philosophy and 'that bigotted silly fellow, Beattie', not even only by Kant, but also by our contemporaries, e.g. by Russell and as we shall see, by Popper. What none of them saw was that Hume's sceptical arguments differ essentially from traditional scepticism.

W. L. Robison has called Hume a Naturalist and a Meta-sceptic.[6] I think this is a good characterisation, although it is not really new (apart from this new-fangled term 'meta-sceptic'). It repeats the central idea of Kemp-Smith's epoch-making interpretation. I would like to formulate the central doctrine of Hume's naturalism as follows: There is nothing like a proof concerning our own rational notions of ourselves and of the world outside. We have experience, but experience only suffices to give us factuality, not necessity. It therefore restricts our knowledge to things experienced, excluding us from any knowledge of things to come. So far, the argument *is* sceptical. But then Hume gives it a naturalistic turn: Although reason necessarily leads us into such an insecure and doubtful position, we need nevertheless have no fear of the experiences to come because 'Nature, by an absolute and uncontrollable necessity has

determin'd us to judge as well as to breathe and feel . . .'.⁷
But then perhaps all our 'natural' judgements are wrong? – We
need not expect this, Hume argues, since all our experience
shows that experience itself and those expectations which are
based on it are very reliable. If, in this situation, the rationalist
sceptic goes on doubting, pointing out that reliability is not in fact
absolute security, then the naturalist develops his central argument, the argument which is always overlooked by those philosophers who identify naturalism with scepticism. It runs like this:
We do not *need* security, it is only *reason* that longs for it. And
'Reason is, and ought only to be the slave of the passions, and can
never pretend to any other office than to serve and obey them'.⁸
The naturalistic turn consists in a reduction of the importance of
reason for human life. This implies that the sceptic, who indeed is
a rationalist *par excellence*, is right in doubting our capacity to
reach security by rational argument. But his fault is to over-
estimate the role of reason. Reason is far less powerful a gov-
ernor of our lives than are the passions. It is only this fact that
explains what I would like to call the sceptical paradox. Hume
formulates it like this: The sceptical arguments *'admit of no
answer and produce no conviction'*.⁹

Kant's misunderstanding of Hume's intentions is a result of the
conservatism of his image of man. Hume's revolution consists at
least partly in interpreting man not as the rational animal, but as
a natural being, a being governed by passion and emotion, not by
reason. Kant's image of man is the traditional one; therefore
naturalism must appear destructive to him, because it destroys
this image. It is not the question of how to look at the principle of
causation that makes Hume's and Kant's thought so fun-
damentally different but this anthropological implication of
naturalism. Kant thinks that a foundation of 'truth' in 'belief',
'custom' and the like does not suffice for a being which is *animal
rationale*. Hume, in contrast, thinks that the major fault of both
traditional scepticism and dogmatic rationalism is to think of
man as the rational animal. From the point of view of this
traditional anthropology naturalism looks like a modified scepticism, because it does not doubt the validity of the sceptical
arguments. From Hume's point of view, naturalism is the only
valid counter-argument against scepticism, because it is only by
doubting the importance of reason that we can deny the significance of the sceptical arguments.

Kant, therefore, is basically wrong in suggesting that Hume
fell back into scepticism. And he is also wrong in making us
believe that he himself brought to a completion what Hume had

merely started. It is transcendentalism itself that falls back, not into scepticism, but into a problematic image of man; and what Kant considers as the fulfilment of Hume's beginning is, in fact, the outcome of denying the central results of Hume's philosophy. Kant is not Hume's rightful heir and I wonder whether Hume's philosophy, any more than that of Kant, ought to be regarded as antiquated and obsolete. For Hume's concept of man seems at least to be more akin to the results of modern anthropology.

This leads us to the final point of this section: Not even Hume's intentions were sceptical. He did not want to destroy philosophy by sceptical arguments; he wanted rather to replace the traditional philosophy, based on prejudices, by a science of man, a scientific anthropology. The sceptical arguments are brought forward merely to clear the ground, not for religion, but for science. And clearing the ground implies giving up one's anthropological prejudices. This is something that Kant did not understand at all. He, too, by the way, was influenced, like Hamann and Jacobi, by Prussian Pietism.

3. The Austrian Renaissance of Hume's Philosophy: The Positivist

George Davie pointed out that just at the same time – the seventies of the last century – when Edinburgh's leading role in Britain's philosophical and scientific life came to an end, the Scottish enlightenment experienced a renaissance in the Austrian empire.[10] There are two different philosophical movements, starting in Austria, that took up the Scottish and, especially, the Humean tradition: Phenomenology and Logical Positivism. One of the reasons why, within the German-speaking countries, it was Austria that revived Hume's philosophy, and why in Austria there is a genuine tradition of reception to British philosophy is surely the fact that here Kantianism and Kant's misinterpretation of Hume's role in the history of philosophy never took root. Austrian philosophy therefore retained an openness to English and Scottish influences that was destroyed in Germany by Kant and Hegelian Idealism. It seems that there is a complementary openness also on the British side: Both Wittgenstein and Popper, who gained world-wide respect, or at least a certain notoriety, while teaching in England, are Austrians by birth and by education.

Now I am sorry that I must spoil this image of harmony between British and Austrian philosophy but I think it is necessary to point out that the positivistic interpretation of Hume's philosophy too is not without misunderstandings.

Popper adopted Russell's crude misunderstandings of Hume's role in intellectual history. In the first essay of 'Objective Knowledge' he quotes Russell's motto: 'The growth of unreason throughout the nineteenth century and what has passed of the twentieth is a natural sequel to Hume's destruction of empiricism'.[11]

While Popper suspects Hume to be one of the fathers of an irrationalism which, in its final consequence, produced the ideology of German National Socialism, other representatives of Logical Positivism, although sharing the interpretation of Hume's philosophy as sceptical, point out that this scepticism cannot be regarded as the source of any kind of irrationalism because it was not unlimited. Thus it did not include logical and mathematical knowledge. These kinds of knowledge were to be regarded as certain. Of course the intention behind this Viennese interpretation of Hume is the attempt to establish some kind of superiority of the logical and mathematical sciences over other sciences.

Now there can be no doubt that Hume, like nearly all eighteenth-century philosophers, was deeply impressed by the new natural sciences, governed by mathematics. But nevertheless he never forgot that these sciences were empirical and therefore could only attain probability in their judgements. Therefore he developed his own theory of probability.

The positivists could, I think, accept this correction without forgoing the general tendency of their own understanding of Hume's thought. But then, I have to draw attention to a very obvious fact, which seems to be overlooked by the positivistic philosophers: Hume admired Newton but he did not want to repeat his doctrines.

What he wanted was to apply the principles of Newtonian natural science to the moral sciences, to the science of man. He wanted to become a Newton of the Human Sciences. The philosophical part of his work was meant to lay the foundations for a new science of man. This being his main intention, it could obviously not be his central idea that only logic and mathematics, and the natural sciences based on them, could be called sciences in the strict sense of that word. Moreover, it is obvious that Hume would not even allow the natural sciences, mathematics and logic to be regarded as superior to or as more important than the science of man. On the contrary, already in the introduction to the *Treatise*, he stressed his conviction that the science of man is the real and necessary basis for *all* our knowledge – including logical and mathematical knowledge and the knowledge of the natural sciences. ''Tis evident, that all the sciences have a relation, greater or less, to human nature; and that however wide any of them may run from it, they still return back by one passage or another. Even *Mathematics, Natural Philosophy, and Natural Religion,* are in some measure dependent on the science of MAN; since they lie under the cognizance of men, and are judged of by their powers and faculties'.[12]

As to 'logic', which is not referred to in this passage, my interpretation is that Hume used the term 'logic' mainly to refer to what we would nowadays call epistemology or theory of knowledge and not to formal logic as this is now customarily understood, i.e. as a science consisting of only analytical sentences about the deducibility relation between one sentence and another. The Humean 'logic' is not referred to in the quoted passage because it does not belong to the sciences depending on the science of man, but to this science itself. Logic is a genuine part of the science of man and not something depending on it. But, on the other hand, neither is it superior to the science of man in the sense that it is the basis for this science. Hume says: 'In these four sciences of *Logic, Morals, Criticism, and Politics,* is comprehended almost every thing, which it can any way import us to be acquainted with, or which can tend either to the improvement or ornament of the human mind'.[13]

These four sciences therefore seem to constitute what Hume calls the 'science of man'. This implies that these sciences and not formal logic, mathematics and the natural sciences may justly claim a superior position within Hume's system of knowledge. I think it is obvious how far distant is such a view of the system of the sciences from the positivistic outlook. If, therefore, Hume did not extend his scepticism to mathematical knowledge and logic, this does not by any means mean that he regarded these sciences as the most fundamental and the most important or satisfying. Such a conclusion rests on the false assumption that Hume gave in to the idea that sceptical doubt was as important as it appeared at first glance to be. But, as was already pointed out, Hume gave his scepticism a naturalistic turn. One of the results of this turn is that for him sceptical arguments did not decide about the security and the relevance of scientific judgements. Exactly this is the core of the positivistic misunderstanding of Hume's philosophy: to think that those sciences which do not fall within the ambit of sceptical doubt have to be regarded as superior to the others or even as their foundations. The source of this

misunderstanding is obvious: it is the lack of a genuine understanding of Hume's basic intention: the foundation of a *science
of man*.

1 Neitzsche, 1969, 718.
2 Horn, 1980, 78.
3 Berlin, 1977.
4 *Ibid.*
5 Hume, 1975, E.H.U., X.
6 Robison, 1876.
7 Hume, 1978, 183.
8 *Ibid.*, 415.
9 Hume, 1975, E.H.U., XII.I; 155n.
10 Davie, 1977.
11 Popper, 1975, p. 1.
12 Hume, 1978, Intro., p.xv.
13 *Ibid.*, pp.xv and xvi.

M. PAKALUK

Philosophical 'Types' in Hume's *Dialogues*

COMMENTATORS ON Hume's *Dialogues* have generally focused on three exegetical problems: that of deciding whom the characters of the *Dialogues* are meant to represent, that of explaining Philo's seeming change from scepticism to belief in Dialogue XII, and that of determining whether belief in God is, for Hume, appropriately classified with those irresistible, instinctual beliefs that Kemp Smith has called 'natural'. In this paper, I shall address mainly the first problem; however, it will be seen that my solution to it entails solutions to the others as well.

Many interpreters of the *Dialogues* have argued that Philo, Cleanthes, and Demea are to be taken as representing philosophers or schools flourishing in Hume's day. A well-known but problematic instance of this would be Mossner's claim that Philo can be identified with Hume, Cleanthes with Bishop Butler, and Demea with Samuel Clarke.[1] Now although I admit that such interpretations broaden our understanding of the issues and arguments raised in that complex work, nonetheless, I hold that, if the characters of the *Dialogues* do represent philosophers or schools of Hume's day, they do so only incidentally. My thesis is that Hume intends that the characters in the *Dialogues* represent what I call philosophical 'types'. It is possible, but not necessary, that these can be roughly identified with one or more of Hume's contemporaries. What I am arguing for then, concerning the *Dialogues*, is for a change in emphasis: I do not wish to deny what is of value in other interpretations so much as to supplement it. In particular, I aim to give a distinctively psychological slant to the *Dialogues,* whose characters I maintain should be taken as representing philosophical 'types'.

I

By 'type' I mean what Hume means when he talks of a 'species', 'sect' or 'character': that is, a particular cluster of traits that can be manifested in different ways, as environment, circumstance, and historical setting change. It is clear that one of Hume's central interests is that of describing the various causes that result in a person's believing and behaving in the way he does. In this respect, Hume is like the modern psychoanalyst who, systematising his observations about psychology, characterises syndromes that manifest themselves in different ways under different conditions. Just as the psychoanalyst may, for example, point to examples of 'anal-retentive personality' scattered throughout the pages of history and literature, so Hume delineates philosophical syndromes that appear many times throughout the history of thought, each time in a different guise.

Hume's quartet of essays – 'The Epicurean', 'The Stoic', 'The Platonist' and 'The Sceptic' – is an example of his thinking in terms of types. The footnote appended to the first of these essays is revealing:

> The intention of this and the three following essays is not so much to explain accurately the sentiments of the ancient sects of philosophy, as to deliver the sentiments of sects, that naturally form themselves in the world, and entertain different ideas of human life and happiness. I have given each of them the name of the philosophical sect, to which it bears the greatest affinity.[2]

Notice how Hume states that these sentiments 'naturally form themselves' – a phrase suggestive of a syndrome of traits. Moreover, Hume's remark that the characters sketched in the essays have an affinity to the ancient sects suggests that these syndromes, if we may call them such, manifest themselves historically in different ways. Incidentally, the quartet of essays does read as a proto-dialogue – a dialogue among philosophical types.

We do not need to look very hard to see sketches of 'types' in other parts of the Humean corpus. Hume's descriptions of sects, denominations and political groups in his *History*, for example, are often descriptions of types. Puritanism, for instance, he calls a 'species of religion', and he explains its different forms in different countries by examining how the same species 'received some alteration, according to the different situation of civil affairs, and the different species of government, which it met with in its progress'.[3] Again, when describing the Catholics, Hume makes explicit his interest in typology: 'The characters of sects may be studied,' he remarks, 'when their controversies shall be totally forgotten'.[4] Other examples of Humean typology include his essay 'Of Superstition and Enthusiasm' and that notorious catalogue of stereo-types, 'Of National Characters'.

Of course, there is ample evidence for Hume's interest in typology in the *Dialogues* themselves. Consider the strange

sketch of the history of theology that we are given in Dialogue I.
The Fathers and Reformers, we are told, adopted the methods
and principles of the Academics; Huet, Cleanthes says, is a
hidden Pyrrhonist:[5] here are examples of similar 'types' that
arise both in pagan and Christian contexts. Again, Philo remarks
that post-Lockean theologians 'talk the language of STOICS,
PLATONISTS, and PERIPATETICS, not that of PYHRRHO-
NIANS and ACADEMICS'[6], thereby comparing the form or
structure underlying some contemporary school with that underlying ancient ones. In a similar manner, at least sixteen such
types or instances of types are compared and contrasted in the
Dialogues in various ways.[7]

It will be seen, during the presentation of textual evidence
below, that my claim that the characters in the *Dialogues* represent philosophical types will be plausible only if one attends, not
only to what the characters *say*, but also to what they *do*. It is
important to look at both, because Hume had a life-long interest
in uncovering hypocrisy, that is, disparity between what one says
and how one acts. Hume, we may say, is specifically interested in
'intellectual hypocrisy,' which is a disparity between what one
says one believes (or what one says are one's grounds for belief),
and what one actually believes (or what actually are the grounds
for one's belief). His interest in intellectual hypocrisy so defined
resembles a similar interest evident in Bayle (*P. D.,* §§ 136, 138,
where he argues that passions, not rationalisations, determine
behaviour). It is most apparent in his sceptical criticisms of
proofs for the causal maxim: the reasons we think, or like to
think, that an effect necessarily follows from its cause, are not at
all the reasons why we actually think this.

We find intellectual hypocrisy vividly portrayed in the *Dialogues*: Cleanthes *professes* principles of causal reasoning, yet he
does not *act* in accordance with these, by following them out to
what, Hume thinks, is their just conclusion; Demea *professes* an
extreme way of negation, but he does not *act* in accordance with
this by denying all knowledge of the Deity. These instances of
'intellectual hypocrisy' draw our attention to the different levels
of the *Dialogues*: the level of profession and the level of action
(here taking thought processes to be actions of a kind). The
Dialogues have these two distinct levels because of a consequence of the principle of verisimilitude: any author who wishes
realistically to depict a character uses the knowledge he has of
human psychology in developing that character. It is to be expected, therefore, that Hume has used his understanding of
human psychology – that is, the conclusions of the *Treatise* – in

developing the characters in the *Dialogues*. That is, Philo, Cleanthes, and Demea are 'designed' not only to articulate verbally
various principles peculiar to Hume's psychology, but also –
since these principles are principles of psychology – to reason
according to them, even when these characters articulate conclusions with which Hume would disagree. Remember that, in the
first *Enquiry* and the *Treatise*, Hume compares his science of
human nature to anatomy, and argues that, just as the study of
anatomy is the only sound basis for accurate painting, so the
study of human nature is the only sound basis for popular mora-
lising. Because of the principle of verisimilitude, as painting
stands to anatomy so the *Dialogues* stand to the *Treatise*: underlying the speeches, changes of mood, and emotions of the characters in the *Dialogues* is the conscious application by Hume of his
principles of the understanding. When one realises this, then one
sees how several of the seemingly 'logical' moves made by the
characters of the *Dialogues* are best viewed as 'psychological'.

II

I now turn to textual evidence for my claim that the characters of
the *Dialogues* represent philosophical types. I shall discuss two
passages, *Treatise* I. iv.3 and § 12 of the first *Enquiry,* and I shall
argue that Hume describes philosophical types in these passages,
that these types correspond to the characters in the *Dialogues*,
and that the dialectical relationship among them is similar to that
among the characters of the *Dialogues*.

Now, many commentators have remarked upon the distinction that Hume draws between what Kemp Smith has
called the 'vulgar' and 'philosophical consciousness.'[8] In
general, it would seem that, for Hume, the vulgar consciousness is the common, unrefined, non-scientific and often superstitious consciousness of the generality of mankind. The philosophical consciousness, on the other hand, is marked by a concern for discovering causes in seemingly chance events and by a
vigorous rigour of mind, which leads the philosopher to trace
chains of causes and effects to great lengths. 'The generality of
mankind,' Hume tells us, 'never find any difficulty in accounting
for the more common and familiar operations of nature.
. . . They acquire, by long habit, such a turn of mind, that,
upon the appearance of the cause, they immediately expect
with assurance its usual attendant. . . . It is only on the discov-
ery of extraordinary phaenomena, such as earthquakes . . . that
they find themselves at a loss to assign a proper cause'.[9] However, Hume tells us that philosophers go further than this:

'proceeding from particular instances to general principles, they still push on their enquiries to principles more general, and rest not satisfied till they arrive at those original principles, by which, in every science, all human curiosity must be bounded'.[10]

Now Hume sometimes adds another 'consciousness' to the two already described – that of the 'false philosopher'. Hume talks about the false philosopher mainly in those passages where he would distinguish his own philosophy, which he considers the true philosophy, from that of his opponents, such as, say, Locke or Berkeley, which he considers to be false, though very much in outward appearance like the true. Perhaps the most striking discussion of this trio of philosophical types occurs in the *Treatise*, I. iv. 3, 'Of the antient philosophy,' where he discusses 'occult qualities':

> In considering this subject we may observe a gradation of three opinions, that rise above each other, according as the persons, who form them, acquire new degrees of reason and knowledge. These opinions are that of the vulgar, that of a false philosophy, and that of the true.[11]

Now, I claim that, roughly, Philo is a true philosopher, Cleanthes a false philosopher, and Demea a vulgar reasoner. This claim acquires greater plausibility when we examine this passage of the *Treatise* in detail.

The first thing to notice is that Hume observes that 'we shall find upon enquiry, that the true philosophy approaches nearer to the sentiments of the vulgar, than to those of a mistaken knowledge'.[12] The true philosophers, Hume tells us, by dint of their intellectual acumen, free themselves from the tangled speculations of the false philosophers, who are such that '[had] they fallen upon the just conclusion, they wou'd have return'd back to the situation of the vulgar, and wou'd have regarded all these disquisitions with indolence and indifference'.[13] But this description of the true philosopher, and his relationship to the vulgar, matches Philo's outlook, and his relationship to Demea. As many commentators have acknowledged, Demea and Philo agree in their sceptical conclusions. In fact, throughout most of the *Dialogues*, Demea views Philo as an ally, and certainly Philo agrees with the substance if not the intent of Demea's scepticism. Philo and Demea are allied in defending 'the adorable mysteriousness of the divine nature',[14] against Cleanthes' philosophical rationalism, but their alliance is an uneasy one, for, one might say, Philo's scepticism is mitigated, whereas Demea's is vulgar.

Again, the true philosopher is said to look upon the systems of the false philosopher with 'indolence and indifference'. Of course, this reminds us of that famous passage at I.iv.7 in the *Treatise*, where, again, Hume compares the false philosopher and his system-building to the true philosopher, who 'will be diffident of his philosophical doubts, as well as of his philosophical conviction,' and 'who studies philosophy in [a] careless manner'.[15] And, of course, this brings to mind Pamphilus' identification of Philo as a 'careless sceptic' – which confirms the contention that the characters of the *Dialogues* correspond to the three philosophical types of true philosopher, false, and vulgar. (When one looks to Johnson's *Dictionary*, one finds that the primary definition of 'careless' is given as 'having no care; feeling no solicitude; unconcerned; negligent;' the secondary definition is 'cheerful; undisturbed;' and the tertiary one is 'unheeded; thoughtless; unconsidered.' It is clear that when Hume describes the sceptic as 'careless' he means not 'thoughtless' but rather 'unconcerned' or 'undisturbed'.)

Consider also what Hume says about the false philosopher at I.iv.3. Instead of 'drawing a just inference' from the observation that all perceptions are distinct and separate, 'they frequently search for the qualities, in which this [causal] agency consists, and are displeas'd with every system, which their reason suggests to them, in order to explain it . . . they seem to be in a very lamentable condition'.[16] However, the false philosophers are 'consoled' by their invention of 'faculties' and 'occult phaenomena'. In connection with his discussion of these false philosophers, Hume discusses two errors of false philosophers, arising from 'a very remarkable inclination in human nature, to bestow on external objects the same emotions, which it observes in itself; and to find everywhere those ideas, which are most present to it'.[17] It is significant that these two errors of false philosophers that Hume here describes – a feckless desire to build systems that lack the authoritative support of common sense and a tendency to anthropomorphise – are precisely the two charges that Philo brings against Cleanthes' brand of natural theology. 'Your theory,' Philo says to Cleanthes, 'implies a contradiction to . . . experience'; and just before this he asks: 'can we ever hope to erect a system of cosmogony, that will be liable to no exceptions, and will contain no circumstance repugnant to our limited and imperfect experience of the analogy of nature? Your theory itself surely cannot pretend to any such advantage; even though you have run into *anthropomorphism*, the better to preserve a conformity to common experience'.[18]

Additional evidence that Hume considers this tendency to

anthropomorphise to be the psychological process that underlies formulations of the argument from design may be found in Hume's March 1751 letter to Elliot: 'We must endeavor to prove that this Propensity is somewhat different from our Inclination to find our own Figures in the Clouds, our Face in the Moon, *our Passions & Sentiments even in inanimate Matter*' (my emphasis).[19] Also relevant is the following passage from the *Natural History of Religion*: 'There is an universal tendency among mankind to conceive all beings like themselves, and to transfer to every object, those qualities, with which they are familiarly acquainted, and of which they are intimately conscious. We find human faces in the moon, armies in the clouds . . . Nay, philosophers cannot entirely exempt themselves from this natural frailty; but have oft ascribed it to inanimate matter the horror of a *vacuum*, sympathies, antipathies, and other affections of human nature. The absurdity is not less, [when we transfer], as is too usual, human passions and infirmities to the deity. . . .'[20]

So, then, we can conclude that the description that Hume gives of the three philosophical types in the *Treatise* seems to correspond to the principles and traits of the three characters in the *Dialogues*.

III

I now want to substantiate further the claim that Demea, Cleanthes, and Philo represent philosophical types by turning to §12 of the first *Enquiry*. In §12, Hume is concerned with delineating the different *species* of scepticism, i.e., he is quite consciously providing characterisations of different 'types' of sceptic. I claim that Philo, the true philosopher, corresponds to the mitigated sceptic; Cleanthes, the false philosopher, to the dogmatist; and Demea, the vulgar, to the vulgar sceptic.

Now, it is clear from a careful reading of §12 of the first *Enquiry* and Part I of the *Dialogues* that these two texts have many common, parallel passages. Perhaps Hume composed them at the same time, or perhaps he drew heavily on §12 when, at a later date, he composed Part I. With regard to these two texts, I shall try to support the following three claims. First, Hume's central concern in §12 of the first *Enquiry* is similar to one of the central concerns of, indeed, the whole of the *Dialogues*. Once this result is established, then the application of the philosophical types of §12 to the characters of the *Dialogues* is to some extent justified. Second, Philo corresponds to the mitigated sceptic; Cleanthes corresponds to the dogmatist; and Demea corresponds to the vulgar sceptic of §12. Third, in Hume's

discussion of the problem of the external world in §12 he characterises three philosophical types, and these correspond as well
to characters in the *Dialogues*.

Now, the very first paragraph of §12 begins as follows:

> There is not a greater number of philosophical reason-
> ings, displayed upon any subject, than those which prove
> the existence of a Deity, and refute the fallacies of *Atheists*;
> and yet the most religious philosophers still dispute whether
> any man can be so blinded as to be a speculative atheist.
> How shall we reconcile these contradictions?[21]

This is a curious paragraph, for, after posing this difficulty,
Hume drops the topic of atheism and does not pick it up again.
Instead, he switches to a discussion of scepticism, even though
the difficulty concerning the existence of atheists is presumably
part of the impetus for the investigations of §12 in the first place.
How shall *we* reconcile these contradictions? Why does Hume
raise the subject of atheism only to drop it immediately?

It is clear from the second paragraph of §12 that atheism is
mentioned in order to develop an analogy between atheism and a
certain kind of scepticism, excessive scepticism or Pyrrhonism.
Although a man may profess to be a sceptic of this kind, in fact
and in practice, nobody can be one. So, the analogy would be:
just as it is possible to profess Pyrrhonism but impossible to be a
Pyrrhonist so it is possible to profess atheism but impossible to be
an atheist. (Here, by the way, we find the distinction, earlier
cited and so important for understanding Hume's philosophy,
between what a person *says* and how he in fact *acts*.)

This analogy between scepticism and atheism is preserved and
mentioned in the *Dialogues,* where Cleanthes states:

> And it is now, in a manner, avowed, by all pretenders to
> reasoning and philosophy, that atheist and sceptic are
> almost synonymous. And as it is certain, that no man is in
> earnest, when he professes the latter principle; I would fain
> hope that there are as few, who seriously maintain the
> former.[22]

Of course, later Cleanthes says that mystics like Demea 'are, in a
word, atheists'[23] and so Cleanthes *embodies* the paradoxical view
mentioned at the opening of the *Enquiry*: for he doubts that
atheists can exist, yet he calls Demea one, and, moreover, tries
to prove the existence of God. Here, Cleanthes embodies in his
manner of arguing and acting a philosophical portrait that Hume
elsewhere describes.

Again, Philo, it will be remembered, twice denies the existence of atheists. In Dialogue XII he says 'I next turn to the

atheist, who, I assert, is only nominally so, and can never possibly be in earnest . . .'.[24] Earlier, he had remarked: 'Could I meet with one of this species (who, I thank God, are very rare) . . .'.[25] Here, the use of the word 'species' is significant, and it hearkens back to Hume's claim in §12 of the first *Enquiry* that there are no living examples of that *species* of sceptic, the Pyrrhonist.

It is clear, then, that analogous concerns direct both §12 of the first *Enquiry* and the *Dialogues*. In §12, Hume states that he is investigating two questions: 'What is meant by a sceptic?' and 'How far is it possible to push these philosophical principles of doubt and uncertainty?'. Likewise, in the *Dialogues*, Hume investigates 'What is an atheist? (or theist?)' and 'How far is it possible to push philosophical principles of doubt and uncertainty in natural religion?'. In the first *Enquiry*, he answers the first question by developing a catalogue of types of sceptic: in the *Dialogues* he answers the first question by having three types of theist (corresponding to three species of sceptic) interact. Again, just as, in the first *Enquiry*, Hume answers the second question by describing how a tincture of Pyrrhonism strips a man's beliefs down to the bare, natural essentials, so, in the *Dialogues*, he investigates how far it is possible to push principles of doubt and uncertainty by actually having Philo do the pushing. Again, we find that a philosophical portrait that is only described by Hume in one place is *embodied* in a character of the *Dialogues*. Philo embodies the portrait of the mitigated sceptic, described in the *Enquiry*, whose method is that of applying the tincture of Pyrrhonism.

So much, then, for my first point, that some concerns of the *Dialogues* are similar to those of the first *Enquiry* §12. Next, I argue that Philo corresponds to the mitigated sceptic, Cleanthes to the dogmatist, and Demea to the vulgar sceptic.

Philo is clearly a mitigated sceptic, both in profession and practice. In §12 Hume in fact mentions two sub-species of mitigated scepticism, and Philo professes and embodies each of these. The first form of mitigated scepticism consists of that state of calm and reasonableness attained only after going through the purge of Pyrrhonism. In the *Enquiry* what Hume recommends is that a person 'be once thoroughly convinced of the force of the Pyrrhonian doubt, and of the impossibility, that anything, but the strong power of natural instinct, could free us from it'.[26] In the *Dialogues*, Philo recommends a similar regimen: 'if a man has accustomed himself to sceptical considerations . . . he will not entirely forget them when he turns his reflections on other subjects' and that a man who goes through this doubt 'is not

obliged to give any other reason [for his opinions and actions]
than the absolute necessity he lies under of so doing'.[27]

Another sub-species of mitigated scepticism is the natural result of a careful investigation into the workings of
the human understanding, after which the 'narrow limita-
tion . . . of our enquiries' is known, and one then learns
'what are the proper subjects of science and enquiry',[28] that is,
the abstract and experimental sciences. This kind of mitigated
sceptic 'justly insists, that all our evidence for any matter of fact,
which lies beyond the testimony of sense or memory, is derived
entirely from the relation of cause and effect':[29] It will be immediately clear that Philo both professes this kind of mitigated
scepticism, in that he is always espousing Hume's principles by
which to judge of causes and effects, and, moreover, he follows
these principles in practice, by reasoning according to them.
Philo, in fact, urges this kind of mitigated scepticism against
Cleanthes. In the *Enquiry* §12 we find the following passage
stating this brand of mitigated scepticism:

> While we cannot give a satisfactory reason, why we
> believe, after a thousand experiments, that a stone will fall,
> or fire burn; can we ever satisfy ourselves concerning any
> determination, which we may form, with regard to the ori-
> gin of worlds, and the situation of nature, from, and to
> eternity?[30]

In the *Dialogues*, we find Philo making a nearly identical point:

> When the coherence of the parts of a stone, or even that
> composition of parts, which renders it extended; when these
> familiar objects, I say, are so inexplicable, . . . with what
> assurance can we decide concerning the origin of worlds, or
> trace their history from eternity to eternity?[31]

Whereas Philo corresponds to the mitigated sceptic, Cleanthes
corresponds to the dogmatic reasoner. According to Hume in the
Enquiry, because dogmatists 'see objects only on one side, and
have no idea of any counterpoising argument, they throw themselves precipitately into the principles, to which they are
inclined'.[32] Philo charges Cleanthes with being such a dogmatist,
urging against his argument from design that 'no system of this
kind ought ever to be received from a slight analogy'[33] since
many counter instances are easy to collect. Cleanthes himself
confesses his propensity to 'see objects only on one side,' for he
responds to one of Philo's sceptical cosmological hypotheses,
saying: 'This theory, I own, . . . has never before occurred to
me, though a pretty natural one; and I cannot readily, upon so
short an examination and reflection, deliver any opinion with

regard to it'.[34] Philo chides Cleanthes for this, and admits that he himself never has any trouble 'starting objections and difficulties'.[35] Now, drawing again the distinction between profession and action, we see that Cleanthes professes the experimental principles of Hume's philosophy, but in 'action' he is a dogmatist. He has grasped, one might say, the letter but not the spirit of Hume's philosophy. This is why Cleanthes and Philo can form an uneasy alliance in agreeing upon the experimental method of reasoning, but why, in fact, Cleanthes is a 'counterfeit' Humean, because he is, in practice, a dogmatist.

It should also be noted that Cleanthes' philosophical type is also expressed in that essay, 'The Platonist'. It will be remembered that the Platonist puts forward the argument from design:

> Compare the works of art with those of nature. The one are but imitations of the other. . . . Can we then be so blind as not to discover an intelligence and a design in the exquisite and most stupendous contrivance of the universe? Can we be so stupid as not to feel the warmest raptures of worship and adoration, upon the contemplation of that intelligent Being, so infinitely good and wise?[36]

If Cleanthes embodies these sentiments, then Philo embodies those expressed in the essay 'The Sceptic'. And it is significant that the opening sentences of that essay criticise the argument from design put forward by the Platonist for precisely the same reason that Philo criticises Cleanthes and the mitigated sceptic criticises the dogmatist:

> There is one mistake to which [philosophers] seem liable, almost without exception; they confine too much their principles, and make no account of that vast variety, which nature has so much affected in all her operations. When a philosopher has once laid hold of a favourite principle, which perhaps accounts for many natural effects, he extends the same principle over the whole creation, and reduces to it every phaenomenon, though by the most violent and absurd reasoning.[37]

Notice the similarity of Philo's point against Cleanthes:

> When nature has so extremely diversified her manner of operation in this small globe; can we imagine that she incessantly copies herself throughout so immense a universe? . . . is a part of nature a rule for another part very wide of the former? Is it a rule for the whole? Is a very small part the rule for the universe?[38]

Finally, Demea embodies the various sketches of 'vulgar' or 'popular' scepticism that Hume provides in several places in §12 of the first *Enquiry*. The objections of the vulgar sceptic, Hume tells us: 'are derived from the natural weakness of human understanding; the contradictory opinions, which have been entertained in different ages and nations; . . . [and] many other topics of that kind'.[39] Hume concludes that such scepticism is very weak, since it is specious. Philo describes vulgar scepticism in similar terms: 'The vulgar, indeed, we may remark . . . observing the endless disputes of the learned, have commonly a thorough contempt for philosophy; and rivet themselves the faster, by that means, in the great points of theology, which have been taught them'.[40]

It is evident that Demea is a sceptic of this kind. Consider Demea's espoused theory of education, by which he imparts religion to his pupils: 'While they pass through every other science,' Demea tells us, 'I still remark the uncertainty of each part, the eternal disputations of men, [and] the obscurity of all philosophy. . . .' Thus taming the minds of his pupils, Demea can 'season their minds with early piety' and 'imprint deeply on their tender minds an habitual reverance for all the principles of religion'.[41]

So, as I noted earlier, Demea is a sceptic and, *qua* sceptic, can, throughout most of the *Dialogues,* preserve an uneasy alliance with Philo. Note the parallels in their scepticism: Philo applies a tincture of Pyrrhonism; Demea stirs up specious sceptical difficulties: Philo, dumping out the basket of apples, keeps only what natural necessity compels him to believe; Demea, having thoroughly confused his pupils, imposes the 'artificial' regimen of 'education'.

So then, it is, I think, plausible to assume that the characters of the *Dialogues* embody several of the species of sceptic that are described in §12 of the first *Enquiry*. My final claim is that the characters of the *Dialogues* correspond to positions Hume describes in his discussion of the existence of an external world in §12 of the first *Enquiry*.

It will be remembered that, in the *Dialogues*, Lord Bacon's famous maxim is cited, that a little philosophy leads a man away from religion, and a little more leads him back again.[42] Now this maxim illustrates a basic conception of philosophical inquiry that underlies many passages in Hume's writings. We have, first, an untutored, unreflective state; next, we have a state different from this, disturbed by an imperfect grasp of philosophy; finally, we have the settled state, resembling the first, the result of a consistent and thoroughgoing use of philosophy. These states correspond to the three philosophical types of vulgar, false, and true philosopher, respectively.

This tripartite characterisation of philosophical dialectic underlies Hume's discussion of the external world in §12 of the first *Enquiry*. The vulgar unthinkingly have a simple faith in their senses, which is soon disturbed by the Pyrrhonist, who raises what are in fact specious difficulties. The sceptic's challenges are answered by the false philosopher, who constructs representational systems that lack the authority of both sense and reason. Finally, the mitigated sceptic appears, who, playing the Pyrrhonist off against the system-builder, retires to the calm repose of natural piety again.

In one paragraph, Hume sums up the dialectical dilemma about the external world as follows:

> Do you follow the instincts and propensities of nature, . . . in assenting to the veracity of sense? But these lead you to believe that the very perception or sensible image is the external object. Do you disclaim this principle, in order to embrace a more rational opinion, that the perceptions are only representations of something external? You here depart from your natural propensities and more obvious sentiments; and yet are not able to satisfy your reason, which can never find any convincing argument from experience to prove, that the perceptions are connected with any external objects.[43]

It is curious that, by transposing and adjusting only a few words, we arrive at the core of Philo's objections to Cleanthes' presentation of the argument from design. 'Do you follow,' Philo might say to Cleanthes, 'the instincts and propensities of nature, in assenting to the purpose, design and intention in nature? But these lead you to believe that nature itself contains an ordering principle. Do you disclaim this principle, in order to embrace the more theological opinion, that order in the world is only a representation of the order in the mind of an invisible Deity "behind" appearances? You here depart from your natural propensities (for surely the universe is not very similar to a house) and yet you are not able to satisfy your reason, which cannot meet opposing hypotheses, and which can never find any convincing argument from experience to prove the attributes of an invisible God from the observed order of nature.' In this way, Philo's criticisms of Cleanthes would correspond to Hume's criticisms of Lockean representationalism.

In a like way, Philo's criticisms of Demea correspond to

Hume's criticisms of Berkeley's idealism. This is what Hume
writes regarding Berkeley's theory:

> The second objection goes farther, and represents this
> opinion as contrary to reason . . . Bereave matter of all its
> intelligible qualities, both primary and secondary, you in a
> manner annihilate it, and leave only a certain unknown,
> inexplicable *something,* as the cause of our perceptions; a
> notion so imperfect, that no sceptic will think it worthwhile
> to contend against it.[44]

By altering this slightly, we can construct a critique of Demea's
position, similar to that voiced by Philo: 'Mysticism goes farther,
and represents theological opinions about God as contrary to
reason. Bereave God of all His intelligible attributes, you in a
manner annihilate Him (and are an "atheist"), and leave only an
unknown, inexplicable something as the cause of order; a notion
so imperfect, that no sceptic will think it worthwhile to contend
against it.' And, indeed, Philo does not.

Here, then, is ample evidence for the 'structuralist' who would
investigate Hume's philosophy. The same 'structure' underlies
several seemingly disparate arguments. My claim is that this
same structure is, in a sense, embodied in the characters of the
Dialogues.

Michael Ayers has kindly brought to my attention a difficulty
in my characterisation of Demea, whom I would have to be both
a vulgar reasoner and a 'popular' sceptic. Now Hume seems to
identify the popular sceptic with the excessive sceptic, or Pyrrhonist, and certainly Hume never thought that the common
man is a Pyrrhonist, or the Pyrrhonist common.

I think that this criticism points to a way in which my hypothesis concerning the typology of the characters in the *Dialogues*
needs to be refined. There is no doubt that Demea is not a
'philosopher' in the 18th century sense of the word, as Philo and
Cleanthes are philosophers. And his views are intended to coincide, I think, with the piety of the average Christian of Hume's
day. In addition, we need to explain Demea's superficial agreement with Philo on so many matters, and all of this supports the
suggestion that Demea is one of the vulgar. On the other hand,
he is also a sceptic. Cleanthes seems to liken Demea's form of
scepticism to Huet's, which, Cleanthes says, is a manifestation of
Pyrrhonism – and I see no reason for saying that this is not also
Hume's view. And, as I point out in the paper, Demea explicitly
professes scepticism – a scepticism which Hume clearly wants us
to think is specious, as is the 'popular' scepticism mentioned in
the *Enquiry.* In sum, I think that Hume means us to see in

Demea 'the union of philosophy with the popular religion,' consisting of an unnatural mixture of natural piety with 'declamations against reason, against the senses, against every principle, derived merely from human research and enquiry'.[45] Demea is then rightfully described as a vulgar sceptic, but, I think, it would be Hume's opinion that such a type became prevalent, that is, became common or 'vulgar', only upon the Christianisation of the Western world.

IV

At the beginning of this paper I stated the three principal exegetical difficulties of the *Dialogues*, and I suggested that the solution I should propose for the first of these would entail solutions to the others as well. I now want to conclude this paper by suggesting how, if we take the characters of the *Dialogues* to represent philosophical types, we can then explain more easily Philo's seeming turnabout in Dialogue XII.

We may look upon this difficulty of Philo's turnabout as both a 'logical' and a 'psychological' change on Philo's part. Logically, Philo in Dialogue XII assents to a proposition – that there is intention and purpose in nature – that he previously has not assented to. Most commentators explain away this difficulty by making two moves: first, by pointing out that Philo's 'confessions' in Dialogue XII actually concede very little to the theist; second, by pointing out that the little that Philo does concede in Dialogue XII is never denied by Philo in Dialogues I through XI. However, this solution to the 'logical' difficulty creates another, 'psychological' one. For these same commentators would admit that Philo concedes nothing about the purpose or intention in nature that he is not compelled to believe by a kind of 'natural belief' in this purpose or intention. But then the 'psychological' difficulty arises of why, if belief in design and purpose is a natural belief, that belief only manifests itself for Philo in Dialogue XII. Philo seems completely oblivious to this belief in Dialogues I to XI; yet, if it is a natural belief, it ought always be a part of his 'original constitution'.

The resolution to this psychological difficulty is suggested by the thesis here defended, that Philo represents a certain philosophical type, and that, consequently, Hume crafts Philo to behave in accordance with Hume's principles of the human understanding. For it is a familiar maxim of Hume's psychology that 'it is always found that a vigorous exertion of the . . . faculties [of reason or imagination], necessarily, from the narrow capacity of the human mind, destroys all activity in [the affections]'.[46] However, Philo, in Dialogues I through XI, is of course exercising his reason and imagination with great vigour. While he argued with Cleanthes, Philo says, 'concerning the natural attributes of intelligence and design, [he] needed all [of his] sceptical and metaphysical subtlity to elude [Cleanthes'] grasp'.[47] It follows, then, that during these vigorous metaphysical discussions, Philo's affections, including the sentiment that there is purpose or intention in nature, would be suppressed, only to resurface in Dialogue XII, when the intense sceptical duelling is over. Hume, the author of the *Dialogues*, in having Philo act in this manner, has merely had his character act, as would any author, in accordance with the principles of human psychology as he understands them.

In the eighteenth century, the English word 'principle' was notoriously ambiguous, for it could mean either a maxim to be consciously cited and followed, such as the principles that serve as premises in a philosophical argument, or a law describing some inexorable process of nature, such as the principles of mechanics. Now, the principles of Hume's philosophy are principles of psychology. It follows that, if they are true, they *may* be followed, in the sense of being consciously cited and obeyed, and they *must* be followed, in the sense that they describe the thought processes of all human beings.

Here a kind of self-containment enters in, for Hume so constructs the *Dialogues* that only one of the characters, Philo, cites consciously the same principles that also describe how he acts. For example, Philo, in argument, follows (consciously) Hume's *philosophical* definition of cause and effect; Philo, in action or thought, follows (descriptively) Hume's *natural* definition of cause and effect. Philo, then, understands the principles by which he acts as a philosopher. He thus embodies what may be considered the Humean equivalent of the Socratic ideal of knowing one's self. By crafting Philo's character in this way, Hume so contrives it that Philo alone is confidently in command of the argument; that Philo's comments, unlike those of Demea and Cleanthes, can never be ironically turned against himself; and that Philo understands and bears with both the dogmatism of Cleanthes and the impetuous scepticism of Demea.

1 Mossner, 1936.
2 Hume, 1875, I, 197.
3 Hume, 1970, 72.

4 *Ibid.*, 96.
5 Hume, 1980, 138–9.
6 *Ibid.*, 139.
7 *Ibid.*, 133–98, passim.
8 Kemp-Smith, 1941, 450 ff.
9 Hume, 1975, 69.
10 *Ibid.*, 6.
11 Hume, 1978, 222.
12 *Ibid.*
13 *Ibid.*
14 Hume, 1980, 144 and –6.
15 Hume, 1978, 273.
16 *Ibid.*, 223.
17 *Ibid.*, 224.
18 Hume, 1980, 186.
19 Greig, 1932, I, 155.
20 Hume, 1963, 40–1.
21 Hume, 1975, 149.
22 Hume, 1980, 139.
23 *Ibid.*, 159.
24 *Ibid.*, 218.
25 *Ibid.*, 215.
26 Hume, 1975, 162.
27 Hume, 1980, 134.
28 Hume, 1975, 163.
29 *Ibid.*, 159.
30 *Ibid.*, 162.
31 Hume, 1980, 131–2.
32 Hume, 1975, 161.
33 Hume, 1980, 186.
34 *Ibid.*, 172.
35 *Ibid.*
36 Hume, 1875, 212–13.
37 *Ibid.*, 213–14.
38 Hume, 1980, 148–9.
39 Hume, 1975, 158.
40 Hume, 1980, 131.
41 *Ibid.*, 136.
42 *Ibid.*, 139; cf. Hume, 1963, 56.
43 Hume, 1975, 153–4.
44 Hume, 1975, 155.
45 Hume, 1980, 138.
46 Hume, 1975, 299.
47 Hume, 1980, 101–2.

TOM CAMPBELL

Adam Smith and the Economic Analysis of Law

WHEN BY natural principles we are led to advance those ends, which a refined and enlightened reason would recommend us, we are very apt to impute to that reason, as to their efficient cause, the sentiments and actions by which we advance those ends, and to imagine that to be the wisdom of man, which in reality is the wisdom of God. – Adam Smith.[1]

A major influence in contemporary legal theory is the school of thought which has been labelled 'The Economic Analysis of Law' (EAL).[2] Richard A. Posner, its best known exponent, states that 'the hallmark of the "new" law and economics is the application of the theories and empirical methods of economics to the central institutions of the legal system, including the common law doctrines of negligence, contract, and property: the theory and practice of punishment; civil, criminal, and administrative procedure; the theory of legislation and of rule-making; and law enforcement and judicial administration'.[3] The novelty of the approach is claimed to be the systematic nature of its commitment to the study of law in the manner of economics. Intimations and instances of EAL are, however, noted both in legal studies of explicitly economic areas of law, such as anti-trust law, and in the work of such forerunners as Jeremy Bentham and Adam Smith.[4]

The citation of Smith as a proto-EAL writer is understandable in view of his significance for neo-classical economists of the Chicago School who have close intellectual and ideological affinities with EAL theorists, particularly as Smith was deeply involved in the study of law both as part of his economic and moral theory and as a subject in its own right. Further Smith was not slow to point out the economic benefits of the efficient administration of justice and the sociological link between legally protected freedoms and economic wellbeing. Also the preference for common over statute law, characteristic of EAL theorists, is equally characteristic of Smith's laissez-faire theory of the state. Nevertheless justice (which for Smith is synonymous with 'law') is, on the standard interpretation of Smith, primarily a moral ideal which provides grounds independent of economic considerations for the regulation of social interactions. Moreover, again on the standard view, Smith is not a Benthamite utilitarian of the sort whose mechanistic approach to social behaviour establishes the sort of economic approach which, in the view of most commentators, is part of E A L. The assumption that Smith is a forerunner of E A L is thus contentious enough to deserve investigation both to assess the justification for his invocation as a respected ancestor of a relatively novel legal theory and as an occasion for looking again at Smith's jurisprudence to see what illumination, if any, is provided by viewing his legal work in this perspective. It is, indeed, an attractive idea that Smith as the father of the science of economics might also be the progenitor of E A L. This would, however, involve a significant, but perhaps not altogether unjustified, revision of the orthodox image of Smith as a natural lawyer whose economic theory was bounded by moral constraints other than those of economic efficiency.

I

E A L is an attempt to provide a perspective on law which enables us both to understand and improve it in terms of economic efficiency. This approach, which has been developed largely in the United States since the late 1960s, follows on the introduction of economic concepts into the study of politics, also a largely American phenomenon, a decade or so earlier.[5] But E A L does not, like, for instance, the economic theory of democracy, simply deploy economic-type concepts, such as market competition, to the social reality it studies; it goes further than this and designates the purpose of law in primarily economic terms. The ultimate legal value is assumed to be wealth maximisation, the measure of wealth being what people are able and willing to purchase.[6] This thesis is partly descriptive in that, at least in the case of common law, decisions are said to be made, consciously or unconsciously, largely on the basis of economic efficiency, and partly normative, in that some judicial decisions and much legislative intervention is criticised for failing to safeguard or express the underlying economic logic of the law.

The basic premises of E A L are spelt out with helpful directness and clarity by Posner, who, characteristically of both economic theory and the analytical tradition of legal thought, sets out his assumptions in the form of a series of definitions. Thus 'efficiency' is defined as 'exploiting economic resources in such a way that

human satisfaction as measured by aggregate consumer willingness to pay for goods and services is maximized'. 'Value' is also
defined in terms of 'willingness to pay'.[7] The path to an efficient
society, therefore, is so to arrange things that resources are
distributed to those who are prepared to pay the highest price for
them; this is to give these resources their greatest value. If A is
prepared to pay £1 for a ticket to the football match for which B is
prepared to pay £2, then the ticket should go to B, thus giving it
twice the value it would have in A's hands. The only test of
whether B is prepared to pay £2 for the ticket is the fact that he
does so, just as the only test of its value to A is the price for which
A is prepared to part with it. Both matters are settled if there
occurs a voluntary exchange between A and B such that A sells a
ticket to B for £2 which A negotiated to buy for £1. In these
circumstances A and B have both gained since A has £1 more than
he started out with and B has the ticket he wants. The fact that
both parties are better off is alleged to be a general characteristic
of voluntary exchanges, for whenever a buyer is willing and able
to pay a sum which the seller is prepared to accept then satisfaction, as measured by willingness to pay, is increased.

This basic assumption about the benefits of voluntary exchanges is developed in the Chicago approach to economics into
a general consideration of how to facilitate voluntary exchanges
in such a way as to maximise value. Such maximisation requires a
free market in which people are able to produce what they will
and offer their products for sale to consumers who are free to
decide what to buy according to their preferences and means.
Adopting the assumption that men always seek to maximise their
satisfaction, it is argued that self-interested consumers, by choos-
ing the type of goods they wish at the lowest price on offer, will
force equally self-interested producers to make and market
goods of the quality and price for which there is the greatest
demand. Given adequate information about available products,
a sufficient range of producers able to enter the market, consumers able to buy, and low transaction costs, the economic system
will tend to a point of Pareto optimality in which no-one, producer or consumer, can improve his welfare in one respect without
reducing it more in another.

EAL, as expounded by Posner, makes the same standard
assumptions regarding human behaviour. Individuals seek to
maximise their utility outcomes so that, by voluntary exchanges,
value will be maximised by allocating scarce resources to those
who are willing to pay most for them. Applying this to law it is
assumed that the behaviour to be regulated by laws is governed

by wealth maximising individuals and that the motivations of those involved in legal processes as litigants, lawyers or judges, is governed by similar considerations. Thus potential criminals, in deciding whether or not to seek the benefits of theft, calculate the likely cost of the outcome and act accordingly, hence the deterrent power of the criminal law which parallels the law of supply and demand in economics, at least when there is a degree of certainty in the detection and punishment of offences. Similarly potential litigants, in deciding whether to take up or pursue a suit calculate the quantity and likelihood of the possible outcomes before making a rational decision on the basis of known probabilities, and in terms of their own wealth maximisation (or, perhaps, the wealth maximisation of all those in similar circumstances). More controversially judges determine the cases which come before them in terms of the most economically efficient way to allocate rights, determine liability and assess damages. Thus the law of tort or delict is a process of deciding upon the most efficient allocation of the hazards of life according to the opportunity costs involved (that is the benefits lost by eschewing more productive uses of the same resources) the general idea being that liability falls on the party who is the cheapest cost-avoider in relation to the losses at issue.[8] Again, property rights are allocated so as to achieve the most economically efficient distribution of possessions. Here as elsewhere the law functions by giving incentives to economically efficient behaviour.

EAL does not go so far as to claim that legal decisions are made consciously and overtly on an economic basis rather than according to distinctively legal reasoning but the claim is that the economic model does provide an effective means for predicting and hence explaining the function and development of laws. This in part is because judges in making law always consider the type of case with which they are dealing and therefore must take into account the consequences of their decisions for all similar situations using their common sense regarding the best use of scarce resources. Thus legal decision making is forward not backward looking, as on the orthodox view.[9]

One theoretical assumption of EAL, derived from the work of R.H. Coase,[10] is that if there are no costs involved in transactions between those in economic conflict, the legal allocation of rights is immaterial as regards the eventual outcome, for the party who values the relevant right most highly will always purchase it from the other party even if that party has been accorded the right in law. This runs counter to the previous held view that 'externalities', that is costs of production for which the producer did not have to pay, were economically inefficient since some of the factors which should affect the price did not in fact do so.[11]

However in real legal life pursuers and defenders of law suits are greatly affected by the costs of litigation just as in normal economic life they are influenced by the cost of entering into agreements with their fellows. Law suits are said to arise where the costs of ordinary voluntary agreements are too high for one or both of the parties but the losses entailed by having no agreement lead them to seek one to be enforced. Hence the recourse to law. The underlying legal attitude to such disputes is, it is alleged, to consider which party would pay most for the controversial right if there were no transaction costs and perfect information. Thus law promotes economic efficiency by making the allocations which would be the product of voluntary exchanges in situations which, however desirable on the free-market model, do not in fact exist. One of Coase's examples relates to the enormous cost of a railroad company making agreements with all owners of fields adjacent to railroad which are liable to be set on fire by engine sparks. In this and other similar allocations of the losses arising from risky activities the most efficient allocation is the one which places the loss on those whose loss-making or cost-avoiding activities are most highly valued by them. This means assigning legal rights to the party who would, if practicable, buy it were it assigned to the other party,[12] a matter which is, of course, affected by the relative wealth of the parties and the relative cost of each party meeting the losses, the allocation of which is being disputed.

Posner's thesis is that in all areas of law 'the common law method is to allocate responsibilities between people engaged in interacting activities in such a way as to maximise the joint value, or, what amounts to the same thing, minimise the joint cost of the activities'.[13] Adherence to 'moral' principles which appear to run counter to this, such as that contracts must be kept, if properly understood, can be seen as themselves ways of distributing the losses which make the behaviour in question immoral in a way which will minimise these losses in future. The basic moral rules of fidelity and honesty, for instance, are themselves economically efficient, or where they are not, are modified in their legal applications.[14]

II

Although Posner identifies his own criterion of wealth maximising with that adopted by Adam Smith[15] and R. H. Coase endorses what he regards as Smith's theory of human nature[16], few proponents of EAL give detailed consideration to Smith's own treatment of law. However Becker, a major influence on EAL theorists, quotes Smith's assertion that 'we are not ready to suspect any man of being defective in selfishness'[17] and he offers a general overview of Smith's jurisprudence to the effect that 'although Adam Smith, the principal founder of the economic approach, in interpreting laws and legislation in the same way as he interpreted market behaviour, even he, without much discussion, largely dismissed others as the result of folly and ignorance'.[18] This expresses the belief that Smith may be considered at least a tentative innovator of EAL and that his account of law is sensitive to [non-]economic factors. Both these connections will be illustrated in the remainder of this essay.

If we take *The Wealth of Nations* (which has a great deal of legal content) as having to do with 'expediency' or wealth maximising and note Smith's emphasis on the economic benefits of the settled administration of justice,[19] his historical studies of the development of law in relation to the economic states of social development[20] and the apparently general assertions he makes about the dominance of self-interest in human motivation,[21] there appears to be much to support the endorsement of the EAL view of Smith's approach to legal study. Further the model of the impartial spectator as judge[22] accords well with the role given by EAL to the common-law judge and the stress on the significance of the common law as the common-sense approach to economic conflict. Moreover Smith's conception of the invisible hand in relation to market equilibrium and other points of social balance[23] coincide with the EAL view of law as a process in which individual self-interest maximises value at least in part through the unintended consequences of the participants' actions.

There are, nevertheless, immediate objections to an analysis of Smith's social theory purely in terms of the interaction of self-interested individuals even within the constraints imposed by Smith's embodiment of the moral point of view, the impartial spectator. Not only are human beings concerned as much with obtaining the good opinion of their fellows as with straightforward personal wealth maximising[24] but they are also concerned with the welfare of their families, friends and countrymen.[25] Moreover the constraints of the impartial spectator, internalised by conscience and imposed by law and public opinion, are the results of actual spectators' efforts to sympathise with or 'enter into' the motives and feelings of those whose behaviour is being assessed. These spectator reactions depend on psychological factors with little direct connection with calculations of utility, either in the form of wealth maximisation or a pleasure-pain account. Rather they arise from instinctive reactive responses to the act, following on the imagining of what it is like to act, and to be acted upon in a certain way. Smith repeatedly denies that such reactions are based on extensive reflection. Rather, he argues, they arise from an immediate perception of agreement or disagreement of sentiments as between the actual agent's feelings and the sympathetic feelings of the spectator, and a spontaneous reaction of resentment or gratitude to imagining what it is like to be at the receiving end of the acts in question.[26] Since, on the basis of these immediate responses, rules are formed to prohibit harmful acts (basically those which generate 'natural' or unreflective sympathetic resentment), and these rules are accepted as limiting the actions of economically rational maximisers, it appears that many of the norms of social existence must be prior to considerations of wealth maximising.

The apparent absence of economic calculations from the sympathy mechanisms of the impartial spectator does not however negate the wealth maximising hypothesis as applied to Smith's account of law. For although Smith denies that the utility of moral and legal rules is the result of the conscious intentions of agents or spectators he equally insistently argues that they have such utility. Participants and observers may feel that their acts and judgements are based on their apprehension of what is right and proper, and it may be that these appreciations are indeed determined by what or what they can 'enter into' by way of sympathetic identification, but this is irrelevant to the end-products or as Smith would say, the 'final causes' of their acts and judgements.[27] Smith sharply distinguishes the efficient causes of human behaviour from its actual effects and, in this context, his thesis is that the cause of moral sentiments, and hence ultimately of a great deal of positive law, is imaginative sympathy, but that the results of this process are moral judgements and legal codes which, by and large, are efficient by utilitarian standards.

Moreover it can be argued that in many cases the success or otherwise of the spectator's effort to sympathise with others does depend on an implicit awareness of the economic value of the material things involved in the situation. Thus the degree of resentment felt by agent and spectator alike, in the case of theft, depends in part on the market value of the goods in question.

In the end much depends on the contentious issue of Smith's alleged utilitarianism, both descriptively (does he believe that social arrangements, including law, do maximise utility? and does he define utility in terms of wealth maximisation?), and

normatively (does he or does he not, in the end, subordinate
sentiments of justice to the general welfare where there is a clash
between them?). Difficulties of interpretation arise here
because of Smith's anti-utilitarian stand on the origin of morality
and law, his repeated claims that there is scarcely any conflict
between justice and expediency and his frequent warnings about
the self-centred abuses of an act-utilitarian approach to everyday
decisions. Thus the issue of whether Smith adopts an economic
analysis of law is part of a broader and more general dispute
about the nature of Smith's social and political theory which
cannot be comprehensively reviewed here.[28] But within this
wider controversy it is possible to explore a little of the evidence
for an economic approach in Smith's treatment of positive law.
No question of a simple Benthamite utilitarianism arises here, at
least from the legislator's point of view, but it has to be asked
whether Smith sees the history of common law as illustrating the
divine intention to protect and further the happiness of His
creatures conceived in wealth maximising terms via the mechanisms of human nature as they operate within specific social and
economic environments, and to what extent these mechanisms
can be construed as enabling men to respond to the incentives for
cooperation with this divine plan which are provided by the
sanctions of positive law.

Smith's *Lectures on Jurisprudence* are an obvious source in
which to quarry for evidence of his economic approach to law.
Both versions of the *Lectures* begin with resounding definitions
of the science of jurisprudence as the study of the rules which
ought to direct the actions of governments and the examination
of how far actual governments abide by these rules.[29] The overall
impression given by Smith, is that, within the limitations imposed by the stage of economic, moral and political development
of the societies in question, there are patterns to be observed in
the laws of all societies and that, by and large but far from totally,
these patterns are founded upon 'reason'.[30] This, at any rate,
echoes the ambivalent but clear enough voice of contemporary
EAL theorists to the effect that their analysis is largely descriptive, particularly in the sphere of the common law, but marginally prescriptive, particularly in relation to statute law. (EAL
theorists, of course, vary in the extent to which they are prescriptive, Calabresi, for instance, being more normative than Posner.)

A significant initial hurdle for the EAL interpretation of Smith
is Smith's clear distinction between the governmental pursuits of
justice and opulence. 'The first and chief design of every system
of government is to maintain justice; to prevent the members of

a society from encroaching on one anothers property, or seizing what is not their own.' It is only once this 'internal peace, or peace within doors', is secured that 'the government will next be desirous of promoting the opulence of the state'.[31] It would, therefore, appear that the law of property (or injury in general) is contrasted with 'police', that is whatever regulations are made with respect to trade, commerce, agriculture and manufacture, in not having to do with the pursuit of national wealth. The impression that the fundamental purpose of law is non-economic is strengthened by Smith's brusque appeal to 'reason' as the foundation of the basic laws which pertain in all societies against injuring others with respect to physical integrity, liberty and reputation:

> That a man has received an injury when he is wounded or hurt in any way is evident to reason, without any explana-tion; and the same may be said of the injury done one when his liberty is in any way restrain'd; any one will at first perceive that there is an injury done in this case. That one is injured when he is defamed, and his good name hurt amongst men, needs not be proved by any great discussion.[32]

Indeed, when Smith does provide the further explanations which he indicates to be largely unnecessary he does so by pointing to the 'natural' resentment aroused by such injuries and the retalia-tory impulses which are triggered by these reactions. Both the criminal and the civil law in these areas are the product of the modified sympathy felt by the non-involved persons in society – the impartial spectators – for those who suffer such injuries. Spectators go along with the natural resentments of the injured, although not to the full extent felt by those who suffer the injuries. They therefore approve of retaliation taken against the agents of injuries and the exaction of reparation where these are limited to the degree which is prompted by their restricted sym-pathy with the injured.[33] All this suggests little in the way of economic analysis for the impulses and reasons involved have no direct bearing on the increase of wealth.

It is true, however, that Smith elsewhere stresses the economic value (as well as the economic cost) of the proper administration of justice.[34] The peace and good order which this brings to a society is a prerequisite of its prosperity, particularly at the commercial stage of economic development. Thus, it could be argued, while justice is the first duty of government it is so only because, until justice is established, opulence is unobtainable. This is compatible with the maximisation of wealth being the more fundamental value or even with the pursuit of justice being dominantly of instrumental significance in the pursuit of wealth. Even if this is allowed however – and in its extreme form it is clearly a distortion of Smith's balanced view of the interrelationship of justice and economics – it does not begin to establish the novel thesis of the EAL, namely that the content of laws, the actual distribution of rights and duties, has an economic rationale. Smith's insistence on the economic utility of justice relates to the need for enforced rules governing those matters which cause resentment. This is not to give an economic explanation of such resentments.

It is always possible, of course, to maintain that since men are resentful of injury, and sympathetic with the resentment of those injured, they value the punishment of those who injure themselves or others and are prepared to pay for this by instituting and maintaining a system of law. In this way everything can be given a price and hence an economic value, including the satisfaction of any attainable moral objective. This way of 'economising' non-economic values can and often is used by those who present an 'economic' analysis of human behaviour[35] but it empties the theory of its original force by collapsing the distinction between wealth and other values. It is more interesting and significant, therefore, to peruse the question of the extent to which Smith sees natural justice as an independent factor in the determination of law rather than, for instance, as a device for wealth maximisation.

I shall return to a consideration of the criminal law later to see how far Smith's more elaborate treatment of this subject in the *Moral Sentiments* accords with Posner's thesis that economic rationality is a dominant feature within it. Remaining with the *Lectures on Jurisprudence,* for the moment, we find there an extensive treatment of the laws of property, a sphere in which Smith notes (and this is probably the reason for his extended treatment of property law) 'the origin of natural rights is not altogether plain'. Perhaps, then, in this more manifestly economic area, Smith's alleged economic approach to law will be more evident.

Initially the evidence is, again, not favourable to the economic interpretation of Smith. The first point Smith makes on the origin of property is that our sentiments concerning its distribution do not appear to coincide with a distribution which reflects the utility of objects to their potential possessors:

> It does not at first appear evident that, e.g. any thing which may suit another as well or not better than it does one,

should belong to one exclusively of all others barely because I have got it in my power; as for instance, that an apple, which no doubt may be as agreeable and as useful to an other as it is to me, should be altogether appropriated to me and all others excluded from it merely because I had pulled it off the tree.[36]

Smith then sets out to explain the traditional 'five causes from which property may have its occasion', namely:

1st, Occupation, by which we get anything into our power that was not the property of any before. – 2nd, Tradition, by which property is voluntarily transferred from me to another. – 3rd, Accession, by which the property of any part that adheres to a subject and seems to be of small consequences as compared to it, or to be part of it goes to the proprietor of the principal, as the milk or young of beasts. – 4th, Prescription or Usucapio by which a thing that has been for a long time out of the right owners possession and in the possession of an other, passes in right to the latter. – 5th, Succession, by which the nearest of kin or the testamentary heir has a right of property to what was left to him by the testator.[37]

Smith's explanation for the legitimacy of these ways of acquiring property is the spectator's approval of them which rests on the agreement felt by the spectator with the possessors' or inheritors' expectations of continued possession and exclusive use, expectations which thereby are deemed 'reasonable'.[38] The basis of this shared feeling lies in the psychological causes of expectations, which do not include the anticipated general utility of such expectations being fulfilled. This is not to say that Smith denies the economic utility of property systems, the protection of which constitutes the chief purpose of government whose activities are ultimately justified by its capacity to maintain the material conditions of human happiness[39] but, characteristically, he rejects the Humean account of the 'artificial' nature of property rules as some sort of human contrivance to further the general good.[40]

In practice the bulk of the material offered in the *Lectures on Jurisprudence* consists of historical narratives and descriptive comparative law rather than an attempt to trace a theoretical explanatory pattern in conjunction with explicit principles. However the clear overall framework of the narrative is the process of economic development through the 'four distinct stages which mankind pass thro: – 1st, the Age of Hunters; 2ndly, the Age of Shepherds; 3rdly, the Age of Agriculture; and

4thly, the Age of Commerce'.[41] Smith alleges that it is 'easy to see that in these several ages of society, the laws and regulations with regard to property must be very different'.[42] Hunters will have little property apart from captured prey, shepherds extend their concept of property to cover flocks, herds and huts; in an agricultural society this is broadened to include land, while in the Age of Commerce complex rules are required to facilitate the processes of production and exchange.

Obviously, then, Smith assumes that there is a close connection between a society's property law and its economic system. Man's claims to the exclusive use of things depend on their economic needs and aspirations. Clearly a pastoral society needs some rules to allocate the ownership of beasts while an agricultural society must regulate the use of land so as to give relatively permanent rights of possession to its users. All this accords with Posner's thesis that 'the legal protection of property rights has an important economic function to create incentives to use resources efficiently'.[43] But, again, the economic imperative of having some property laws with respect to productively significant items does not go so far as to demonstrate that the actual laws adopted are maximally efficient from an economic point of view. Nevertheless Smith's analysis of and comments on property rights do have much in common with Posner's in that both refer to the significance of exclusivity (the owner may prevent others using his property) and transferability through voluntary exchange. Posner says that exclusivity and transferability, combined with universality (when all resources are owned by someone), are the 'three criteria of an efficient system of property rights'[44] and in particular he says that 'if a property right cannot be transferred, there is no way of shifting a resource from a less productive to a more productive use through voluntary exchange'.[45] Smith similarly argues against a property system that limits transferability. Thus he notes that providing for perpetual entails is 'not only absurd in the highest degree but is also extremely prejudicial to the community, as it excludes lands entirely from commerce', while 'the right of primogeniture and the power of making entails have been the causes of the almost totally bad husbandry that prevails in these countries where they are in use. – When land is in commerce and frequently changes hands it is most likely to be well managed'.[46] These prescriptive comments have a clear EAL ring about them, but in his account of the actual laws prevailing there is little suggestion that economic factors are always decisive. In the case of primogeniture, for instance, the social needs which it met were primarily military not economic, since estates divided into small parts were unable adequately to defend themselves.[47]

One interesting example of an apparently EAL analysis in the sphere of property is Smith's treatment of the English rule making stray animals the property of the lord of the manor which is 'so constituted as to make people more careful in preventing strays and more attentive to claim them in due time'.[48] This explanation obviously assumes the role of law in providing incentives to economically efficient behaviour. As such it is to be compared to the application of EAL to the allocation of liability for losses caused by straying animals in which the duty of owners of land to users of the highway to maintain adequate fences is seen as providing incentives to prevent accidents. However a more typical EAL approach to this type of issue is to speak in terms of the least cost-avoider and the party best able to initiate market transactions.[49] Of this type of calculation there is no sign in Smith's jurisprudence.

Perhaps the most explicit example of EAL in Smith relates to his comments on exclusive privileges, such as the hunter's exclusive privilege to the beast he is in pursuit of, and the rights of patents and copyrights. These he notes are mainly 'greatly prejudicial to the interests of society,'[50] by which he means the wealth of society, and argues that 'the greatest part however of exclusive privileges are the weakness of the civil constitutions of the country', thus revealing a characteristic EAL distrust for statute as against common law. One example of an exclusive privilege which he exempts from such criticism, perhaps, as himself an author, in a self-serving manner, are laws of copyright, which he remarks, in an economic sounding vein, may 'encourage the labours of learned men',[51] an interesting exception since it is justified in terms of the provision of incentives.

This is, however, no more than a prelude to the critical account Smith gives, principally in *The Wealth of Nations*, of the evils of exclusive privileges in manufacture or trade, that is, of monopolies, which, he argues, have the effect of reducing supply and raising prices. Smith's persistent attacks on the mercantile system whereby each country sought to protect its own manufactures by tariff controls so as to maximise its holdings of gold, may indeed be considered as the most evident example of his economic interpretation of law, for his attack on government-imposed restrictions on trade and his preference for 'the obvious and simple system of natural liberty'[52] are directly linked to his avowed goal of increasing national wealth as measured in terms of consumer satisfaction, as is his support for those laws which restrain those who try to thwart open competition in manufacturing.[53]

Although this is removed from the assumptions of modern EAL theorists in that Smith measures national wealth by the quantity of consumer goods, or the necessities and conveniences of life,[54] while his modern counterparts make capacity to pay the measure of value, there is a very close parallel in their hostility towards state interference in the operations of the free market. Moreover the explanation given for the prevalence of such restrictive laws, namely the political influence of self-interested combinations of manufacturers and traders, is broadly similar, for Smith, too, realises that politicians and legislators more than courts are open to the manipulation of the pressure groups.[55]

Smith's defence of natural liberty in manufacture and commerce has to be viewed in the context of his overall economic theory in which he seeks to chart the causes of and the hindrances to the growth of national and multi-national wealth. It is neither necessary nor desirable to expound this theory in any detail here[56] but, as is well known, it results in his advocacy of a market economy which he views as a mechanism for translating man's normal desire to obtain the maximum return for his labour, capital and land, into the greatest possible output of 'the annual produce of the land and labour of society'.[57] This is achieved when men's economic choices are not influenced by laws which seek to alter these choices, so that resources are deployed 'naturally' in terms of the relative economic advantages of the commercial options open to individuals. This does not mean that there are no laws relating to economic behaviour, for the spectator's sympathetic resentments prohibit inter-personal injuries, but it does mean that, by and large, there should be no laws to restrict fair competition, which means no monopolies, restraints or prohibitions which affect market prices so that they detract from the 'natural' prices to which, in a condition of liberty, actual prices are 'continually gravitating'.[58] This situation of laissez-faire is approximated to in the common law because spectators do not sympathise with laws which prevent individuals deploying their resources as they wish and enjoying the fruits of their labours. However actual laws may be affected by the influence of faulty economic theories (such as mercantilism), the intervention of foolish politicians who bow to the demands of sectional interests and a variety of other historical and accidental factors.[59]

This thesis concerning natural liberty is clearly more of a

normative than a descriptive form of economic analysis, when applied across the board, although Smith contends that there are always 'natural' pressures which encourage the liberty which aids commerce, at least at the appropriate stage of economic development.[60] He does, however, make the assumption, essential to EAL, that the participant individuals act in the light of the incentives that economic opportunities and legal restrictions present. Law is assumed to alter economic behaviour by making certain commercial prospects less or more attractive to the maximiser of personal wealth. This type of social control hypothesis is a central ingredient of EAL. But it should be noted that the incentives in question are not always economic ones (in the shape of fines or loss of material goods) but include the other sanctions of the law which, although they may be given arbitrary economic equivalents, are not themselves economic, as in the case, for instance, of the threatened loss of liberty. Interestingly, EAL is ambiguous as to what counts as an incentive for the purposes of the theory, sometimes restricting 'incentives' to obviously economic or material factors, such as goods and services, and sometimes taking in any objects of desire or aversion provided we can make sense of the individual putting a cash value on them. In this looser conception of 'incentives' EAL tends to be reduced to uninformative tautologies regarding human behaviour which insufficiently distinguishes the economic from the moral aspects of human aspirations.[61] In Smith's case there is, perhaps, reasonable consistency, in the discussion of natural liberty at any rate, in that he treats the incentives which affect trade primarily in genuinely economic terms.

There are, nevertheless, major issues of interpretation at stake here for it has been argued that Smith's real interest in these matters is the furtherance of liberty for its own sake.[62] Certainly Smith is at pains to stress the fact that natural liberty is just as well as efficient. Thus to restrict the woollen trade is 'evidently contrary to that justice and equality of treatment which the sovereign owes to all the different orders of his subjects'.[63] And laws which prevent manufacturers from becoming shopkeepers are 'evident violations of natural liberty, and therefore unjust; and they were both too impolitick as they were unjust'.[64] The question as to which takes priority – justice or opulence – would be more readily solved if Smith allowed that there might be serious clashes between these two governmental goals. But, for Smith, such conflicts are rare, so that there is an unsettled question in many commentators minds regarding the relative significance of Smith's main principles, justice and efficiency.[65]

One inherent difficulty in resolving this issue relates to the point at which economic efficiency comes into Smith's own calculations of the value of laws. Evidence that he takes the overall benefits of free trade, for instance, to be satisfaction maximising, does not entail that he regards this as more than one aspect of its justification. Often his appeal is to the sentiments of the impartial spectator as not only causally prior but as in general superior to the explicit forward looking calculations of judges and legislators, although there is evidence that in his own practical reflections, Smith tended to adopt a more consequentialist approach to the political issues of his day.[66] But it is clear that Smith was not prepared to recommend this approach to anyone who did not have the stature of a statesman rather than that of a mere politician.[67]

Here we do seem to have a major difference between EAL and Smith's jurisprudence. The system of natural liberty, as we have seen, consists of an absence of laws which do not gain the approval of the spectator and the existence of laws which do gain that approval. The approval and disapproval of the spectator is based on psychological factors regarding the emotions and imagination and is not the outcome of the sort of rule-utilitarian reasoning attributed to common law judges in hard cases by some EAL theorists. Smith's spectator, in considering how to distribute rights, imagines how he would feel in the place of the various contending parties and does not ask himself which rules will be most conducive to economic progress. Thus laws prohibiting free entry into the woollen trade are unjust because the spectator cannot but share the frustrations of those excluded, and they are tyrannical because the spectator shares the resentment of those who are punished for illegal trading in wool. And we have already seen that in the *Lectures on Jurisprudence*, for instance, property rights are based in the spectator's capacity to enter into certain expectations of the parties concerned.

Equally in the case of the obligation to keep contracts this is based on the expectations aroused by entering into a formal agreement and the consequent resentment following upon a breach of contract.[68] Little direct reference is made to the economic utility of any specific laws of contract in explaining its origin and force, these being a matter of the degree of resentment aroused by the disappointment caused to those who rely on contracts which are broken. It should, however, be noted that in his account of the historical selection of those types of contract which could sustain legal actions, Smith notes that 'All contracts which were necessary for the carrying on of business . . . were considered as sustaining action'.[69]

Nevertheless, since the weight of Smith's material is used to convince us that the spectator theory is the key to the development of law and hence the practical basis for establishing a positive legal system which approximates to ideal of natural jurisprudence, it is easy to assume that Smith is presenting a theory of natural rights, which accords ill with the more utilitarian schema of the EAL.[70]

III

To appreciate the nature and extent of the EAL aspects of Smith's jurisprudence it is necessary to examine further his concept of the 'invisible hand'[71] whereby the sentiments of man, as they operate in different economic and political circumstances, do in fact produce a result which accords with God's intention to see to the happiness of all sentient creatures.[72] From this perspective it appears that justice is basically instrumental to an ulterior utilitarian purpose, although not one which is captured in purely wealth-maximising terms. On this topic Smith is more sophisticated in his analysis than Posner's simple appeal to the role of general rulings and the immorality of wasting scarce resources,[73] for he does have a concern for fair distribution as well as economic efficiency. The rough equality in the distribution of the essentials of life which he observes to be a feature of commercial society[74] comes about only in part from the recognition of man's basic natural rights[75] and has more to do with the growth of the division of labour and the manufacturing enthusiasms of those who are inspired by their (largely unfounded) anticipations of the pleasures of wealth and greatness and their delight in the workings of complex industrial systems[76] which lead them to produce far more of the necessities and conveniences of life than they can themselves use. This is a process which Smith argues is relatively unaffected even by bad commercial laws since 'The natural effort of every individual to better his own condition, when suffered to exert itself with freedom and security, is so powerful a principle, that it is alone, and without any assistance, not only capable of carrying society to wealth and prosperity, but of surmounting a hundred impertinent obstructions with which the folly of human laws too often incumbers its operations'.[77] It is this overall view of the divine economy, expressing God's concern for the happiness of *all* his sentient creatures, that provides the context in which Smith makes his remarks about the sacred rights of man.

The political implications of such an approach are that laws should be confined to the formal expression of the sentiments of natural resentment in inhibiting injury, plus such positive measures as are required for defence, revenue raising and the 'erecting and maintaining certain public works and certain public institutions, which it can never be for the interests of any individual or small number of individuals, to erect and maintain'.[78] One institution required for the pursuit of these objectives is a judiciary, independent of the executive, which because of its separation from the every day world of commerce and positions, has the impartiality to heed the voice of the spectator and hence apply the rules of natural justice.[79] That these rules turn out to be happiness maximising is not the result of judicial foresight but of impartial judgment and a capacity to apply general rules to particular circumstances.[80] Thus although judges are not intentional utility-maximisers they do have their part to play in the divinely organised social system.

A good example of this divine economy operating in relation to law is to be found in the *Moral Sentiments* where Smith discusses liability for negligent actions. Smith notes that in the case of gross negligence, as when 'a person should throw a large stone over a wall into a public street',[81] this is punished even if no injury results, but it is punished more severely if there is a resulting injury. Similarly in less blameworthy cases where a person's acts cause harm to others there may be liability to pay compensation even though the act would not normally be considered particularly blameworthy and even when no blame attaches to it. This Smith notes is an 'irregularity' in that it does not seem rational to take accidental considerations into account in this way[82] but it does accord with the sentiments of the spectator whose imaginative feelings are influenced more by actual than by possible consequences of acts. This is evidenced in similar laws in different jurisdictions. Sympathetic resentment is, therefore, the efficient cause of this aspect of the law of delict but the final cause of this, 'irregularity of sentiment' whereby 'the world judges by the event, and not by the design' is the 'happiness and perfection of the species',[83] for it prevents the uncertainties and disturbances which would arise from punishing mere intentions and makes men attentive to the actual consequences of their acts so that they take care to avoid damaging others. Thus the sentiments of the spectator, irrational as they may appear to be, teach man 'to reverence the happiness of his neighbour',[84] a clear example of the influence of law on behaviour through the incentive effects of the allocation of liability for loss.

Similar points can be made about the EAL approach to criminal law for here there are some interesting parallels between Posner's and Smith's analysis. At first sight it may seem a difficult task to apply the EAL to the criminal law outside the area of theft, fraud and destruction of property since the economic loss involved in physical injuries and death are not immediately apparent, unless loss of earnings or the cost of hospitalisation or funeral expenses are thought to be the central features of the losses inflicted by violent crime, although it is feasible to think of what victims would have been prepared to pay in order to avoid the injuries they sustained and to avoid the fear of assault and murder, thus enabling us to compute the social cost of crime. However the central focus of Posner's analysis of criminal law is on the behaviour of the potential criminal who as a utility-maximiser must be threatened with greater costs than he would gain from criminal acts:

> People engage in the acts that yield them the most value net of costs and can be deterred from criminal activity by a punishment system that makes the cost of criminal activity greater than the value of the activity to them.[85]

While, in the case of civil law the object of deterrence is limited to those cases where the costs to the victim of the tort are greater than the benefits which accrued to the perpetrator of the wrongful act, in criminal law the objective is to prevent all performance of the forbidden behaviour except, perhaps, where the disvalue of the punishment outweighs the harm done by the putative criminal behaviour. In view of the potential criminal's prospects of concealing his act the penalties threatened must take this risk factor into account and be correspondingly higher as the chances of detection are less. The most obvious measure of the level of sanction is the quantity of a fine, but equivalences can be found for the penalty of imprisonment, particularly if the relative wealth of offenders is taken into account in fixing the monetary equivalent of a period in jail.

Thus, on the economic analysis, the basic legal method of reducing crime is the effective imposition of penalties sufficient to deter criminal behaviour, although this requires to be supplemented by reducing the poverty which makes property crimes attractive and giving incentives to potential victims to take steps to avoid victimisation (which could itself be achieved in part through legal sanctions).

The economic model of crime control is, as Posner notes, a Benthamite one, and as such runs counter to Smith's insistence that while rational calculation is a feature of economic life it is no more than an after-thought in the mind of the impartial spectator as he is embodied in the person of the criminal judge. The spectator imagines himself to be the victim of the crime and to the extent he shares in the resentment and desire to retaliate felt by the victim, so far does he approve of criminalisation of injurious conduct and the infliction of a degree of punishment equivalent to the extent of his sympathetic resentment: 'in all cases the measure of punishment inflicted on the delinquent is the concurrence of the impartial spectator with the resentment of the injured'.[86] No calculations of utility are involved, at least in normal cases. Those exceptions that Smith allows, such as the military law which lays down the death penalty for sleeping on watch, have special justifications not present in ordinary criminal activities. Equally unnatural are crimes, such as smuggling, created by statute despite the absence of any spontaneous resentment against smugglers.[87]

Yet, before Smith's theory of the criminal law is classified as non-economic, it is necessary to take account of his insistence that criminal punishment does in fact deter criminal acts and that, through an invisible hand mechanism, the degree of punishment is apparently fortuitously but actually through divine pre-arrangement, sufficient for the purposes of deterrence. In practice, 'the punishment which resentment dictates we should inflict on the offender tends sufficiently to deter either him or any other from injuring us or any other person in like manner'.[88] Moreover Smith, arguing in a very economic style, explains the severe punishment for piracy, for instance, as being due to the greater opportunities there are for committing that crime undetected.

Smith's line of reasoning here seems to imply that agents, if not spectators, do act as rational maximisers of their own utility, which conflicts with some of his statements about the limited capacities of human beings in this regard. These limitations are most in evidence in the moment of action and for this reason Smith commends that we govern our behaviour by general rules and not by on-the-spot reckoning of consequences, for fear that in the heat of the moment the temptations of partiality and short sightedness (for which our conscience will punish us thereafter) will lead us into ultimately irrational acts. It is not therefore altogether clear how this squares with Smith's sanguine belief in the efficacy of deterrence. But there is little doubt that he had such a belief and that gives his theory of criminal law considerable affinity with Posner's more explicit and direct economic analysis.

Conclusion

It is possible to argue that, despite Smith's appeal to the mechanisms of the impartial spectator's non-intellectual judgements and the implications this has for the model of judicial judgement, there is no fundamental divergence here between EAL and Smith's apparently more socio-psychological theory of law. EAL theorists are not always clear as to how the efficiencies of the common law come about. Some assume that there is a large element of common-sense economic reasoning at work, but others give no real account of the process of common law judgement[89] or are ready to fasten on something like Smith's concept of a blind social mechanism of which the beneficial results are not the intended consequences of rational human choice.[90] In contrast, Smith may be said to have provided a general theory to explain the efficiency of the common law, something which is lacking in the modern EAL. On Smith's view, consideration of the general good is too weak a ground for human beings to act upon and judges to reason about. God does not therefore leave attainment of the general happiness to human rationalisation but implants strong instincts and sentiments which properly socialised man can follow in his every day affairs and use in the judgement of his fellows and thus unwittingly play his part in achieving God's utilitarian goal.

There are clearly many significant points of detail in which Adam Smith and modern EAL theorists such as Richard Posner differ. Specifically Smith does not attempt systematic analyses of law in terms of the cost-benefit approach and other techniques of modern welfare economics. Moreover there are major differences in general outlook between the theological functionalism of Smith and the secular individualism of fully-fledged EAL theorists. However the apparently massive difference between Smith's natural rights apparatus and the amoral instrumentalism of modern EAL theorists diminishes on closer examination. Smith's natural rights are not immune from revision in the light of consequentialist reflections and many of those reflections relate to the maximisation of national wealth. Moreover, as I have argued, at the level of explanation Smith's perspective of the divine economy relates his endorsement of natural rights to their divinely intended role of securing the safety and prosperity of mankind. Further, EAL theorists do not claim that laws are never affected by non-economic criteria such as fairness and propriety; what they argue is that efficiency is normally the dominant factor in the determination of the common law, particularly in the nineteenth century.

Even Smith's rather wider use of 'utility' to cover the happiness of all sentient creatures, and his idiosyncratic minor theme in which the admiration of 'utility' is equated with man's wonder at the nice adjustment of means to ends, particularly in the operations of complex mechanisms,[91] does not present a sharp contrast with EAL theory which tends to drift from pure economic utility involving the use of scarce resources which serve material satisfactions into a more general value which covers any object of human desire, including the fulfilment of moral goals. Smith is at one with EAL theorists in that, when considering laws which have direct economic relevance, it is the maximisation of wealth that is man's chief measure of utility.

Finally it should be noted that, for all Smith's rejection of human consequentialist reasoning as a major factor in the causal explanation of legal and other social phenomena, he does presuppose that individuals act in relation to laws in an instrumental way by refraining from disobeying the law in order to avoid the unpleasant consequences of liability. Men are rational enough to be deterred by the prospect of economic loss and punishment. This is far from the whole picture for Smith, since laws which are based on the sentiments of the spectator will be supported and approved by the bulk of a population, although men may be tempted to break the law when it is to their advantage to do so. Rational self-interest is therefore reinforced by individual conscience and social pressure. For this reason there are strict limits to the flexibility of law reform since laws which do not express the reactive feelings of the impartial spectator, however beneficial they may appear to be, will lack the normal moral supports and will therefore fall short of the level of compliance required to produce their desired effects.[92] Yet the effective enforcement of laws also requires sanctions and in so far as it is the sanctions that Smith has in mind in his comments of the beneficial effects of good laws, to that extent he manifests one of the chief characteristics of EAL, the idea that law is a means for diverting self-interested individuals towards a mutual accommodation in which clashes of interest are settled at least over all cost to the community, thus contributing to the market pursuit of maximal efficiency.

References to Smith's *Theory of Moral Sentiments* are to Smith, 1976a and take the form 'TMS page number' or 'TMS pt.sect.chap.para.'

1 TMS II.ii.3.5.
2 See Calabresi, 1970 and the Chicago based journals *Journal of Law and Economics* and *Journal of Legal Studies*.
3 Posner, 1975, 757.
4 See Bowles, 1978, Coase, 1976, Posner, 1979, Becker, 1976, p. 12, Terrebone, 1981, Buchanan, 1976 and Partlett, 1982, 65.
5 Downs, 1957.
6 Cf. Keenan, 1981.
7 Posner, 1972, p.4.
8 Recommended in Calabresi, 1875.
9 Cf. MacCormick, 1978.
10 Coase, 1960, p.1. Cf. Cooter, 1982.
11 See Pigou, 1932.
12 Posner, 1972, 36.
13 *Ibid.*,178.
14 *Ibid.*, chs 1 and 28.
15 Posner, 1979, 105–35.
16 Coase, 1976, 529–46.
17 Becker, 1976, 282.
18 *Ibid.*, p.12.
19 See Smith, 1976c, v, iii, 7; also TMS II.ii.3.3–4.
20 Smith, 1978, A, i, 26–35; B, 149–50; 1976c, v, i.a–b.
21 TMS II.ii.2.2; 1976c, I, 11.2.
22 See Haakonssen, 1981, 100.
23 See Campbell, 1971, 69–79.
24 TMS III.1.3.
25 *Ibid.*, VI.ii.3.6.
26 See Campbell, 1971, ch.5.
27 TMS II.ii.3.5 and iii.intro.6.
28 See Campbell, 1975 and 1981; Lindgren, 1973; Haakonssen, 1981, ch.4; Buchanan, 1976.
29 Smith, 1978, A, i.1.
30 See Campbell, 1971, 116–52 and 197–9.
31 See Smith, 1978, A, 1.2. and B, i.5.
32 *Ibid.*, 1.24.
33 TMS VI.ii.intro.2.
34 See Smith, 1976c, IV, vii, 6.2. & v.i.6.
35 See e.g. Becker, 1976.
36 Smith, 1978, A, 1.26.
37 *Ibid.*
38 *Ibid.*, i.35–7 and B, 150; also Haakonssen, 1981, 104.
39 TMS IV.I.11.
40 TMS II.11.3.6n and Hume, 1975, E.P.M., III.
41 Smith, 1978, A, 1.29.
42 *Ibid.*, 1.33.
43 Posner, 1972, p. 10.
44 *Ibid.*, p.11.
45 *Ibid.*, p.13.
46 Smith, 1978, A, i.166.
47 *Ibid.*, i.134.
48 *Ibid.*, i.58.

49 See Kenny, 1982, 46ff.
50 Smith, 1978, A, ii. 34.
51 *Ibid.*, ii, 32.
52 Smith, 1976c, IX, ix, 51.
53 *Ibid.*, I., xi, and IV, ii.39.
54 *Ibid.*, I, intro.4.
55 See Smith, 1978, B, 328 and 1976c, I, xi, p; also
   I.x.c.61; IV, ii, 43; IV, vii, b.49.
56 See Campbell, 1977.
57 Smith, 1976c, I, intro.9.
58 *Ibid.*, I, vii.15.
59 See *ibid.*, III, passim.
60 See *ibid.*, IV, ii, 43.
61 See Leff, 1974.
62 See Lindgren, 1973, 82 and Macfie, 1967, 48.
63 Smith, 1976c, IV, ii.43.
64 *Ibid.*, IV, v.b.16.
65 See Haakonssen, 1981, 87–9.
66 See Campbell, 1981.
67 See Smith 1976c, VI, ii.2.12 and 14.
68 See Smith 1978, A, ii.56.
69 *Ibid.*, ii.69; see also 71.
70 See Fried, 1978.
71 See TMS IV.i.10; also 1976c, IV, ii.9.
72 See TMS III.5.7.
73 Posner, 1972, pp.6–7 and 393f.
74 See TMS IV.i.10.
75 See Smith, 1976c, IV, iii.b.16 and 44.
76 See TMS IV.i.9–10.
77 Smith 1976c, IV, v.b.43.
78 *Ibid.*, IV, ix.51.
79 *Ibid.*, v, i.b.25.
80 See TMS III.4.
81 TMS II.iii.2–8.
82 See Campbell, 1971, 41–5.
83 TMS II.iii.3.1–2.
84 *Ibid.*, II.iii.3.4.
85 Posner, 1972, 357.
86 Smith, 1978, A, ii.89.
87 See *ibid.*, ii.92 and TMS II,ii, 3.11.
88 Smith, 1978, A, ii. 156.
89 See Posner, 1972, p.6.
90 See Rubin, 1977, 31 and Priest, 1977, 65.
91 See TMS IV passim.
92 See Campbell, 1977, 523–34 and 532ff.

V. HOPE

Smith's Demigod

UNTIL RECENTLY Adam Smith's moral philosophy was sadly neglected. Fortunately appreciation of its importance is now growing as it is seen to be no minor variation on the spectator theories of Hutcheson and Hume, but rather a major improvement on them.

Professor D.D.Raphael comments:

> The positive advance that Smith made in moral philosophy was as great as Hume's . . . and represents the culmination of an important movement of empiricist ethics . . . The concept, though not the precise name, of an impartial spectator is there already in Hume. What is original in Adam Smith is the development of the concept to explain judgments of conscience made by an agent about his own actions.[1]

As Hume improves on Hutcheson, so Smith improves on Hume. He points out what neither of his predecessors realises – that there is no virtue which is not conscientious and that the feeling of conscientiousness is a sense of being expected to act impartially as one expects others to act.

Hutcheson thinks that all virtue is the spontaneous benevolence of the individual (aided by calculative reason). Hume thinks that some virtue is natural and some 'artificial' or conventional. Smith goes further – he thinks that all virtue is conventional, the conscious observance of mutually agreed principles, which, because they are moral, are impartial.

The first part of the following discussion considers his views on the relation of conscience to external or public expectation. The second considers his theory of moral propriety. The concluding section deals with his assumption that virtue is identical with propriety.

1: The man within and the man without

Smith describes conscience as an internalised spectator. He refers to this imagined person as 'the man within'. There has been

considerable discussion about just who this person is and what
his qualities are. Some believe him to be an idealised critic.²
Others feel that Smith means him to represent a kind of social
consensus.³ Professor Raphael takes him to be the agent himself
measuring his behaviour by his own ideal of impartiality, and he
shows how, with the progress of editions, and especially in the
sixth, Smith alters his conception of 'the man within' who seems
finally to enjoy a kind of apotheosis.

In the sixth edition, Raphael notes, Smith is at pains to declare
the independence of individual conscience.

> Here (in *The Theory of Moral Sentiments*, sixth edition,
> III.3.29), as elsewhere, Smith distinguished the impartial
> 'supposed' spectator from the 'real' one. The rudimentary
> stage of the virtue of self-command, found in the child or the
> man of weak character, depends on the feelings of actual
> spectators. The higher stage, reached by the man of con-
> stancy, depends entirely on conscience.⁴

Smith has come to see that the conscience of the man of virtue if
not of lesser mortals, is above convention. Later in the sixth
edition, for the first time he distinguishes 'the idea of exact
propriety and perfection' from 'the approximation to this idea
which is commonly attained in this world.' The sense of virtue
draws on the former, though its original model is the latter. The
individual, he says in the sixth edition, begins by respecting 'the
man without' but ends by acknowledging the supremacy of 'the
man within', his own conscience.

> But though man has, in this manner, been rendered the
> immediate judge of mankind, he has been rendered so only
> in the first instance ; and an appeal lies from his sentence to a
> much higher tribunal, to the tribunal of their own con-
> sciences, to that of the supposed impartial and well-informed
> spectator, to that of the man within the breast, the great
> judge and arbiter of their conduct. The jurisdiction of those
> two tribunals are founded upon principles which, though in
> some respects resembling and akin, are, however, in reality
> different and distinct. The jurisdiction of the man without, is
> founded altogether in the desire of actual praise, and in
> aversion to actual blame. The jurisdiction of the man within,
> is founded altogether on the desire of praise-worthiness,
> and in the aversion to blame-worthiness . . .⁵

Smith realises that public standards can be too low for virtue and
is impressed by the possibility of private heroism. He sees that if
he attaches overmuch importance to virtue's need to please the
public, virtue will seem no more than fashion.

Raphael suggests, however, that if he changes his emphasis from the social to the private aspect of conscience, he continues throughout to give each its place. Conscience evolves an ideal of impartiality from reflection on actual practice.

> Throughout the development of Smith's concept of the im-
> partial spectator, his fundamental position was unchanged.
> In the first edition he stressed the effect of men's social
> situation more than the work of the imagination; in the
> second and sixth editions, he reversed the emphasis.[6]

It is clear, then, that Smith comes to regard 'the man within' as a model for improvement on convention, as the voice of an ideal, standing for excellence and perfect virtue.

Before his change of emphasis he describes conscience as an inner representation of real people. Though imagined, the spectator is not imaginary. In judging ourselves, he says in the first edition,

> we must imagine ourselves not the actors, but the spectators
> of our own character and conduct, and consider how these
> would affect us when viewed from this new station . . . We
> must enter, in short, either into what are, or into what ought
> to be, or into what, if the whole circumstances of our con-
> duct were known, we imagine would be the sentiments of
> others, before we can either applaud or condemn it.

> A moral being is an accountable being. An accountable
> being, as the word expresses, is a being that must give an
> account of its actions to some other, and that consequently
> must regulate them according to the good-liking of this
> other. Man is accountable to God and his fellow-creatures.[7]

We are told here that conscience constructs what are or 'ought to be' the sentiments of our fellow-men, 'ought' here being descriptive, not prescriptive. The imagined spectator stands for external attitudes, not for subjective responses on the part of the person who imagines him. Even in the sixth edition Smith repeats his original statement of the first edition, that virtue regards the feelings of real spectators.

> To be amiable and to be meritorious; that is, to deserve love
> and to deserve reward, are the good character of virtue; and
> to be odious and punishable, of vice. But all these characters
> have an immediate reference to the sentiments of others.
> Virtue is not said to be amiable, or to be meritorious,
> because it is the object of its own love, or of its own grati-
> tude; but because it excites those sentiments in other men.[8]

Indeed, the main claim of his theory is that propriety only attaches to someone's behaviour insofar as someone else can

sympathise with it. Propriety, or virtue (since Smith usually
thinks they are the same) is intersubjective and is not a quality
one's behaviour has in itself or merely because one approves of
oneself. Echoing what he had said in the first edition, he says in
the sixth,

> We either approve or disapprove of the conduct of another
> man according as we feel that, when we bring his case home
> to ourselves, we either can or cannot entirely sympathize
> with the sentiments and motives which directed it. And, in
> the same manner, we either approve or disapprove of our
> own conduct, according as we feel that, when we place
> ourselves in the situation of another man and view it, as it
> were, with his eyes and from his station, we either can or
> cannot entirely enter into and sympathize with the senti-
> ments and motives which influenced it. We can never survey
> our own sentiments and motives, we can never form any
> judgment concerning them; unless we remove ourselves, as
> it were, from our natural station, and endeavour to view
> them as at a certain distance from us. But we can do this in
> no other way than by endeavouring to view them with the
> eyes of other people, or as other people are likely to view
> them. Whatever judgment we can form concerning them,
> accordingly, must always bear some secret reference, either
> to what are, or to what, upon a certain condition, would
> be, or to what, we imagine, ought to be the judgment of
> others. We endeavour to examine our own conduct as we
> imagine any other fair and impartial spectator would ex-
> amine it.[9]

The test of propriety, we are told, is one of sympathy between
real people. We must appeal to 'the judgment of others'. The
'inner man', then, even if he represents an ideal, must, in some
way, also represent the sympathies of actual people when they
consider motives and sentiments from a disinterested point of
view. On this understanding Professor T. D. Campbell says,

> The spectator is 'ideal' in the sense that he excludes all those
> features of actual spectators which relate to their special
> interests as particular individuals involved in the actual
> situation which they are observing; he is 'empirical' in the
> sense that once this abstraction is made, the responses of the
> spectator are identified with the consensus towards which
> any actual group of persons can be observed to approximate
> in their attitudes to the behaviour of their fellows.[10]

Professor Campbell disagrees with the view that Smith wants us
to understand the spectator as someone who 'represents certain

normative standards which go beyond those to be found in the average spectator'.[11]

On the one hand, then, Smith's original theory describes conscience as the feeling of being watched by some representative of real people to whom one feels accountable. On the other, he comes to modify the representational significance of the imagined spectator, with the object of freeing him from convention. This modification implies that the standards of the virtuous are higher than those of 'mere propriety'.

However, he feels uneasy about this alteration and is uncertain about the relation of conscience to convention. If conscience is conventional, the ordinary man can be conscientious, but duty is the slave of fashion. If conscience requires perfection, duty is freed from public opinion, but the ordinary man cannot be conscientious. His confusion is indicated, perhaps, by his reference in the second edition to 'this inmate of the breast, this abstract man, the representative of mankind'[12], the latter phrases suggesting someone who is not real, yet somehow epitomises real attitudes.

His discomfort shows when he considers the effect on conscience of violent public criticism.

> We scarce dare to absolve ourselves, when all our brethren appear loudly to condemn us. The supposed impartial spectator of our conduct seems to give his opinion in our favour with fear and hesitation ; when that of all the real spectators, when that of all those with whose eyes and from whose station he endeavours to consider it, is unanimously and violently against us. In such cases, this demigod within the breast appears, like the demigods of the poets, though partly of immortal, yet partly too of mortal extraction . . . when he suffers himself to be astonished and confounded by the judgments of ignorant and weak man, he discovers his connexion with mortality, and appears to act suitably, rather to the human, than to the divine, part of his origin.[13]

He is admitting, in other words, that conscience cannot go against the weight of total public opposition.

But these theories of conscience, as prescriber of conventional duty and as advocate of perfection, can easily be reconciled. Conscience demands that one does one's conventional duty, providing one is in sympathy with it. But conscience sees this as a *minimum* that must be done, beyond which lies virtue. The virtuous, then, while agreeing with sound convention, naturally aspire to doing more than is needed to avoid being blameworthy. Smith unfortunately, confuses mere dutifulness with virtue, of which, indeed, it forms a part, and hence precludes the possibility of being more than dutiful. But, seeing that great virtue transcends conventional requirements and even capabilities, he tries to make room by loosening duty from convention. Instead he should recognise the difference between mere dutifulness and true virtue, between meeting an obligation and acting supererogatively. There is no inconsistency between conscience agreeing with a minimum laid down by convention while advocating that more be done. How much more the individual does is up to him and his natural virtue.

Smith is surely correct in basing duty on external expectation and the sense of duty on the feeling that one should meet that expectation. To accept something as one's duty means agreeing to be reliable in doing something which is useful. It is conventional in the weak sense that it presupposes agreement to be dependable, on the part of the agent, and to be dependent, on the part of the person to whom the duty is owed. One cannot acquire or dissolve duties simply by making personal decisions. There must always be a factor of external dependence, even if the duty is a moral one. 'The man within', the voice of duty, has to speak for someone other than the agent, that is for the dependent.

If the agent agrees to be dependable, the man within voices a consensus between him and his dependent. This is the case with conscience. Conscience implies one's agreement to be dependable. The agent, the man within and the man without then have a common sympathy.

2: Smith on Propriety

'The man within' continues the career of the disinterested spectator found in Hutcheson and Hume. However, he plays a much more active role than they give him. By contrast Smith believes that *any* virtue is partly owing to his active supervision in his role as conscience.

Both Hutcheson and Hume admit the existence of the sense of duty and its power to guide action, but neither sees its exercise as necessary for virtue. They both think that a person can be virtuous without any direction from the man within. For both, the moral good of a virtuous act is quite incidental to its aim, though the aim is not, they think, incidental to its goodness.

Virtue, Hutcheson says, is benevolence insofar as it is pleasing to a disinterested spectator. There is no need for the agent to aim at being thus pleasant and it is no moral loss if his only purpose is to do good to some other being.

Hume's conception of virtue is more sophisticated. Yet his

position is essentially the same. Virtue is behaviour which is pleasing to the disinterested spectator because it is useful or agreeable. He stresses that moral good is irrelevant to aim and devotes himself to explaining how behaviour, especially of the just, has happy results, including causing disinterested pleasure.

Smith considers this a trivialisation of virtue, reminding us of the difference between being a good person and being a good chest of drawers (a remark which is somewhat unfair to Hume who allows moral virtue only to sentient beings).

He writes at length on the sense of duty, insisting that there is no virtue without it and ending the third part of *The Theory of Moral Sentiments*, which concentrates on duty, by saying, 'No action can properly be called virtuous, which is not accompanied with the sentiment of self-approbation.' He is referring to the approval of the imagined spectator. This is an important correction to the Hutchesonian theory of moral sense and Hume's version of it.

His greater achievement, however, is his theory of moral propriety, that it attaches to behaviour which is intentionally impartial so as to earn the sympathy of 'the man without'. The essence of propriety, he thinks, is mutual sympathy between an agent and his critic. The distinguishing feature of moral propriety is that it aims at the sympathy of the impartial, who are not just in sympathy with impartiality *but are also in sympathy with aiming at having such sympathy*.

He thinks that two forms of moral propriety are conscientious action for which gratitude is appropriate and conscientious action for whose omission resentment is appropriate. These actions are directed at others. But as well as these responsibilities there are, he believes, duties to self. These three kinds of moral propriety have their corresponding virtues of beneficence, justice and prudence. The master virtue is self-command which ensures that one does whatever one thinks morally right.

Smith's notion of sympathy is akin to Hume's, though with important differences. Hume says that the moral sense relies on sympathy with those happily or unhappily affected by agents. Being sympathetically pleased because someone has been made happy by someone, he says, one feels pleased with the agent and that feeling is a perception of his virtue. Or, feeling sympathetically displeased because someone has been made unhappy by someone, one feels displeased with the agent and the feeling is a perception of his vice. Smith thinks along similar lines. The sense of moral propriety depends on sympathy with the gratitude or resentment of those affected by agents, but he adds that approval

of virtue also depends on *sympathy with the agent*, while disapproval of vice depends on being out of sympathy with him.
This a vital supplement to Hume's views.

He attaches two slightly different meanings to the word 'sympathy', one weaker than the other. He illustrates the weaker by
reminding us that we can see that something is funny without
ourselves being amused.[14] We realise that we would laugh, were
we in the mood. The weak notion of sympathy is thinking that,
given one's present character, though not one's mood, one
would behave like someone else were one in their circumstances.

His stronger idea is that sympathy is the mild replication of a
passion or feeling which one believes someone to have, in consequence of thinking that one would feel a certain passion were one
in that person's shoes. Accordingly, those who have just eaten
their fill cannot sympathise, he says, with the famished, because
they cannot feel hungry.[15]

If he uses both notions, it is perhaps fair to say that the core of
his theory is that in sympathising one knows that one shares with
someone else a common response to some kind of situation. He
then says that approval of behaviour is finding that one sympathises with it and disapproval is finding that one is out of sympathy.
Hence, in his view, propriety and impropriety are relative to the
joint character of agents and spectators—who are also agents.
Where there is a common character there can be mutual sympathy, approval and propriety; where there is a positive dissimi-
larity, there is no sympathy but disapproval and impropriety.

The joint character of the dutiful and those who approve of
them is not obvious from Smith's theory because he stresses the
critic's role as a spectator. But his theory of sympathy makes it
clear that he regards the critic as an agent in the position of
observer. He is meant to be an impartial agent as well as an
impartial judge. In approving of duty he feels he would do the
same himself. He would mean to engage just such sympathy as
his were he in similar circumstances.

The need for impartiality arises, Smith thinks, from the need
to avoid conflicts of interest which inevitably occur when one is
dealing with friends, family and associates. Realising that an
action will offend some, while pleasing others, one appeals to a
disinterested spectator from whose viewpoint all interests are
given equal importance.[16]

Equality of interest does not mean, however, equality of attention by one person to others, Smith suggests. Each person should
look to himself first, then to his family, friends and associates.
Impartiality asks that everyone's interests are open to the same

means of satisfaction, though each person gives prominence first
to himself, then his family and so on. So self-interest combines
with altruism under the general direction of sociableness.

The main-spring of virtue, he believes, is man's natural desire
for 'mutual sympathy', the realisation by two people that each
sympathises with the other. Virtue guarantees a certain kind of
mutual sympathy, sympathy with deliberate impartiality. It
guarantees mutuality among those who are prepared to consider
each as important as any. Selby-Bigge describes Smith's theory
well when he says, ' . . . the essence of his system is that it is a
closed circle of reciprocal sympathy.'

In this there is a further advance on the moral psychology of
Hutcheson and Hume, for by postulating natural pleasure in
mutual sympathy Smith is observing that man is not simply a
compound of benevolence and self-interest, since he enjoys sharing for its own sake. Neither Hutcheson nor Hume recognises
this for both ignore the satisfaction of sharing.

However, advanced as it is, this account of moral propriety
needs correction. In the first place it implies that one's responsibility is to a disinterested spectator. But those to whom one is
morally responsible always have a certain interest in what one
does, though not necessarily *self*-interest. They are not *mere*
spectators. Only if one has some interest at stake has one any
reason to complain if duty goes undone. Moral responsibilities
are not owed to mere spectators but to those with whom one
shares a common good. What Smith means to convey is the
impartiality of the moral viewpoint.

Secondly, while propriety does indeed depend on mutual sympathy with impartiality, it is not sympathy as Smith conceives of
it. A confirmed bachelor can be in sympathy with the institution
of marriage. Someone who cannot suffer a phobia can have
sympathy for someone who does. But neither possibility is
allowed by Smith's theory, for that requires that a sympathiser
thinks that he, with his present character, would choose marriage
for himself and would himself be terrified in the manner of the
phobic. (This interpretation of Smith's notion of sympathy is
unusual; and is based on I. ii. I & 2. On the other hand see VII.
iii. I.4.) However, sympathy is not thinking that one shares the
same personal reaction. Rather it is *either* thinking that someone
is in a bad way and should be helped (or should have been helped
to avoid his distress) *or* thinking that certain behaviour is right
and should be supported. The sense of duty depends on the
latter. Both forms imply value-judgments moreover. And this is
a further omission from Smith's account which lacks any mention

of the worth of one reaction compared with another. So on two scores his idea of sympathy is out of step with commonsense.

However, moral propriety *is* to be explained by mutual sympathy. To have moral propriety behaviour needs to be that of an agent on whom someone depends so to act, both being in sympathy with the principle that, in the interest of impartiality, one such person should depend on such another. For example, the moral propriety of dress rests on clothes-wearers and potential dependents agreeing that in the common-interest it would be impartially best if certain types of clothes be worn. Once there is agreement wearers can then accept responsibility from dependents.

3 : Propriety and Virtue

Smith distinguishes at one point between virtue and mere propriety.

> Virtue is excellence, something uncommonly great and beautiful, which rises far above what is vulgar and ordinary. There is in this respect a considerable difference between virtue and mere propriety; between those qualities and actions which deserve to be admired and celebrated, and those which simply deserve to be approved of. Upon many occasions, to act with the most perfect propriety, requires no more than that common and ordinary degree of sensibility or self-command which the most worthless of mankind are possest of.[17]

But this is an uncharacteristic admission for one who tries to explain virtue simply through propriety. The bed-rock of his whole theory is his analysis, first of propriety, then of moral propriety, whose test is the sympathy of the impartial spectator.

On many occasions he refers to conscience as 'the sense of propriety', as he does, for example, when he says that the virtues of self-command are recommended to us 'by the sense of propriety, by regard to the sentiments of the supposed impartial spectator'.[18]

That he regards virtue as a form of propriety is implied by his comparison of his own account with that which values virtue by utility.

> That system which places virtue in utility coincides too with that which makes it consist in propriety . . . According to this system (of utility) therefore, virtue consists not in any one affection, but in the proper degree of all the affections. The only difference between it and that which I have been endeavouring to establish, is, that it makes utility, and not

sympathy, or the correspondent affection of the spectator, the natural and original measure of this proper degree.[19] But propriety is not identical with virtue. It consists in doing what is conventionally expected, *whether the convention is right or not.* One can act with perfect propriety, but wrongly, because people are mistaken about what they should be relied on to do.

Virtue, on the other hand, cannot do what is wrong. It is the quality of being good for being reliable in doing what one really ought to be relied on to do. In being virtuous one is not only conventionally right but actually so. The convention is itself right. But even if a convention of reliability is sound, true virtue is more than mere propriety. To be truly virtuous one has to be good beyond the point of simply being blameless, though any conscientiousness has some virtue if the action is morally right.

References to Smith's *Theory of Moral Sentiments* are to Smith, 1976a and take the form 'TMS page number' or 'TMS pt.chap.para.'
1 Raphael, 1875, 85.
2 Firth, 1952.
3 Campbell, 1971.
4 Raphael, 1975, 93–4.
5 TMS III.2.32.
6 Raphael, 1975, 94.
7 TMS IIIn.
8 *Ibid.*, 113.
9 *Ibid.*, 109–10.
10 Campbell, 1971, 127.
11 *Ibid.*
12 TMS 130n.
13 *Ibid.*, 131.
14 *Ibid.*, 17.
15 *Ibid.*, 27.
16 *Ibid.*, 129.
17 *Ibid.*, 25.
18 *Ibid.*, 262.
19 *Ibid.*, 305–6.

GEORGE MORICE

Opinion, Sentiment and Approval in Adam Smith

HERE IS Adam Smith's initial account of what it is to approve of the sentiments of another.

> When the original passions of the person principally concerned are in perfect concord with the sympathetic emotions of the spectator, they necessarily appear to this last just and proper, and suitable to their objects; and, on the contrary, when, upon bringing the case home to himself, he finds that they do not coincide with what he feels, they necessarily appear to him unjust and improper, and unsuitable to the causes which excite them. To approve of the passions of another, therefore, as suitable to their objects, is the same thing as to observe that we entirely sympathize with them; and not to approve of them as such, is the same thing as to observe that we do not entirely sympathize with them.[1]

In the immediately succeeding paragraph, Smith somewhat abruptly introduces the topic of approval of opinions and makes the following claim:

> To approve of another man's opinions is to adopt those opinions, and to adopt them is to approve of them. If the same arguments which convince you convince me likewise, I necessarily approve of your conviction; and if they do not, I necessarily disapprove of it: neither can I possibly conceive that I should do the one without the other. To approve or disapprove, therefore, of the opinions of others is acknowledged, by everybody, to mean no more than to observe their agreement or disagreement with our own. But this is equally the case with regard to our approbation or disapprobation of the sentiments or passions of others.[2]

The construction of this paragraph and its placing in the argument of Chapter III suggest the following account of Smith's procedure here: having expounded what he believes is a new and perhaps controversial theory of the approval of sentiments, he aims to elicit acceptance of this theory by appeal to a matter on which he expects agreement; namely, the character of our approval of opinions. This interpretation is suggested by the unheralded introduction of the topic of opinion and its approval, and by the easy transition to the claim that this reading of approval of opinion is universally acknowledged. The conclusion is then swiftly drawn that approval of opinion does not differ essentially from approval of sentiment.

One therefore expects approval of opinion, as briefly delineated here, to be a common and commonly-remarked phenomenon. But it is certainly not immediately clear to the modern reader what approval of opinion is. There is also some evidence that Adam Smith's contemporaries were puzzled by the phrase. A student of Thomas Reid's represents that philosopher, who had an ear for such matters, as holding that 'men's opinions are no proper objects of moral approbation or disapprobation, but when it is applied to opinion *to approve of an opinion* indeed only signifies that I am of the same opinion'; and that when 'our author says "to approve of an opinion is to observe the agreement with my own," this one would think has some meaning but I really can see none in it'.[3]

Although Reid, if indeed these are Reid's sentiments, is puzzled by the expression, he acknowledges that no man would approve of an opinion contrary to his own 'for this would be to suppose him to have an opinion & to have it not, at the same time'.[4] I agree with this. I understand the expression 'approval of opinion' to mean at least that there is a necessary connection between approving of an opinion and oneself holding it. As Smith himself says: 'If the same arguments which convince you convince me likewise, I necessarily approve of your conviction; and if they do not, I necessarily disapprove of it; neither can I possibly conceive that I should do the one without the other'.[5] Whatever Smith may mean by 'necessarily', the reference to necessity is apt.

What interests me is the question whether the parallel that Smith draws between approval of sentiment and approval of opinion is a just one. I find the parallel intriguing because of its evident implications for the objectivity of morals. So far, I have drawn attention to two somewhat divergent features of Smith's argument. In the first place, he appears to support his characterisation of approval of sentiment by appeal to a generally acknowledged feature of approval of opinion. But, in the second place, it is not a simple matter to say what approval of opinion is. I shall approach the problem of the validity of Smith's parallel from the opposite direction. Taking it that Smith has a generic notion of approval, which he is presenting in these early chapters, I shall ask what approval of opinion is likely to be, given this generic notion. This will uncover certain problems about approval of opinion. I shall then consider the implications of the suggestion that by 'approval of opinion' Smith means no more than assent to opinion.

Smith's primary interest, of course, is the approval of sentiment. I shall not, in general, comment on the analysis he offers of this. Rather, I wish to ask if it *is* the case, whether or not 'acknowledged by everybody', that 'to approve or disapprove. . . . of the opinion of others [means] no more than to observe their agreement or disagreement with our own'.

> A. N. Prior makes the following comment on Smith's claim:
> The trouble with this argument is, of course, that it is *not* 'acknowledged by everybody' . . . that 'to approve or disapprove of the opinions of others' *means* no more than 'to observe their agreement or disagreement with our own'. It would probably be acknowleged that we would in fact approve of all opinions coinciding with our own, and of no others; but *why* would we? Plainly, many would say, because to make an opinion 'our own' is to regard it as true, i.e. as a perception or representation of a fact beyond the opinion itself. . . . The coincidence of another man's opinion with ours we take to be a sign of its truth, but we do not identify this coincidence with its truth. On the other hand, Smith does identify the 'propriety' of another man's feeling with its coincidence with our own. The supposed analogy between such propriety and the truth of an opinion therefore disappears.[6]

In the end, I will have little to add to this. But I wish to understand Smith's parallel. I find it an attractive parallel, since it brings together phenomena that much recent philosophy has sharply separated; namely, believing and approving. (An exception is Bambrough, 1979.)

Essentially, according to Smith, to approve of another's sentiments is to be pleased by the observation of a concord of that person's sentiments with one's own. This concord arises, where it does arise, out of an attempt on the spectator's part to imagine what he would feel were he in the situation of the agent. If, on thus imagining himself in the agent's shoes, the spectator experiences a feeling similar to that felt by the agent, then he sympathises with the latter; there comes into being a 'correspondent affection' in the spectator, who is pleased by this coincidence of sentiments. This pleasure, generated in the said fashion, Smith calls 'approval'.

In Smith's account of the moral sentiments, both these phenomena appear to be necessary, viz. *sympathy,* or a correspondence of affection in agent and spectator that is brought about by the act of the imagination whereby the spectator distances himself from his own situation, and the *pleasure* generated in the spectator by his observing this sympathetic concord: for 'nothing pleases us more than to observe in other men a fellow-feeling with all the emotions of our own breast; nor are we ever so much shocked as by the appearance of the contrary'.[7]

I say that both these phenomena appear to be necessary; but two qualifications to this claim may be noticed immediately.

Smith observes that there are cases of approval where there is no sympathetic duplication of the agents' sentiments;[8] so that, in these cases, approval would appear to need another account. But even where, as a matter of fact, there is no imaginative generation of a correspondent affection in the spectator's breast, approval, he argues, is 'ultimately' founded upon such a correspondence. The explanation of this is that we learn from experience what sorts of phenomena are apt to generate sympathetic feelings in us; so an association is formed between the agent's sentiments and our approval. This association does not always require to be mediated by the imaginative exercise of transposing ourselves into a situation not our own. It is, perhaps, enough that on identifying a situation as one of a type we have already encountered we judge that if we were in that situation we should feel thus-and-thus. We need not actually experience a correspondent affection.

The other preliminary qualification is that forced by Smith's acknowledgement that, as spectators, we often sympathise with an agent who does not have that sentiment the similitude of which arises in our breast when we survey his situation. Such cases include those of the insane and the dead.[9] Here, we often feel for another a passion 'of which he himself seems to be altogether incapable'. Although this type of case is puzzling, its possibility is a direct consequence of Smith's insistence that sympathetic feelings are not directly transmitted from agent to spectator, but arise from the act of the imagination whereby the spectator transfers himself into the situation of the agent. So central to the theory is the agent's *situation*, that reflection on this situation can arouse in the spectator sentiments whose originals do not exist in the agent. And this phenomenon requires us to make a distinction. For Smith, 'sympathy' usually means correspondence of sentiments (whether actual or hypothetical). Sometimes, however, 'sympathy' is used by him to refer to the power of the imagination by which such a correspondent affection is brought about. We must, that is, distinguish sympathy as an achievement and sympathy as a power.[10]

The first of these qualifications, and Smith's explanation of it, pose a question about his comparison of approval of sentiment and approval of opinion. It seems sufficiently clear that to approve of an opinion is to share it. That is to say, if I approve of what another thinks I actually hold the same belief. There is nothing in the least hypothetical about my doing so. Although Smith does not use these words, it is clear that he means that such approval implies endorsing the opinion as true. And doing this is the same thing as holding the opinion. But, as we have noticed, to approve of another's sentiments is not necessarily to feel the same or similar passions. There is pleasure in the concord of sentiments, but this concord does not have to be actual. What my approval of another's sentiment commits me to is a judgement that *if* I were in his situation I should feel likewise. This observation pleases me; that is, I approve of his sentiment; but I am not, and may never be, in his situation.

However, approval of another's opinion commits me to actually holding it, and not merely to the judgement that if I were in his situation then I should believe what he believes. This is, obviously, a consequence of the difference between an opinion and a sentiment. If two people share an opinion, there is one, and only one, opinion that each believes. Whereas, if two people share a sentiment it seems clear that there are two, qualitatively similar, sentiments. I suspect that Adam Smith could not have recognised this distinction.

Now, we know that Smith represents approval of sentiment as the taking of pleasure in the observation of a concord of agent's and spectator's sentiments, this concord being brought about by the spectator's imaginative transposition of himself into the situation of the agent. And this imaginative transposition is necessary to the account. One thing that appears to be wrong with the comparison of approval of sentiment and approval of opinion is that the mechanism of sympathetic identification, as one may call it, is quite irrelevant to the approval of opinion. In order to approve of another's opinion 'as agreeable to truth and reality' it is not in the least necessary to suppose myself in his situation and view the matter as I should then see it. It is not required that I consider the evidence available to him, and review the arguments that are to his hand. To do this might well be to cut myself off from a source of evidence that is available to me but not to him. If the question is 'Is his opinion *true*?' we have no business to – and we commonly do not – ignore evidence that, for one reason or another, he did not consider.

The attempt to imaginatively identify with another, in order to reach a view about his opinions, is relevant, however, to a different exercise: that of considering whether I approve of *him* for holding these opinions. In this case, I am less interested in the question whether his opinions are true than in the question whether they are *justified*; that is, in the question whether *he* is justified in believing these opinions, given the evidence that is available to him. And, naturally, I can think that he is justified, and that had I been in his situation I should have held exactly the same opinions, without therefore concluding that these opinions are true. One may, for example, approve of a juryman for believing that the defendant did not do the deed, although one believes, perhaps even knows, that he did what he was accused of. One may think that the juryman has correctly drawn his conclusions from the evidence that was presented at the trial. And we think it important that juries be capable of reaching decisions from correct appraisals of the evidence, even if this sometimes leads to verdicts that are at variance with the facts.

So there is a parallel between approval of sentiment and approval of opinion but *this* parallel is not of the kind that Smith imagines. What he seeks is a parallel between approval of opinions and approval of sentiments; what we have at present is a parallel between approving of someone for holding an opinion and approval of someone for having a sentiment. It remains a question whether there is a parallel of the sort he proposes.

At this point, it is necessary to notice a qualification to the claim that approval implies a sympathetic identification, of spectator with agent, in the sense so far explained. Smith distinguishes two sorts of occasions on which judgements of propriety or impropriety are made. There are those occasions when the objects that excite our sentiments are considered 'without any peculiar relation, either to ourselves or to the person whose sentiments we judge of', and there are those occasions when the objects 'are considered as peculiarly affecting one or other of us'.[11]

The kinds of object that belong to the first category comprise a somewhat heterogeneous lot. They are 'the beauty of a plain, the greatness of a mountain, the ornaments of a building, the expression of a picture, the conduct of a third person, the proportions of different quantities and numbers, the various appearances which the great machine of the universe is perpetually exhibiting, with the secret wheels and springs which produce them', which Smith sums up as 'all the general subjects of science and taste'.[12] But the important feature of judgements of propriety of this kind is that you and I look at the objects of these judgements from the same point of view. Since the objects of such judgements bear no peculiar relation to your interests rather than to mine, or to my interests rather than to yours, we are both spectators. And the implication of this is that there is no need for sympathetic identification; that is, there is no occasion for the imaginary change of situation that forms such a central part of Smith's distinctive theory of approval.

Where, however, the object of judgement is such as to affect differently our interests, it is much more difficult to arrive at correspondence of sentiments, and at the same time it is much more important. Your indifference to my injury or adversity is intolerable to me; and, conversely, my passion and my violence are repugnant to you. Each of us, therefore, has a motive for seeking an accommodation of sentiments, and the mechanism of sympathetic identification is brought into play.

There is a further point about judgements of the former kind. Although we occupy the same vantage point in relation to the objects of such judgements or sentiments – it is significant that, here, Smith uses the words 'judgement' and 'sentiment' indifferently – this does not imply that we always agree in our judgements about 'the general subjects of science and taste'. Of course, we do not. But where we are 'differently affected' this is because we differ in the degree of 'natural acuteness in the faculty of mind', and also in the amount of attention we give to the matter in hand. And where we differ, where 'your judgements in matters of speculation, [or] your sentiments in matters of taste, are quite opposite to mine, I can easily overlook this opposition'.[13] Indeed, if I have any spirit, this very contradiction may afford our conversation some extra piquancy. Smith even says, in the same paragraph, that when we disagree about this picture or that poem or some system of philosophy, we can neither of us 'reasonably be much interested about them. They ought all of them to be matters of great indifference to us both'.

The distinction between the two sorts of judgements of propriety, those that require and those that do not require the effort of sympathetic identification, appears to be less a distinction between types of subject-matter (morality as opposed to speculative thought, for example) than a distinction between matters that do and matters that do not affect our interests. The need for sympathetic identification is most evident in the domain of what we are accustomed to call morality, although even here experience will often enable us to dispense with an actual effort at identification, as Smith has agreed. On the other hand, even judgements about numbers and proportions may give rise to differences of interest, for example in applied mathematics, say in questions of money and inheritance. It seems to me that the difference is between those situations in which there is an agent and a spectator and those in which there are only spectators. In the sorts of case that do not necessitate sympathetic identification, Smith includes 'the conduct of a third person', in relation to whom you and I are both spectators and are not divided by interest. And I wish to follow up this thought.

But first let me note the implication of this distinction for the criticism I earlier made of Smith. My original interest was in his comparison of two sorts of approval. In both sorts, to approve is to observe, or to be pleased by the observation of, a certain kind of agreement between approved and approver: an agreement of sentiments or of opinions, as the case may be. And I argued that the comparison is defective, inasmuch as in the case of opinion there seems, in general, no need for an imaginary change of place to bring about the sympathetic affection. That seemed relevant to a different question; namely, whether I approve of the agent for being affected as he is. It now appears that Smith has an answer to this. In the case, speaking generally, of opinions, there is indeed no need of sympathetic identification, and the reason for this is that there is, normally, no agent in such cases. Those who approve and those who are approved of are both spectators, they occupy the same standpoint, and there is no potential conflict of interest.

I am not, however, persuaded by this, and that for two reasons. In the first place, I think that Smith's explanation of the dispensability of sympathetic identification in matters of science and taste necessitates a revision of his principle that mutual sympathy is always pleasing to us.

The principle of the pleasure of mutual sympathy is presented and explicated in *The Theory of Moral Sentiments*, 1.1.2. Here, Smith insists that 'whatever may be the cause of sympathy, or however it may be excited, nothing pleases us more than to observe in other men a fellow-feeling with all the emotions of our own breast; nor are we ever so much shocked as by the appearance of the contrary'. It is fundamental to Smith's theory that a correspondence of affection between oneself and another, whether the affection itself be intrinsically pleasing or displeasing, is always agreeable. Indeed, approval itself *is* the pleasure that we take in observing such coincidence.[14]

Now, as we have seen, there is a class of judgements of propriety, or of occasions for such judgements, where we approve without the need for sympathetic identification. The correspondence of sentiment (and, I repeat, in *The Theory of Moral Sentiments,* 1.1.4, sentiment and judgement are not distinguished) is brought about without the imaginary translation of the spectator to another place. Nevertheless, what we have here is fellow-feeling, which should yield pleasure, according to Smith's principle that nothing gives us more pleasure than coincidence of affection, however it is brought about.

It is not merely that, when we concur in opinion, this frequently does not provoke any very lively sense of pleasure; for Smith offers an explanation of this. Rather, it is his insistence that the objects of science and taste are, and ought to be, matters of great indifference to us; 'so that, though our opinions may be opposite, our affections may still be very nearly the same'.[15] And it is his further insistence that, if we are people of any degree of temper, we may derive entertainment from opposition and difference. What, in that case, becomes of the principle of the agreeableness of mutual sympathy? The very idea that coincidence of taste ought to be a matter of indifference to us seems almost to sustain verbal contradiction when, rebutting the egoistic explanation of the agreeableness of mutual sympathy, Smith insists that this pleasure is always felt so instantaneously, and often on such frivolous occasions, that it cannot possibly be founded on nice calculations of self-interest.[16]

I have another reason for being dissatisfied with Smith's claim that approval of opinion does not require the characteristically Smithian mechanism of sympathetic identification. If approval of another's opinions does not require an imaginary change of situation, what then remains of the comparison between approval of sentiment and approval of opinion? It seems to me that, bluntly and crudely, what is left is this: I approve of another's opinions if they agree with my own. And what is wrong with this is that, while it is true that I approve of another's opinions if they agree with my own, clearly something is left out if we say that to approve of another's opinions *means no more* than that they agree with my own. This, of course, is Prior's criticism.

We thus arrive at an old debate between commentators on Adam Smith, one on which I have here nothing fresh to say: this is the debate about the difficulty that Smith has in bridging the gap between sentiments as praised and the same sentiments as praiseworthy; or again, the debate about the connection between the sentiments of an actual, indifferent spectator and those of an ideal Impartial Spectator.

At one time, I viewed these early chapters of Smith's book as if he were there engaged in writing a kind of natural history of approvals; a natural history that required to be amplified in the light of the later introduction of the Impartial Spectator, and of Smith's generalisation of the latter's role into a norm for all judgements of approval and not merely for judgements of self-approval. But it does presently seem to me that the early chapters resist this interpretation, and that Smith is here making more or less categorical statements about *what it is* to approve. One reason for thinking this is that, while he has a continuing concern with our 'original' judgements of approval, this concern cannot be solely with our earliest, and perhaps no-longer typical judgements. He writes, for example, that 'originally. . . . we approve of another man's judgement, not as something useful, but as right, as accurate, as agreeable to truth and reality'.[17] But it is clear that he does not think that agreement with truth and reality is properly replaced, in the development of the moral sentiments, by utility. This placing of utility is reinforced and amplified in the fascinating second chapter of Part IV; here, he asserts that our sentiments of approval 'are originally and essentially different' from the perception of utility. 'The usefulness of any disposition of mind is seldom the first ground of our approbation; and . . . the sentiment of approbation always involves in it a sense of propriety quite distinct from the perception of utility'.[18]

When, therefore, Smith says that to approve of the opinion of another means no more than to observe its agreement with our own, indeed that it is acknowledged by everybody to mean no more than this, and that the case is the same with the approval of another's sentiment, I cannot treat this characterisation as simply a moment in the developing history of the phenomena of approbation and disapprobation.

Essentially, my difficulty with Smith, here, is this: he is right in thinking that approval implies a position of detachment from the biased situation of an agent; an assumption of the role of spectator. But he does not accurately specify this detachment. Briefly, he appears to think it enough that a spectator is indifferent in the sense of being uninvolved (I am aware that, later, he speaks with a different voice; aware, too, that an attractive feature of his system is his reluctance to depart very far from the stance of actual spectators) whereas what he requires is that a spectator be indifferent in the sense of being impartial.

In order to approve or to make a judgement of propriety, it is necessary that he who judges be impartial. One might then think that the last thing that a spectator or judge ought to do is to imagine himself in the agent's shoes; surely, the more successful this act of imagination is, the less impartial will be his judgement? The spectator must depart from his private and particular situation in order that he properly judge the agent's sentiments. But this is not to say that he must entirely adopt the agent's situation. For then he will merely have exchanged one private and particular stance for another: he will not be a genuine spectator.

However, it is, I think, an essential feature of Smith's theory that it is as spectator that I judge. (There are contrasting suggestions. In particular, v. TMS VII. III. 1.4.) I enter into the agent's *situation*, but it is with *my own eyes* that I judge; the exercise of imagination in detaching me from my present, actual situation does not destroy my spectatorial impartiality. It is supposed, I think, that the combination of taking *his* place and looking at it with *my* eyes produces impartiality. This comes out particularly sharply in his discussion of the insane and the dead, where the attempt to see their plight with their eyes would result, in the case of the insane, in a surrender to their happy idiocy, and in the case of the dead, in no judgement at all. The spectator, therefore, has to 'retain some consciousness of his own self as that which sympathises'.[19]

However, my difficulty remains. In seeing the agent's situation with my own eyes, I still view that situation from a private and particular standpoint. I am detached in that I do not submerge myself to the degree that I forget I am a spectator; but I am not detached in the sense that I adopt a general and impartial position that is neither his, nor mine, nor his as seen by me.

When Smith avers that to approve of another's opinion is to observe its agreement with our own, and that sympathetic identification is unnecessary for judgements of science and of taste, he has forgotten that in the case of 'the various appearances which the great machine of the universe is perpetually exhibiting' we do *not* look at them from the same point of view. Indeed, he denies it. He has forgotten, or he has not yet realised, what he was to write later (significantly, after the introduction of the Impartial Spectator) that

[even] to the eye of the body, objects appear great or small, not so much according to their real dimensions, as according to the nearness or distance of their situation. . . . In my present situation an immense landscape of lawns, and

woods, and distant mountains, seems to do no more than cover the little window which I write by, and to be out of all proportion less than the chamber in which I am sitting. I can form a just comparison between those great objects and the little objects around me, in no other way, than by transporting myself, at least in fancy, to a different station, from whence I can survey both at nearly equal distances, and thereby form some judgement of their real proportions. Habit and experience have taught me to do this so easily and so readily, that I am scarce sensible that I do it. . . .[20]

In the succeeding paragraph, Smith makes the parallel claim for judgements about objects that are differently related to my interests and to those of another. 'We must view them, neither from our own place, nor yet from his, neither with our own eyes nor yet with his, but from the place and with the eyes of a third person, who has no particular connexion with either, and who judges with impartiality between us.'

I am, therefore, inclined to conclude that Smith's parallel between approval of opinion and approval of sentiment is not a valid one. The dispensability of sympathetic identification raises a serious question about his fundamental principle of the pleasure of mutual sympathy; and the reduction of approval of opinion to the observation of agreement in opinion (or to the pleasure evoked by such observation) is unjustified.

However, I cannot firmly conclude that the parallel drawn by Smith is unwarranted until I have noticed another suggestion about what is meant by 'approval of opinion'. Consideration of this suggestion will also help to explain Smith's easy persuasion that the ground of such approval is agreement in opinion.

The suggestion that I have to consider, briefly, is that when he writes of approval of opinion Smith means merely assent to (an) opinion. (That Smith may have meant, by 'approval', assent or *approbatio*, was pointed out to me by my colleague Peter Jones.)

This is certainly how he was understood by some of his contemporaries; for example, by Adam Ferguson, who, indeed, represents Smith's theory of approval, in one place, as the theory that the distinction of right and wrong is 'the Sympathy or want of Sympathy, that is, the Assent or Dissent of some two or more persons. . . .'[21] Here, Ferguson writes of sympathy rather than of approval, but what he is discussing is Adam Smith's theory of approbation. In this dialogue (which its editor, E. C. Mossner, was inclined to regard as a report of an actual conversation that took place in 1761), Ferguson represents Robert Clerk as saying to Smith,

You endeavour to explain away the distinction of Right and Wrong by telling us that all the difference is the Sympathy or Want of Sympathy, that is, the Assent or Dissent of some two or more persons of whom some one acts and some other observes the action and agrees or does not agree in the same feeling with the actor. If the Observer agree, sympathise, go along with him, or feel that he would have done the same himself, he cannot but approve of the Action. If, on the Contrary, he does not sympathise or agree with the Actor, he dissents & cannot but disapprove of him; and you seem to mean that where there is neither assent nor dissent there is neither Right nor wrong. . . .[22]

Perhaps, then, in *The Theory of Moral Sentiments,* 1.1.3, Smith is merely saying that to assent to or to dissent from the opinions of another is acknowledged by everybody to mean no more than to observe their agreement or disagreement with our own. This will not save the parallel but, for a reason I shall give immediately, it casts some light on Smith's belief that his claim will be generally accepted. 'Assent' can be, and, I think, normally was, used as the name of an act of the mind, in which I accept a proposition as true. This act need not find expression in words. It is sufficient that, on the proposition's coming to mind, I take it to be true.[23] On the other hand, 'assent' can be used as the name of a public, usually verbal, performance, in which I declare my agreement with a proposition or opinion. Similarly, 'approval' can be the name of an act or state of mind, in which I note, and am pleased by, concordance of another's opinion with my own; and it can be used of a public performance in which I declare or express my pleasure in the agreement of another's opinion with my own. Now, in the public sense, it is reasonable to hold that, in assenting to or approving of another's opinion, I am doing no more than signifying that I concur. I need have no more substantial reason for *saying* that I approve or assent than that I agree with the other. It does not follow from this that in approving of or assenting to another's opinion, that is, in believing it to be true, I am doing no more than thinking that his opinion agrees with mine. Nor, of course, is it true.

It is clear that, sometimes, when Smith writes of approval, what he says is plausible only of the interior act of mind. Only of this can it be true that, if the arguments that convince you convince me, I *necessarily* approve of your conviction. Obviously, when I am persuaded of the truth of a proposition, I do not necessarily express my approval. But I cannot help believing the proposition. At the same time, the fact that, from the first,

Smith's theory of approval is a spectator theory, that the objects of our first approvals are *other people's* sentiments and opinions, exerts some pressure on him to think of approvals in terms of public performances. It would be no surprise, and no uncommon error, if the ambiguity of 'approval' misled Smith.

I conclude, therefore, that the parallel between approval of opinion and approval of sentiment is not justified. I do not infer that there is, therefore, no analogy between approval of a sentiment as proper, just or suitable to its object and belief in an opinion as true or agreeable to reality.

References to Smith's *Theory of Moral Sentiments* are to Smith, 1976a and take the form 'TMS pt.sec.ch.para.'

1 TMS I.I.3.I
2 *Ibid.*, I.I.3.2.
3 Baird, 1977, 517; for the authorship of the notes see Norton, 1980.
4 Baird, 1977.
5 TMS I.I.3.2.
6 Prior, 1949, 66–7.
7 TMS I.I.2.I.
8 *Ibid.*, I.I.3.3.
9 See TMS I.I.I.II–13.
10 Cf. Campbell, 1971, 96.
11 TMS I.I.4.I.
12 *Ibid.*, I.I.4.2.
13 *Ibid.*, I.I.4.5.
14 See *ibid.*, I.III.I.9n.
15 *Ibid.*, I.I.4.6.
16 See *ibid.*, I.I.2.I.
17 *Ibid.*, I.I.4.4.
18 *Ibid.*, IV.2.3. and 5.
19 Haakonssen, 1981, 49; cf. TMS I.I.I.13.
20 TMS III.III.2.
21 Ferguson, 1960, 228.
22 *Ibid.*
23 Cf. Locke, 1975, IV.xv.3.

PETER JONES

An Outline of the Philosophy of James Hutton
(1726–97)

Introduction

JAMES HUTTON is considered by many as the founder of
modern geology. In two papers delivered to the Royal Society of
Edinburgh in 1785, and augmented in his *Theory of the Earth,*
published in 1795, he argued that the earth is continuously
subjected to the processes of deposition, consolidation,
elevation and erosion.[1] Consolidation and elevation are both
effected by intense subterranean heat, and the whole cycle
occurs in a time scale of indefinite extent. In 1792 he published a
volume of papers under the title *Dissertations in different subjects
in natural philosophy,* and two years later he published a huge
philosophical treatise, in three quarto volumes which ran to
almost 2200 pages of text, and which bore a suitably impressive
title: *An Investigation of the Principles of Knowledge, and of the
Progress of Reason, from Sense to Science and Philosophy.*[2] A
few commentators have referred to this treatise, or even quoted
from it, but to students of philosophy the work is completely
unknown.[3] In this paper I shall outline some of its main theses; it
will be necessary, on occasion, to depart from Hutton's own
sequence of argument, in order to bring together widely
separated reflections. In brief, Hutton saw himself as remaining
more rigorously faithful to Lockean premises than anyone else
had done, and as pursuing a Humean account of causation to its
limit.

Knowledge of Hutton's life derives mainly from the
affectionate account delivered to the Royal Society of Edinburgh
in 1803 by his first biographer, and disciple, John Playfair.[4] After
attending the High School, Hutton entered the University of
Edinburgh in 1740 'as a student of humanity'. Like many other
students he is said to have always spoken warmly of Maclaurin's
lectures, and of Professor John Stevenson, 'not so much,
however, for having made him a logician as a chemist'. Hutton
began to study medicine in 1744, completing his studies at
Leyden, and graduating there in 1749.[5] For the best part of

twenty years after that, he devoted himself to the practice and
theory of farming, undertaking study in Norfolk and in the Low
Countries of methods which might be adaptable to his own farm
in Berwickshire. During this period he deepened his interests in
mineralogy, geology and meteorology, all of which were to be of
service in his various enterprises, such as his sal ammoniac
business and his extensive involvement in the construction of the
Forth and Clyde canal. He also began a series of tours through
Britain to study their geological and mineralogical features.[6]
From the early 1770s he apparently assisted his close friend
Joseph Black, then Professor of Chemistry at Edinburgh, in a
number of chemical experiments.[7]

Playfair reports that Hutton 'left behind him an incredible
quantity of manuscript',[8] the result of thirty years and more of
sustained study and reflection, and truly polymathic interests.
Playfair also records the fact that even before Hutton's geological theory was made known to the Royal Society of Edinburgh, in
1785, he had already completed separate treatises on physics and
metaphysics.[9] The silence which greeted the eventual publication
in 1794 of the metaphysical treatise was, and has remained,
almost complete.

Playfair's own brief summary of it, in three pages, is accurate
but necessarily incomplete; he was fully justified in regretting
'the author's peculiar notions of arrangement', as well as the
vocabulary, style and length of the work.[10] In spite of inordinate
repetition throughout the work, Hutton gives surprisingly few
clues to the pre-supposed context of his reflections and allusions.
In fact, however, his strategy was simple and straightforward:
almost invariably he defined his own position in relation to
Locke, Berkeley and Hume, following their routes, discussing
their topics, but modifying their arguments in the light of his own
criticisms and theoretical disagreements. The central concept in
his metaphysical armoury is causation and he always compares
and contrasts his own views with those of Hume. On the issues of
ideas, conception and abstraction, on the other hand, he understandably contrasts his position with those of Locke and Berkeley. Explicit references to other philosophers are infrequent.
Hutton had clearly studied Reid, especially on the notion of
powers, although he disagreed with Reid over common sense; he
referred briefly to Smith on sympathy, chastised Gregory for
misunderstanding Hume, commended Montesquieu in entirely
orthodox fashion, and had obviously read many French and
British works on the origins and nature of language. It is not
known, however, whether he corresponded with his contempor-

aries on philosophical matters or whether he knew the work of
Leibniz and Kant whose ideas his own sometimes resemble.
Playfair's remark that Hutton 'read but few speculative books'
should be treated with caution, if only because absence of
evidence is not evidence of absence.[11]

Hutton's *Investigation of the Principles of Knowledge and of the
Progress of Reason, from Sense to Science and Philosophy*
1 : Aims

The three main parts of his *Investigation,* more or less
corresponding to the three separate volumes, are entitled 'The
Instinctive Faculties which lead to Science', 'Of Science, or the
Conscious Principles which lead to Wisdom', and 'the Proper
End of Science and the Means of Happiness'. In fact this unusual
terminology denotes respectively a study of the nature of ideas,
the nature of reasoning, and the nature of morality.

In the Preface, he announces that his work is written for the
enlightened few who are 'qualified to study the nature of their
own thoughts', and who 'form the taste, the morals, and the
politics' of the civilised world (I. iii). He entirely disagrees with
James Gregory, who had recently claimed that 'no discoveries
ever have been or ever can be made' in metaphysics (I.v).[12] On
the contrary, a proper study of metaphysics will reveal '*how* we
came at' the generally accepted but profoundly mistaken
'opinion of external things', namely, '*That matter is inert,
extended, solid, and impenetrable*' (I.xvi, xxi). In order 'to find
an opinion which we shall not doubt of', we should 'turn our eyes
inward', for then we shall discover 'the order in which our
knowledge had been acquired, and *how* we had arrived at false
opinions' (I.xx).

He sets out to show that man progresses from a primitive
animal stage, in which sensory data are passively received and in
which he judges 'merely for the sake of acting', to higher stages in
which he actively and self-consciously processes the original
sensory data, and judges 'for the sake of knowing' (I.xxiv). In
brief, 'the mind is a thing that grows' and proceeds through
stages which can be sharply distinguished only in abstract
analysis. The stages are labelled 'knowledge, understanding,
science, and philosophy' (II. 527). It must be emphasised at once
that in Hutton's vocabulary the term *science* is to be taken in a
special sense: it denotes 'knowledge attained by means of
analysis', and distinguished by its 'generality' (I. 29, 32). More
specifically:

   natural appearances consist of sensation and perception;

and, in order to make this knowledge science, it must be
first analysed, in abstraction, so as to procure elements,
on which reason operating again synthetically finds a similarity, or a generality which then constitutes a principle.
(II. 19)

It should be recorded that for Hutton 'knowledge' denotes
'whatever is known by the immediate action of matter upon
mind, which is sensation, or by the undistinguished action of
mind, as is perception' (I. 431). In other words, when used in a
restricted sense, the term covers only the proper objects of the
mind in its first stage of development, namely, unprocessed
sensory data together with data processed only in a primitive,
involuntary, unselfconscious way. More generally, however,
'knowledge' (I. 90) denotes the proper object of the mind, in
whatever mode it is functioning. (As a general term 'knowledge'
denotes 'a progress of the mind'; however, his present concern is
not with 'what is and what is not knowledge', but rather with
'sensation' as 'the first information of a mind' (I. 90–94).)
Hutton proposes a five-fold division within 'science': physics,
mathematics, morality, logic and metaphysics. He means that
analytical reflection appropriate to any one of these areas must
not be conflated with that appropriate to any other, although
certain features are constitutive of all analysis:

In science, reason is that faculty of mind by which truth or
principles are known; argument is that process of intellect
by which the steps of reasoning, for the knowledge of truth,
are reviewed in the mind which reasons, and are signified or
enunciated for the information of another mind. . . . In
scientific reasoning, knowledge is produced by steps; in
each of these a principle is required on which to proceed in
reasoning, and thus acquire a further step. It will thus
appear, that, in science, there is no certainty without seeing
every step. (II. 284–5)

No proposition can 'be received as a principle', that is, as a
premise, until it is itself traced 'up to the first principles on which
it is ultimately founded' (II. 286).

Like most European philosophers after Bacon, Hutton is self-
conscious about method. Some issues, for example, are outside
the philosopher's domain or cannot be pursued fruitfully: 'to
inquire *how* we reflect or *how* we think, are unreasonable questions or fruitless speculations', because 'we are totally ignorant
of the manner in which any organ produces sensation in the
mind'. Accordingly, our concern ought not to be with 'the cause
of our perception' but with what 'in perception is the ground or

foundation of our forming a relation, or of our judging in comparison' (1. 57, 99, 119). Mind and body are for ever distinct, and all we have access to through consciousness is mind. We must always specify what kind of discussion we are engaged in:

> Sensation, considered physically or according to our ideas of material things, will appear to consist entirely of motion and mechanism; whereas, considered metaphysically, that is according to our ideas of mind, sensation is immaterial and not mechanical, it is knowledge. (1. 94)

2: Knowledge, 'science' and scepticism

Hutton views his account of the acquisition of knowledge as a crucial modification of Locke's theory: we can never know matter in itself and there is no distinction between primary and secondary qualities. The mind becomes active only after it has been passively 'affected in sensation', but it can be said to act in two ways; 'first, in attending to sensation' merely, and secondly by both attending and 'moving matter so as to change the sensation' (1. 129, 135). We have 'immediate knowledge', by 'being conscious of this transaction', that 'the mind thinks, reflects and conceives'; the task is 'to distinguish conceptions from sensations, to observe the relation and affinity that may be found to subsist among the various conceptions of the mind' (1. 194). Emphatically:

> One thing is certain, that the more we inquire into the nature of our mind, the more we shall find the operation of judgment, or the discerning faculty, actually employed, in the knowledge which we had thought similar to sensation as being instinctive, and in which we had not suspected judgment or reason to be concerned (1. 216).

Ideas, as copies of sensations, 'are gradually obliterated in the mind, when not renewed' (1. 265), but healthy people never mistake or confuse even strong ideas with weak sensations (1. 262). Hutton claims Hume's 'difficulty in distinguishing truth and fiction, reality and fancy' stems from his treating impressions and ideas 'as things of the same species, and only differing in degree'; whereas one must sharply distinguish ideas from their physical source 1. 321). Locke and Berkeley, on the other hand, illicitly appeal to God: 'Mr Locke founds his ideas ultimately upon the power of God acting by the mediation of matter, whereas Dr Berkeley founds his ideas upon the power of God immediately.' But, 'to say that God is the cause of every thing ultimately, is only saying that there is nothing without a cause' (1. 333–4).

Abstraction poses no particular problem. 'There is no more difficulty', Hutton declares, 'of imagining magnitude and figure without sensible ideas, than it is [sic] to form sensible ideas without those of extension and figure':

> In forming the abstract idea of extension, we leave out every consideration by which the general idea may be limited or circumscribed; this idea is then infinitely divisible, and contains an indefinite number of parts of this conceived magnitude, or particular conceived extent. . . . The infinite divisibility of a finite line, which the Doctor [Berkeley] considers as a mathematical absurdity, is truly the perfection of mathematical accuracy, in considering ideas perfectly abstract and distinct from each other, for the purpose of the science. (I. 164, 166)

There is, Hutton insists, 'a wide difference betwixt the having and the knowing an idea', and the 'distinction of conscious and unconscious or instinctive knowledge, is of the utmost importance in the philosophy of mind' (I. 287, 347). Although 'all operations are ultimately simple', and 'animal knowledge grows, from more simple principles, by composition', 'the first ideas that are known are compound'. That is, 'the mind, advancing in scientific knowledge, proceeds in the opposite order, from natural ideas, which are compound, to abstract ideas which are simple' (I. 290, 291, 295). Locke's reasoning about ideas is only applicable to conscious, not instinctive, ideas, and his account of primary and secondary qualities is confused, as Berkeley (inadequately) demonstrated (I. 345, 327, 357). Hutton insists that primary and secondary qualities of body are on precisely the same footing, in being conceptions of the mind which have no resemblance to their external causes. His position is obscured by the additional claims that although matter is imperceptible in itself, body is perceptible in virtue of its qualities; nevertheless such qualities are also said to be merely conceptions of the mind.

It is essential to record a fundamental distinction between 'knowing different things, and knowing that things are different'. But although there can be no doubt about the mind's ability to acquire the conceptions of identity and diversity, there is a question about 'the conditions in which the operation is performed' (I. 381, 382, 384). Hutton, like Hume, claims that the 'comparing operation' of the mind is 'instinctive, so far as it is absolutely necessary in order to the proceeding of mind in knowledge'; but his traditional explanation of the process seems to generate the equally traditional infinite regress, since he postulates 'a mean', in this case an idea in the mind, whereby things 'different in reality may be compared in the mind' (1. 392, 385).

He maintains that 'the two opposite excesses of a mind not sufficiently enlightened by philosophy', are credulity, which results from mistaking imaginary for proper evidence, and scepticism, which arises when 'a species of evidence is demanded, beyond what is natural to the subject' (1. 441). This view is elaborated in the second volume. There, he reaches a conclusion very like Hume's, although by a different route. Although 'a mind may be said to judge instinctively, that is necessarily', it is crucial to grasp that 'doubting is an operation of reason', and cannot be performed 'instinctively'. In the sense that it involves 'questioning truth ' in its desire to know, 'science, properly so called, is founded upon doubting'. In the context of analytical reflection (*science*, in Hutton's special sense) 'doubt is no conclusion'. But although the 'foundation of science is thus laid in doubting, it is only in resolving doubts that science is promoted' (II. 75–78):

> scepticism, or general and unreasonable doubt, is founded upon this proposition, That there is no evidence. But, such a proposition as this would certainly require some species of demonstration, that is, some positive evidence. . . . scepticism may be truly dogmatical, in having founded misbelief upon a wrong principle of evidence. But, no degree of doubt or inquiry, which is the opposite of dogmatism, can be prejudicial to philosophy. (II. 78–79)

Because of 'a mistaken notion' of evidence, that is, scepticism makes people deny what is true. Moreover, there is no general or 'universal principle of disbelief', and to the extent that scepticism is allegedly grounded upon such a principle, it is incoherent (II. 80, 296).[13] Like many of his predecessors, Hutton holds that 'there is a natural principle of credulity in mankind'; 'every natural source of knowledge is implicitly believed' because at the ground level of experience, so to say, no error is possible. There is no 'constitutional error' in man's 'natural faculties' (II. 293–4, 235; cp. I. 432, 442). The philosopher is distinguished from other men by his method:

> he thus arrives at principles, for judging of things which otherwise he could not understand; and, instead of doubting like the sceptic on every occasion, he forms a determined judgment with regard to what is false, as well as what is true. His principles, on every occasion, serve him in order to form his judgment; and, his judgments, not his doubts, serve to confirm as well as to correct his principles. (II. 298)

'Inordinate scepticism', in brief, 'ends in absurdity, and prepares a triumph to the common sense of mankind, in opposition to the abstract reasoning of science' (II. 299). The sting in the tail of this claim separates Hutton as much from Hume as from Hume's critic Reid.[14]

3: Causation

'Knowledge of cause and effect,' Hutton declares, 'is the most important object' of his inquiry (II. 162). Since Hume's account of causation was a constant topic among Scottish scientists in the second half of the eighteenth century, it is inevitable that Hutton defines his own position in relation to it. Like Hume, however, he prefaces his discussion by reflection on our ideas of space and time, and it is appropriate to summarise his conclusions here.

In the first volume Hutton had argued that 'body with magnitude and figure exists not in reality', and he now claims in the second that

> if the ideal nature of knowledge, which we acquire in perception, necessarily implies the ideal nature of space and time, the negation of reality to space and time will be then more than supposition or conjecture. (II. 122)

The traditional query about the origin of those ideas must be faced, however:

> Properly speaking, it is our existence that subsists, and from thence we form the ideas of past and future time; but, present time is only an idea formed by abstraction, a negative idea, being, like a point in mathematics, a conceived or supposed distinction between two several things of which we have a positive idea. (II. 127)

His elaboration of this view is striking:

> these three ideas, space, time, and number, which are so manifestly conceptions of the mind itself, and not things existing independent of that being, are necessarily required in the operations of the mind, concerning those things that are conceived as existing externally and independent of our thought. They are, therefore, constituent principles of those conceptions of external things; and were these three ideas abstracted from our mind, it does not appear how any such conception, as that of an external thing, could be formed in the mind. (II. 139)

There is no evidence of his acquaintance with Kant's work, and he does not further explain what he means by a constituent principle of a conception. But he is anxious that his idealism should not be misunderstood. He is not claiming 'that the mind of itself produces knowledge without being influenced by any thing external'; rather that, strictly speaking, when 'in philosophy we speak of a state of things, this properly implies a certain order in our thought' (II. 167, 169).

At the outset of his discussion of causation he declares his allegiance to several traditional claims (among his premises are these: 'that the laws of nature are established, that all things are mutually related, and that every effect has its proper cause' – II. 303). It 'cannot be doubted' (II. 178) that every event has a cause, and that similar causes have similar effects; moreover, it is only 'in polished nations' that people speak of the abstract ideas of cause and effect (II. 158). He claims that 'cause and effect only exist in action', and in external things cause is never 'known immediately, but is only known by means of effect; and effect is only known by means of action and order in change' (II. 162, 173–4). In this sense, cause and effect are relative and not absolute, since one cannot exist without the other; moreover, because causation flows 'in the order of time', 'things eternal and immutable are not the subject of causation' (II. 182). This last consideration is central to his account of a First Cause, as we shall see later. With reference to Hume's observations on necessity, he declares that 'every event, which necessarily precedes another, is properly a cause in relation to the succeeding event', and in any 'necessarily consecutive' series of events, 'every individual event, is properly both a cause and an effect' (II. 183) (he never defines 'event', but see II. 241). He insists that Hume mishandles the famous billiard-ball example, borrowed from Malebranche, because it is not merely passive observation that takes place. On the contrary, knowledge of the causal relation 'is truly produced by means of reasoning as well as by means of sensation' (II. 185). It should be asked what, precisely, is observed:

> it is only effect which is the proper subject of observation, as having followed something already known; this past thing is then in reason attributed to the present, or is inferred as the cause of that which is then observed. (II. 186)

The 'compound knowledge of the relation of cause and effect' 'requires a process in the mind', although all such 'operations of the mind . . . are commonly overlooked':

> the knowledge of cause and effect, or the relation of things existing in succession, is discerned in the mind, where, without any form of argument, a judgment is formed, or a new species of knowledge is produced, in an operation called reason. (II. 187–8)

Such reasoning is not 'a priori', but it is reasoning, and Hume was wrong to impute the inference to custom or habit, Hutton claims. (In fact, there is little difference between them, since Hume explicitly attributes such reasoning to animals, and the notion of custom, in the context, serves mainly to mark the absence of self-conscious reflection.) Nevertheless, Hutton's conclusion is predictable. 'Observation itself cannot discover either effect or cause', and although 'there is no reason to doubt of the natural succession of events, or of the necessary connection of cause and effect' observation alone cannot establish the connection. On the contrary, the idea of necessary connection, like the ideas of cause and effect themselves, are not innate and not directly derived from observation, but are the product of reasoning (II. 194–5, 215):

> in external things, (which are the proper subject of physics as a science) causes properly speaking are not known, but are judged in reason to be. (III. 138)

He is anxious to make himself clear. 'Physical causes and effects' 'are infinitely removed from sensation, which is no physical event', since mind and body are for ever distinct, and any interaction between them could not be straightforwardly causal:

> That a physical cause should produce a metaphysical effect, that is to say, that a material thing should affect an immaterial substance, is inconceivable to us; it is an expression which either has no meaning at all, or has a meaning which is evidently absurd. (III. 140; cp. I. 273–4)

The sequence of the argument is this:

> The cause of sensation is external; because, it is not from within. Not that we know what is without the mind, but because we are conscious that sensation is not from a cause which is in or proper to the mind. Sensation is the last step to which we can ascend in the investigation of our proper knowledge by reflection. (III. 139)

In addition, since mind and body are distinct,

> some action is necessarily conceived as interposed between the last physical effect of light and the first event in knowledge, when the sense of colour is excited. This action, therefore, is not properly a supposition, for it is judged necessarily; and, although it be a thing judged or known in no other way but that of reason, it is not therefore uncertain in any degree, for, it is necessarily inferred from that which is known. (III. 141)

It is impossible to doubt, and absurd to prove, 'that we are, that we have been, and that we will be'; other truths deduced from such absolute knowledge are equally immune from doubt, although there is, as it were, a hierarchy even among certainties – certainty of the existence of other minds 'is of an inferior order' to certainty 'of our own existence' (III. 161). In the end, however,

> We are now arrived at this conclusion, That external things, as we conceive them, do not exist independent of our mind, and that our mind, of which we have a conscious knowledge, exists independent of those external things. At the same time we are certain, That there is something existing independent of our mind, being properly the cause of our information; which thing, though not known, is known not to be body. (III. 163)

Hutton understandably challenges one feature of Hume's account of probable reasoning, arguing that the probability of an occurrence cannot alone depend on the number of times it has been known to occur in the past; 'any number of times that can possibly be observed, bears so exceeding small a proportion to an indefinite number, or those in which similar things may have happened otherwise'. Probable beliefs cannot be formed 'without the use of reason', and, in any case, 'reason has not its force increased by repetition' (II. 212).

The notion of powers, integral to Locke's position and, more recently from Hutton's standpoint, to Reid's, is equally important to Hutton himself. For him, powers are 'neither perceived nor imagined, but judged in reason and concluded as causes, from events their effect'; of course 'we know not what that thing is in itself which we call power', but 'we form the idea of power from that activity of which we are conscious in our mind' (II. 396, 336, 399). Such overt disagreement with Hume is tempered somewhat by endorsement of a view Hume certainly canvassed:

> Material things must necessarily act, in relation to our mind, in order to produce sensation; but, farther than this, we know nothing with regard to the nature of that external thing to which we affix the name of matter, and which, in the common opinion of mankind, is confounded with the things conceived by our mind, which are therefore the proper or only subjects of our understanding. (II. 400)

He carefully explains his own position: 'we know *a priori*, or we are conscious, that we design; we therefore say, that we have will; we know, *a posteriori*, or by observation, that our will takes effect in action'. The crucial point, however, is that power 'is not necessarily conceived' as coexisting with design:

> For, though we are conscious of design, we are not con-

scious of power; we only judge our having power, because we observe the execution of our will; and, we are certain of our power being limited, in relation to our will. (II. 412–13)

He does not develop his moral system until the third volume of his *Investigation*, but during his discussion of causation in the second volume he introduces his notion of moral agency, primarily as a means to illuminate the differences between man and brute – a theme which runs throughout the whole work. He begins by remarking that 'without an agent knowing the end to which his acting is to lead, that action could not be properly attributed to this ignorant mind'; and it is 'only from the end' that we 'conclude wisdom as instrumental in bringing about that end' (II. 457–8). Perhaps to dissociate himself from the views of Erasmus Darwin and Monboddo (whose work on language he alluded to), Hutton asserts that the 'wisdom' of man and brute are not 'the same in any degree', are 'totally different, and cannot be compared' (II. 473). Although he agrees that animals adapt to their situation, he claims that they cannot be guided in the present by thoughts of the future (II. 486). (It is known that Hutton corresponded with Erasmus Darwin, and agreed with him in some respects: 'Perfect wisdom may appear in the imperfectly adapted state of individuals, always tending to change their constitutions according to the requisite conditions of their sustenance and propagation. . . . [I]n conceiving an indefinite variety among the individuals of that species, we must be assured, that, on the one hand, those which depart most from the best adapted constitution, will be most liable to perish, while, on the other hand, those organised bodies, which most approach to the best constitution for the present circumstances, will be best adapted to continue, in preserving themselves and multiplying the individuals of their race.' (II. 500)) The question to ask is whether an animal 'reasons in order to promote his knowledge':

> unless, therefore, the dog puts the question to himself, *What shall I do in order to attain this end?* he has not reasoned scientifically like man, who on this occasion knows the motive by which he is determined to act. (II. 577)

The central point is exemplified in two common errors: the assumption that, if man is a rational creature, animals are incapable of reason; and the assumption that, if brutes are capable of reason, the mind of man must 'be a thing of the same kind' (II. 569). Hutton argues that man must transcend the level on which he first, and necessarily, reasons in the same way as brutes:

> the brute animal reasons in all respects as the man of common sense, properly speaking; that is to say, he reasons

more immediately from experience, without science, or the formation of general principles, by which our judgments in particular cases may be led or conducted. It is in like manner that children always tell the truth, and understand every thing that is said in the literal sense, before they have learned jesting and deceit, which cannot be known but in science, or on general principle. (II. 532)

Reflective analysis shows, therefore, that a distinction in kind separates haphazardly successful actions from those resulting from ability to follow a rule:

there will appear to be an extreme disparity between a mind that only can invent according to the occasional circumstances or situations of things by which it is immediately actuated or influenced, and a mind which, having in itself the principles of knowledge, may set about invention, without the immediate co-operation of external things. (II. 495)

4: Moral System

In turning to the moral system, Hutton insists, like many philosophers before and since, that 'it is as a brute animal, that an infant man is to be trained'. The pains and pleasures used as 'rewards and punishments' in training are effective because they act as 'instinctive motives that constrain a mind to act'. But they are useless for the profoundly more important purposes of persuading 'a mind to will, in seeing the reason for that conduct' (III. 102, 105). Because of this, 'a man, actuated only by sensual motives, is a slave, and, a slave is to be trained no otherwise than a brute'. What 'constitutes the character of a slave', sensual or intellectual, are not fear and hope themselves, but 'the objects of the hope and fear' (III. 104–5).

Virtue, understood as a 'sentiment, thought, or opinion of the human mind', is neither innate nor instinctive, but must be learned and practised. Moreover, actions

are voluntary, as having followed conscious thought; and, they are conscientious or moral, as being followed by a conscious feeling of good or evil, of approbation or disapprobation, and of happiness or misery. (III. 124)

Moral deliberation calls for reflection on both motives and consequences, and an important role is assigned to spectators. First, however, Hutton observes that:

There are two ways in which a person may be virtuous or esteemed such; for, first, a person may be virtuous in practice in either having no temptation to transgress the rules of virtue, or, in obeying implicitly rules of conduct in which he

had been educated, but without seeing the reason or acquiescing in the truth or justness of these rules. . . . Such a
virtue is actual, and it may be termed practical, in order to
distinguish it from that which, on the other hand, may be
termed virtue upon principle, which is the second kind. (III.
124–5)

Because morals can be looked on as 'a state of mind', readers
will appreciate 'of what importance is the education of the youth'
and, Hutton adds, 'how difficult a task it is to change a nation,
whether from barbarism to be civilised, or contrarily from a civil
to a barbarian state'. Moreover, readers will also grasp 'how
dangerous for the practical virtue of a nation it may be to take
away superstition, from minds incapable of philosophy sufficient
to procure a virtuous disposition' (III. 131–2).

It is important to Hutton that independent spectators act as
checks upon our judgments and behaviour, and in this context he
may have been initially guided by Hume, not least because
Hume's name occurs on the following page.

> The judgment of another person concerning that which I
> think either right or wrong, true or false, is to me of the
> utmost importance. It is a source of information from with-
> out, from the operations of another mind. Now, though that
> mind be of no more authority than my own, it still must have
> its proper weight in my opinion, as coming from a source
> which is in things, and not in thought alone. Without this
> testimony of reality, our opinions would have nothing but
> the authority of a thought; and, our thought might then be
> in some measure like a dream. (III. 214)

Even here, however, he barely avoids arguing for a merely
contingent need of others, who will help an individual who
cannot alone find a secure foundation for his judgments, and who
might succumb to the worst excesses of solipsism.

Gregory had recently argued against Hume's account of free-
will, on the grounds that motives 'obey laws different from those
observed with regard to physical causes'.[15] Hutton finds Gregory's claim unconvincing, and agrees with Hume both that motives are causes of actions, and that 'motive and action, like cause
and effect, are always conjoined' – in our own case we know of
the conjunction by conscious reflection, but for other people we
have to draw inferences from their physical actions:

> Now, though a wise person may thus judge often right, he
> cannot do so always; because, he has not always proper data
> whereon to form a judgment. It is only by supposing motives
> regularly conjoined with their actions or effects, that an

intelligent mind is to form a judgment, from the sensible or perceptible effects, what had been the cause, or conversely, from a known or supposed cause, what will be the actual effect. (III. 216–19)

He also agrees with Hume that there are 'secondary sensations, and proper passions in the mind', such as the sense of joy and grief, which are 'excited in consequence of ideas' (III. 247). Although he finds Smith's account of sympathy generally helpful, he disagrees that it is 'a first principle', and insists that it is 'artificial', in the sense of being 'highly improvable' by education. To explain his own view he uses a distinction much favoured by, although not original to, Reid:

I feel for my neighbour in his pain or in his grief; and, for this purpose it is necessary that I should fancy what he feels. But, when I fancy in order to feel for him in his distress, I certainly do not fancy that I feel with him in his pain or grief. On the contrary, in the height of my distress, I have full possession of my mind; my feeling is called forth, at the same time that I am conscious of being in a state of ease and happiness. (III. 253–4)

Hutton was clearly aware that this view had been canvassed for almost a century by writers, French and British, puzzled by the question of proper response to stage tragedies:

Upon the stage, indeed, the well acted scene betrays my judgment or assists my imagination of the distress; and the imagination of this distress is absolutely necessary to my sympathetic feeling; but neither my judgment nor my imagination can explain the suffering of my mind in feeling for another's woe. . . . But, while on these occasions I am in reflection conscious of feeling pleasure or pain, I am also conscious that I feel independently of any natural delusion of my mind; for, it does not in the least relieve my feeling for another person, that I am conscious I do not feel with him in his agony. (III. 253–4)

In both the aesthetic and moral domains, and despite individual differences in taste, he insists that 'there are certain rules, by which the general sentiments of good and evil are formed in every mind', and that these rules 'conduct the moral sense':

in the consideration of virtuous and vicious conduct, we are not to examine what may be esteemed such by particular persons, or even particular nations; but, we are to look for that which is general to mankind, and will always be esteemed virtuous and vicious by the species, independent of the opinion that may be occasionally entertained by particulars, either in an arbitrary manner, or in opposition to the general rules.

His point here is that

in every actual existence there is system, rule or principle; which rule forms the basis of that thing; But, every rule of this kind admits of varieties, which, though they produce perpetual differences in things, never transgress the rule of which they only form a modification in the strictest order. (III. 286–8)

Earlier philosophers, such as Hobbes and Mandeville, who argued for man's essential selfishness have failed to draw a crucial distinction between 'the instinctive self-love of the animal man, by which the individual is preserved and the species continued' and 'the conscious self-love of minds reflecting scientifically upon the motives of their conduct and the consequences of their will' (III. 263). In a very special sense only can a wise man be described as 'selfish, in providing a source of self-enjoyment, from his disinterested conduct in relation to his species'. But

it is only by undervaluing our proper animal desires in a rational reflection, and inflaming our sympathetic feelings with all the power of virtuous contemplation, that a mind can be brought to suffer itself in order that others should enjoy or should not suffer. (III. 330–2)

Of course, Hutton does not think that 'mankind are always just enough to see things in the proper light, nor happy enough to consult their true interest'; that fact precisely underlines the need for study, learning and practice, since 'the highest degree of merit that can be attributed to an action, is to proceed from no personal motive, but from the idea of general good' (III. 336, 343). Virtue resides in the observance of general rules, and the degree of virtue is proportional to the degree of temptation to transgress it (III. 380): but 'without virtue, a man travels on ambition, amidst the quicksands of crime, blindfold' (III. 404). In an interesting parenthesis which links with his subsequent reflections on economics and politics, he declares that two human failings 'baneful to political society' are 'undistinguishing benevolence' and 'romantic virtue'. The former reveals itself in the profligate distribution of the limited charity available, and the latter in the 'superstitious admiration of heroic operations' (III. 388–9).

Writing as he was, during the period of the American and French revolutions, it is not surprising that he refers to the topic of justifiable revolution: 'In the most oppressed state of political society, there may be good reason for individuals endeavouring to change the state of government, in order to bring about a reformation' (III. 438). While discussing the nature of society, he suddenly launches off into an apostrophe, addressed, by implication, to George III and the Prince of Wales (III. 442ff; cp. 536). He reminds the reader that he has argued throughout that 'man is not naturally a moral agent', and that since 'society is nothing but extended family' leadership is crucial (III. 490, 502). He agrees with Hume and Smith on the stages of man's progress out of a savage state, and on the fundamental importance of peace and security:

> In how much as it is necessary for the prosperity of the state and the happiness of the people, that the persons of the subjects should be safe and their property secure, in so much is it required that the government of the state be steady, and preserved on the one hand from the ambitious contest for supreme power among the great, or, on the other, from the anarchy of a popular invasion. (III. 532)

Of course, Hutton does not deny that political states change: 'they have their beginnings, and they have their end; but, while they are conducted with public virtue and general wisdom, it is not in human science to set a period to their subsistence' (III. 539). Like Hume, therefore, he agrees that, in retrospect, revolutions can sometimes be seen to have had beneficial consequences; but that no general rule can be formulated which justifies one in starting a revolution. He expresses his own fear that

> when science is despised in the nation, and philosophy confined to idle speculation, internal regulation [of the state] is neglected, or injustice, the source of every disorder, will prevail; and then, with all the impotence of a diseased constitution, the body politic will act with the vice of ignorance and folly. (III. 540)

Indeed, 'in a general depravity of political manners, philosophy alone can form a system whereby may be reformed the disorder of the state, and public justice be restored in a nation'. Although at the very time of his writing one 'great commercial nation' proclaimed '*liberty* and *equality*' as its 'rule for governing their conduct', those words, in context, turned out to 'mean no other than *violence* and *injustice*' (III. 544, 547).

He believes that 'men are made by nature equal; but, in being artificially accomplished, they necessarily become unequal' (III. 563). He strongly opposes the view that in civil society there is no freedom and that only in a savage state is man free; the view, in other words, that

> in proportion as man, from brutish ignorance, proceeded on

his intellectual course, he lost his freedom, and became a slave. The opposite of this, however, is true; but the apparent contradiction arises from the occasional opposition, betwixt man's sensual affections, and his rational desires; betwixt his passionate desires, and his intellectual affections. (III. 566)

Man, understood as 'the scientific animal, is always free in some respect, and in some respect he is restrained' (III. 567).

Like almost all writers in the Enlightenment Hutton declares that the importance of social intercourse cannot be overestimated:

> by communicating their ideas, men improve their knowledge; and, it is only by the enlarged knowledge of the species that the science of individuals is brought to that perfection which does honour to the race, in exalting human nature as the chief intention of the First Cause. Thus society is necessary to the human understanding; and, a proper education is required for the accomplishment of man. (III. 581)

'The rules of succession or inheritance' should be monitored and modified to meet changes in the wealth and political nature of a society. In a golden age no pecuniary reward can attend the discharge of duties, but when 'acquired wealth gives a title to pre-eminence, money will be sought merely for the sake of riches; riches will compensate for the want of virtue; and then, nothing but philosophy can suspend the vilest degradation of mankind' (III. 586). There is no fruitful analogy between man and 'the oeconomy of ants and bees' (III. 589), because the political state is not a natural form of government:

> in the artificial or political state, where the general interest of the whole independently of any particular should be consulted, the wisdom of the individual leads not immediately to the happiness of the whole; the common good is only promoted, by each person sacrificing some part of private interest. (III. 589)

Although those who become rich through their skill and industry 'may find a luxury in relieving those that want', 'those that want must not claim a *right* to participate with those that have' (III. 591). Hutton believes that 'the natural course of things is for the industrious labourer to become wealthy, and not for the wealthy to become laborious'; those who benefit by the labour of others should certainly be taxed, but in taxing the so-called 'necessaries of life' the greatest care is needed to establish what the necessaries are, and for whom. Above all, taxation must not discourage industry – not least because industry is an indivisible capacity in the individual, and not a divisible commodity like wealth (III. 600–5). He points out that direct taxation of wealth requires knowledge of the true wealth of each person, whereas indirect taxation on commodities can be levied only with moderation without defeating its purpose by reducing demand (III. 607). An inescapable problem confronting law-makers is the difficulty in predicting the consequences of any restraining law; 'the slow operations of a diversity of causes, influenced by the indefinite circumstances and gradually changing state of human beings', make such predictions hazardous (III. 606).

One feature of his reflections in this context is worth noting, namely, his views on the education of women. Traditionally, he remarks, women have been considered 'as only fitted for domestic service, and for the idle entertainment of the little tyrant, in the thoughtless moments of his life'. They ought to be educated, however, not in reading Latin and Greek, nor in abstract science, but 'in useful knowledge, and in the purest principles, both of private and of public virtue'; and 'in that art of government which is the means of making mankind happy', and 'in every species of learning that may lead to amiable and useful manners' (III. 587–8).

5: Religion: First Cause and Design Argument

Throughout the *Investigation* he has referred to a first cause, and in the third volume he explains the special features of the notion, as he has been using it:

> although we may be convinced that there is a first cause, which has been always, this is only because we cannot conceive an event to happen without a cause; and, therefore, we suppose that the first cause is no event, but has been always, and will be without end. Now, this opinion, although a supposition, is a conclusion that we are in reason constrained to make; but, it is a species of argument that is in its nature perhaps *unique*: The proposition and its contrary are both inconceivable.

He reminds the reader that he has earlier argued that space and time are 'mere conceptions in our mind', and that view has an important bearing on the present issue:

> there is no reason to conclude the first cause, as being limited by space and time, this cause being a thing not known, but judged from all that is known, from every thing that happens in time, and space. Therefore, the first cause, although acting and efficient, is no event, and has not come

to pass; and, although this first cause is necessarily concluded from all that is known, it is in like manner concluded
as infinitely different from every known thing.

Thus, the 'first cause is known, not by conceiving what it is, but
by finding in reason what it is not' (III. 134). On several previous
occasions he has characterised a 'negative' concept (eg. 'conception', I. 200; 'present time', II. 127) and assigned it explanatory
force. In the present context he claims that denial of a first cause
'necessarily implies' understanding 'how things could be produced without a cause'; and to base the denial on the confession
that '*the first cause is unknown*', would be as absurd as for
someone 'to deny his own existence, because he knows not how
he had a being'. Therefore:

> we will be justified in affirming, That the first cause is
> absolute, self-existing, efficient, and final. All other causes,
> again, are only apparent, as happening in the order of our
> thought, and occasional as having come to pass in conse-
> quence of a preceding action; it is therefore only relatively,
> that they can be considered as either efficient or final. (III.
> 136)

After explaining his view of the political system, he rightly
observes that, so far, 'no motive taken from religion has been
supposed to actuate the moral opinion, or influence the principle
of his action' (III. 615). Here, he follows the route taken by
earlier Deist writers, and by Hume in *The Natural History of
Religion*, in speculating on the growth of religious belief.[16] A
savage state, in which man is 'subject to the highest degree of
superstition', yields to the next stage, in which 'an invisible being
is still considered as controlling the ordinary course of nature and
the will of man':

> upon the natural superstition of mankind . . . is ingrafted
> artificial superstition, founded on the imposition of the
> crafty, and the credulity of the simple. It is here that are
> employed, the arts of divination, and the pretended revela-
> tion of the will of the controlling spirits. (III. 618)

But a general confusion arises between 'religious and moral
duties' precisely because civil policy 'employs superstition for the
purpose of imposing obedience to social laws, and preserving the
order of government' (ibid.).

The vulgar cannot grasp the nature of the infinite and perfect
wisdom and benevolence of the divine mind, because they are
restricted to reasoning 'from common sense alone'; it is necessary, however, to 'have reasoned in moral philosophy, after
having in the science of metaphysics carefully examined our

principles' (III. 620). Sceptical philosophers, 'who are always
reckoned atheists' by the ignorant, may well expose superstition
whilst failing to discern its roots in 'true religion'. Moreover, just
as superstition is incompatible with philosophy, so scepticism
may be incompatible with the practical needs of the community,
and the happiness of the individual – since 'it is impossible for
mankind in general to see those truths of science which require
the investigation of many steps' (III. 626). Only the philosopher,
therefore, sees the force of the design argument:

> in the contemplation of this world, so beautiful is the order
> and arrangement of things, so plain and simple are the
> means, so deep and complicated the design, so secret every
> cause, and so certain the effect, we must conclude that
> nothing but a wisdom without defect had been employed,
> and that such wisdom is infinite or incomprehensible to
> man. (III. 645)

In addition,

> systems of illuminated spheres, rolling every where, or
> through infinite space and endless time, must give an idea of
> power that has no bounds; and this indefinite complication
> of system within system, for the production of an animal,
> enjoying sense and acting by reason, must appear to us as
> filling the measure of perfection, in that wisdom by which
> power infinite or endless is employed. (ibid.)

He contrasts 'natural religion', considered 'as being synonimous
[sic] with philosophy', and 'revealed religion', which men receive 'upon authority'. The main problem for revelation concerns the criterion: without a test 'How could a reasoning man
have any confidence in what were called revelation, but which,
for any thing that he knew, might be no better than deception?'
(III. 650–1). In fact, he had discussed a similar point much
earlier when explaining why faith has no place in science (in his
sense) (II. 286).[17] Aside from the practical advantage it might
have in 'regulating the conduct' of the unlearned, 'the supposition
of an oracular information, different from the voice of nature'
must strike any philosopher as 'absurd' – and for this reason:

> To a reasoning person, who knows nature and examines
> principles, a supernatural information would defeat its
> proper intention; for, it would only serve to confound the
> understanding, by representing either the testimony of na-
> ture as fallacious, or the faculty of reason as deceitful. To a
> philosopher, who sees the evidence of this principle, *that all
> things have been ordained in perfect wisdom,* a preternatural
> event is a contradictory proposition. (II. 310)

He insists that in the theological context, no less than elsewhere, one must observe a sharp distinction between denying a proposition, and 'not acquiescing in certain arguments'. As many earlier writers pointed out – Shaftesbury is an obvious example Hutton might have mentioned – failure to observe such a distinction may mislead

> a philosopher to believe himself an atheist, when in reality he was only a rigorous inquirer into the validity of certain arguments; in like manner as they have also thought themselves sceptics with regard to physical objects, when, at the same time, they truly believed in the same manner as other men, and might be even what is termed credulous on other occasions. (II. 312)

He maintains that every religion must be founded on two points: man's duty to his fellows, and 'ideas with respect to the Deity'. Hutton defines as Deity a '*A Being possessed of infinite wisdom, benevolence, and power*', but he is anxious to explain that 'the infinite wisdom of God is not to be compared with the wisdom of man, although our conception or idea of the one is only founded on that of the other' (III. 652; cp. II. 305). (Hutton insists that 'the omnipotence of the supreme Being must, in our reasoning, be restricted to that which is in conformity with our conceptions' – II. 305.) He echoes numerous predecessors in declaring that there can only be three opinions about a deity: atheism, polytheism and theism. And he runs rapidly through the routine *ad hominem* arguments against polytheism and scepticism: the former cannot say how many gods there are, nor how he knows, and the latter merits no hearing since he cannot decide whether he knows anything.

In conscious opposition to Hume, perhaps, he insists that

> it is not, therefore, as only explaining a known effect by an unknown cause, that we say, God is the cause of this universe we know; it is a necessary inference of reason which we cannot withhold, after observing beauty, order, wisdom, and design; for, these we must necessarily attribute to the operations of a mind. (III. 654)

Since I am conscious of not being the cause of the knowledge I have, something else must be the cause of it; Hutton therefore stipulates that 'this external operation, by which I am informed, I call the work of God, the supreme ruler or the first cause'. He concedes, however:

> That there is a deity or first cause, is a proposition or a truth which man has not necessarily, as he has his sense and reason; it is a proposition which is not instinctive, but must

require a proof or principle on which it is to be founded; and
this proof may be more or less convincing. (III. 656)

At this point he agrees with Hume in holding that 'before we can
understand the nature of our religion, we should examine into its
history, and see its origin or progress'; and he also agrees that in
his first savage state, man 'never can look up in contemplation of
a First Cause' (III. 658–61).

Incorporating the one truth of the Hebrew code, that there is
one God, 'the cause of all things', Christianity made itself distinctive by adopting the 'sacred principle of morality – benevolence'
(III. 664–5). On the basis of these premises he sees the essence
of Christianity as 'pure religion':

> the knowledge of this pure religion requires no metaphysical
> reasoning, either with regard to the nature of God, or to the
> essence of our thinking principle; it is adapted to the com-
> mon understanding of mankind; and it is founded upon the
> rational principles of human nature. (III. 665)

Like earlier Deists, he argues that 'pure religion' was corrupted
by 'speculative opinions', that 'miracle and mystery have been
employed, to the disgrace of human reason', and that one result
was a 'domineering hierarchy of an ignorant or designing priest-
hood'. Of course any man 'enlightened with the progress of
science and knowledge of religion, must abhor mystery' (III.
666–70). Remarkably, he suddenly introduces a new notion,
also from the Humean canon, namely, history; this turns out,
however, to be the generic term for all causal inquiries. With
reference to the different levels of thought, he declares that
'philosophy being founded upon science, and science upon history, we ought to see, in history, the origin of the several bran-
ches of science'; the three kinds of history each involving a study
of change, are labelled natural, metaphysical and moral (III.
676).

Only one other claim from Hutton's discussion of religious
topics need be recorded here. He uses his principle that disbelief,
no less than belief, requires evidence, to bolster his view that
there is no evidence for death. For, there is 'not an instant in our
life without a thought, and not an instant in our thought without a
change'; in addition, 'every thing in nature subsists in continual
change', and things 'cannot of themselves cease to act, or to
proceed'. And since 'no rest or inactivity is found in any thing',
there is no evidence for death – in the sense of 'a stop to the
natural progress of thought, and an end to all reflection' (III.
170–1). Of course, 'in the constitution of our being, there is a
sensual part, which is temporary or a finite thing, as being neces-

sarily connected with those which are material; but this is not the part which properly constitutes man. Man is an intellectual being, who . . . does not necessarily depend upon material things, neither for the progress of his intellectual being, nor the existence of his conscious principle'; in brief, 'what is proper to man has nothing in common with the animal' (III. 207; II. 583).

6: Other topics: taste, and language

During discussion of Hogarth's views on beauty, he asserts that 'the scientific pleasure of beauty has, for its principle order, regularity, – such as the mind is able to comprehend, or to pursue in contemplation'. Regularity gives pleasure because its detection involves 'the perfection of truth' (I. 522–3). As 'the knowledge of that which pleases' taste is 'natural to man' as distinct from brute, but it is not instinctive; on the contrary, taste must be learned by means of 'thought and scientifical reflection' (I. 530). He adds, however, that one must distinguish *a priori* from *a posteriori* taste:

> a person, who is knowing in those subjects of our pleasant speculation, must be esteemed a man of taste. But, though he be a man of taste according to this rule, as knowing *a posteriori* what in general is esteemed pleasing, he must not be considered as a man of true taste, in knowing *a priori*, or from a principle within himself, what will please or displease in general. . . . [O]ne who is to be considered as a person of true taste, must have the scientific principle of what is beautiful and pleases, independent of fashion or habit; although, at the same time, he may not be able to describe that general principle in which things pleasing may be found to agree. (I. 532)

He observes that 'a person may be a man of true taste, without being one who has an universal taste, as understanding the principles of beauty in every subject' (ibid.).

He devotes almost two hundred pages, at the end of the first two volumes, to a discussion of language. Although his starting point is Locke, he refers to the work of his own contemporaries, such as Smith, Monboddo, Charles de Brosses and Gebelin. He agrees with those who maintain that language properly belongs only to man, and that 'children are taught, in imitation, to express articulate sounds, the corresponding ideas of which they have not then attained' (I. 577–9). His traditional premise is stated explicitly:

> language is truly a record, in which the operations of a mind, proceeding to communicate its thoughts, may be legible;

therefore, in seeing the elements of language, we shall trace the original thoughts of men; and, it is by examining what has passed in the mind, that the nature of our knowledge may be understood. (1. 575)

Although language is a complex system of signs adapted to 'a regular order of thought', signs alone do not produce a language (1. 594). He agrees with the generally held view of the time that there is no 'necessary connection between the thought and any particular expression of that thought in language', no 'natural relation between any object to be expressed, and the means employed, or the sound by which the thought is to be typified in speech'. Speech, therefore, 'must be considered as an arbitrary sign for our thought', although it is unnecessary to decide 'whether or not the first speech was made of natural signs' (1. 600, 608). These views, of course, barely differ from those of the Port-Royal writers, more than a century earlier.[18] Moreover, for Hutton, naming ideas constitutes the essence of language. 'Nothing can be named but an idea', and 'all composition, inflexion, conjugation, and declension of words, ought to be construed in no other view than as a regular nomination of thoughts'; and 'nomination is no other than the expression, in language, of a natural definition' (1. 632, 617, 619). He insists that it is more important to know what is meant by words actually used, than to determine 'what had been the invention of the word' (1. 604); in the speculative question of 'how language must begin', however, he finds 'no difficulty':

> because every effort of man, to express to another what he feels himself, would, in that state of man, serve the purpose of the intention. He could not, on this occasion, utter a sound which would not have a signification; and, this connection of things would be recorded, in the mind of him who understood the occasional expression. Here, artificial language is begun. (1. 600)

Conclusion

The distinctive features of Hutton's philosophy, as he would have admitted, are the comprehensive nature of his whole system, and the rigour of his method. A casual reader who only dipped into the text could be forgiven for thinking that here was the work of a latter-day Cartesian – especially if the reader was unaware of the extent to which otherwise hostile British writers adopted Cartesian elements; or perhaps the work of someone, impressed by d'Alembert's reflections on system, who intended a direct challenge to well-entrenched British antipathy towards metaphysics. We have seen, however, that Hutton, who repeatedly described his position as 'idealist', saw himself as starting at the same point as Locke, but as remaining more rigorously faithful to Lockean tenets than anyone else had done; Berkeley, Hume, and to some extent Reid, had all contributed essential improvements, but none had followed their insights consistently or integrated them into a comprehensive system.

'Science', he states in his Introduction, 'is the distinguishing of those opinions which are properly founded upon knowledge, and those which are only founded upon supposition or conjecture' (I. xxi), and later he says that the proper philosophical method 'is that of definition, axiom, and proposition' (II. 28). He insists that 'it is necessary, first, to have the most clear and distinct ideas of our principles, and secondly, to employ them only in the subject to which they properly belong' (II. 425). Because all our claims must be referrable to what

> is absolute, evident, or certain, it is necessary that there should be some principles which are true in themselves, or a certain species of knowledge which is ultimate, and therefore cannot be either farther analysed, or compared with any other, in order to try its consistency or truth. (III. 7)

For earlier philosophers, mathematics provided the ideal or standard; but that model is profoundly misleading, not least because 'mathematicians are employed in contemplating things which strictly speaking never did, nor ever will take place'. Moreover, 'it is the consideration of mathematical speculations that gives occasion to regret an imagined imperfection, or reproach physical measurement with a supposed defect'. It should be emphasised that,

> in comparing the real differences and apparent equalities, we come to form certain conclusions, which, though not absolutely unconditional, are true under the known conditions. This is philosophy, or the perfection of human knowledge; not as meaning that human knowledge is perfect and absolutely unconditional, but that it is perfect for our purposes if properly pursued; and, it has not in it any uncertainty, although it be limited in the imperfection of our senses. (III. 44–6)

Hutton's main point here is that 'things may be either considered physically or metaphysically, without any inconsistency'; inconsistency arises from using notions proper to one domain in another domain (III. 59). He has argued that 'physical investigation does not consist in measuring things that truly are':

> so far as the nature of things consists in action, the condi-

tions of those actions are the proper subject of investigation;
so far as external things consist in power to change, the
proper object of philosophy is to know the relative identity
of those powers, and the general direction by which the
effect is regulated. (III. 47)

Material things, Hutton has maintained, 'exist in power and
energy':

> external things are not truly or absolutely extended and
> impenetrable; but . . . they are only virtually so, in having
> the power to excite in us sensation as the cause of our
> perception, and in thus leading our imagining faculty to the
> conception of things with magnitude and figure. (III. 48)

We have seen that, for him, the causal relation cannot be
observed and can only be 'discerned in the mind' by a process of
reasoning, although 'without any form of argument' (II. 188);
on the other hand, by 'a necessary inference of reason' we are
able to formulate the 'negative' concept of a first cause (III. 654,
134), by contrast with which 'all other causes . . . are only apparent, as happening in the order of our thought, and occasional as
having come to pass in consequence of a preceding action' (III.
136). Strictly,

> first causes are things which cannot possibly appear either to
> the sense or intellect, at least in relation to external
> things. . . . and secondary, or subsequent causes are only
> perceived as such in the intellect, where they are connected
> with events perceived, and thus actually known in sense,
> after the first event which had been perceived is really past.
> (II. 200)

Like Locke and Hume, he offers no clear account of memory,
although it obviously plays an important role in his account of
knowledge, not least because on his view, 'it is only the present
state that we can know with certainty', although 'we only judge
of that which is past in our knowledge' (III. 177, 167).

Hutton criticised both Locke and Berkeley for grounding their
accounts of ideas 'upon the power of God', and for doing so in a
trivial way; since, 'to say that God is the cause of every thing
ultimately, is only saying that there is nothing without a cause' (I.
333–4). He himself, however, grounds his whole system on a
first cause, and although he augments his discussion by appeal to
the design argument, it should be asked whether he avoids his
own strictures. His published works appeared within the space of
a decade, and almost all of them allude to a first cause at some
stage, without indicating any details of his views on the topic. At
the outset of the *Investigation*, however, he announces that 'we

shall so far understand the nature of external things, in knowing what they *are not*; and we shall so far understand our own nature, in knowing what we actually *do* in order to *perceive*'. He declares that

> instead of making . . . metaphysical investigation subservient only to physical science and natural philosophy, I discovered a much more important end for metaphysical inquiry; this was, the making natural philosophy subservient to a general system, in which the nature or constitution of *things* must be considered as the proper means of *intellect*. (I. xxxii)

That is why

> we may therefore define philosophy, as being not only the perfection of science, but the proper end or final cause of human knowledge, and as being, in like manner, not only the completion of happiness, but the way in which happiness may be best attained. (III. 10)

'The ultimate accomplishment of the human mind is to know supreme good' (II. 550).

His reflections on moral and political philosophy belong to the context of Hume and Smith, and represent contemporary interpretation and criticism of their views; his work on language is very much of the period, and his Deism is not dramatically distinctive. Historians would do well, nevertheless, to examine the detail of his position because of his attempts to 'rationally deduce first principles' pursuing the Lockean way of ideas and extending Humean notions of causation to their limits:

> it is not given to man to know what things are truly in themselves, but only what those things are in his thoughts.[19]

1 White, 1973; Hutton, 1788, 1794, 1795, 1899; Craig, 1978; Playfair, 1805.
2 Hutton, 1974.
3 Bailey, 1967; Ellenberger, 1972; Eyles, 1972; Galbraith, 1974; Gerstner, 1968; Heimann and McGuire, 1971; O'Rourke, 1978.
4 In White, 1973; cf. Eyles, 1972.
5 Donovan and Prentiss, 1980.
6 Jones, J., 1982, 1983; Craig, 1978.
7 For Black,. see Donovan, 1975.
8 In White, 1973, 197.
9 Hutton, 1792.
10 White, 165, 189.
11 *Ibid.*, 196.
12 Gregory, 1792.
13 See Jones, P., 1982 on Hume.

14 For his views on 'common sense' see II.530; for Reid,
    see Heimann and McGuire 1971 and Laudan, 1970.
15 Gregory, 1792.
16 Jones, P., 1982, ch.2.
17 See Dean, 1975.
18 See Jones, P., 1982, ch.4.
19 In White, 1973, 121.

KNUD HAAKONSSEN

From Moral Philosophy to Political Economy:
The Contribution of Dugald Stewart

1. Introductory Remarks

FOR THE first time since Adam Smith died we can now study his jurisprudence in some detail and in its full scope, thanks to the recently published accounts of his lectures on the subject.[1] And it turns out that it plays a role at least as crucial as one might have suspected on the basis of the already available, brief account. It builds on the moral philosophy put forward in *The Theory of Moral Sentiments,* and it is the organising theory for his political and economic thought, of which *The Wealth of Nations* is only one branch. For the first time we are, therefore, also in a position to judge the way in which those younger contemporaries who were close enough to Smith to have a similarly comprehensive view of his only partly published system of thought compare with him. Of these none is more important than Dugald Stewart.

Put as briefly as possible, Smith's basic idea is that in order for moral, including legal, reasoning and discussion to take place, it must adhere to some elementary principles, of which the most important are impartiality and consistency.[2] To the extent that such principles are deviated from, moral discourse will tend to break down and be replaced by other methods of ordering the relationships between people. These principles are constitutive of that famous fiction, the ideal impartial spectator, and when they are supplemented with the substantive moral principle that avoidance of harm or injury to other people is the primary moral duty, we have Smith's theory of justice as a 'negative virtue', and hence the basis for his jurisprudence.

His suggestion is that these principles should be used to criticise existing law, and as far as this normative-critical intention goes, he clearly sees a kinship with the natural law tradition. But at the same time he thinks that his *theory* of law has to be supplemented with a *history* of law, for it is through an understanding of the development of our present legal institutions that we will get an appreciation of the task of criticising and reforming those institutions. The history of 'law and government' is for Smith basically the story of mankind's successes and failures in approaching and institutionalising the standpoint of the impartial spectator under widely different circumstances. And as I see it, these circumstances include not only economic, but a whole host of other factors. Finally, these attempts through history are themselves formative for subsequent periods. At the same time the study of history will confirm and illustrate the theoretical knowledge we can have of the intractability of matters social and hence imbue us with a proper scepticism and caution concerning our abilities to carry out reforms.

It is this delicately balanced set of ideas that Smith – with or without tongue-in-cheek – called 'the science of a legislator'. And although this peculiar form of 'natural jurisprudence', as he called it, was never published in full, it was nevertheless influential, partly through his lectures; partly through his brief outlines in *The Theory of Moral Sentiments* and the *Wealth of Nations*; and partly through his personal influence on a number of contemporaries, including Dugald Stewart. No-one, however, got it right, and consequently the world was deprived of a line of argument in the great debate of the 1790s and beyond which was not only distinctively different from Burke's old Whiggism and the opposed varieties of radicalism, but also had an interesting theoretical foundation. A study of those who should have understood Smith, but did not, is thus perhaps of more than antiquarian interest.

2. Dugald Stewart's programme

The Smithian concept of a science of legislation is clearly carried on in the work of Dugald Stewart, and yet the content of the discipline as well as its philosophical presuppositions undergo changes which we from hindsight can see amount to its dissolution. Viewed in narrowly disciplinary terms, Stewart identifies the science of a legislator with political economy, but he then reconstitutes the content of political economy by making jurisprudence part of it.[3] At the same time he virtually excludes what he calls politics proper, i.e. the theory of government, from the discipline and, more or less, from scientific treatment at all.[4] Finally, he makes it plain that he considers political economy in this sense to be a direct extension of moral philosophy and he makes it clear that he sees himself in this respect as continuing a tradition which had so far reached its height in the Scottish academic tradition.[5] But despite his awareness of his intellectual ancestry, he finds no theoretical function for history in his political economy, as we shall see. At the level of disciplinary history it is this explicit rejection of history and the less explicit reduction of jurisprudence to a subsidiary role within a more comprehensive discipline which are characteristic for Stewart as compared with Smith.

Behind these changes in the idea of how to study human beings in their social aspect lies a metaphysics of social phenomena and a theory of the historical process which are significantly different from those of Smith. The key to this is, however, to be found at an even more fundamental level, namely in the profoundly different theory of moral knowledge to which Stewart – following Thomas Reid – subscribed. The broad perspective suggested by the following argument is, therefore, that the moral theory of the Common Sense philosophy contributed in an important way to the dissolution of Smith's science of a legislator.

The most basic objective of Stewart's moral philosophy is to counter the subjectivism and the relativism which he saw as the dangerous legacies of much of the moral philosophical tradition; at the same time he wanted to avoid the kind of rationalism which he found in Clarke, Cudworth, Wollaston, and others.[6] The subjectivism with which Stewart was principally concerned was that inherent in the various eighteenth-century theories of the foundation of moral judgement in some form of sensing or feeling – the theories of such philosophers as Shaftesbury, Hutcheson, Hume and Smith. And the objects of his attacks on relativism were philosophers, such as Mandeville, who taught that moral judgement is formed by education and political indoctrination.[7] Normally the two lines of argument were, of course, combined and the second furthermore developed from a crude conspiracy theory of moral and social phenomena to increasingly sophisticated developmental theories, a process which in most respects reaches its climax in Smith, where the relativism is furthermore transcended by his ingenious theory of the abstract normative principles inherent in the ideal Impartial Spectator.[8] The interesting thing is that while Stewart recognises these new developmental theories as of the greatest importance in modern philosophy, he is unable to accommodate them in his own moral and social philosophy.

3. Elements of a Theory of Morals

The central argument in Stewart's moral philosophy proceeds along two complementary lines, one concerning the understanding of moral qualities, the other concerning the reality of moral values as objects of understanding.[9] The latter argument is simply meant to show that moral qualities are irreducible attributes of actions which are analogous to the primary qualities of matter. (On this point Stewart is explicit, whereas Reid never made the analogy clear, as Raphael points out. But then Stewart is quite happy to talk about moral attributes as *qualities*, whereas Reid explicitly denies this and maintains that they are relational. It would seem that this creates more difficulty for Reid's analogy between aesthetic and moral attributes than those Raphael points out, and it makes it hard to see how the primary/secondary quality distinction can be of much help in understanding him, as opposed to Stewart. In this matter Stewart may well be taking up a point from his other teacher, Adam Ferguson, who in his lectures criticised Lord Kames for having 'started a question, whether moral excellence be not a secondary quality'. However, what Kames had in mind was an analogy between primary and secondary qualities on the one hand, and the determinism of human behaviour versus the appearance of free will on the other.) Moral qualities are thus immutable and have real existence independent of their perception by any human mind. Corresponding to this, the human mind has a certain ability to perceive such moral qualities, and these 'moral powers' of the mind are original and irreducible in the sense that they are as much part of human nature as the rest of our mental faculties. The traditional attempts to analyse the moral powers in terms of such principles as 'a regard to character', 'sympathy', 'the sense of the ridiculous', 'taste', or – most importantly – 'self-love', are thus futile and of course dangerous in as much as they tend to obscure the permanency and reality of human morality.[10] Stewart does not want to identify the moral powers with a separate moral sense, nor does he want them understood as an aspect of reason if by reason is meant the ability to draw logical inferences. The moral faculty is a complex of reason and feeling, in as much as it partly consists in the ability to recognise and form judgements about the special attributes of actions which are called moral, and partly in experiencing certain feelings which accompany such judgements.[11] While the ability to judge is, in a sense, of primary importance, the moral faculty or the moral power is a single original feature of our intellectual nature which it does not make sense to try to analyse any further. (In keeping with his general eclectic tendency Stewart allows the four principles of 'a regard to character', 'sympathy', 'the sense of the ridiculous' and 'taste' to be supportive of the moral powers, but insists that it is this very circumstance which has misled philosophers to think that one or another of them constituted the moral powers.)

The most obvious objection to a doctrine of this nature is that human morality at different times and in different places has taken on so many diverse and often incompatible forms that it is exceedingly difficult to see what is permanent and immutable in them. Stewart deals with this kind of objection at some length, pointing out that

> it is necessary to attend to a variety of considerations which have been too frequently overlooked by philosophers; and, in particular, to make proper allowances for the three following: – I. For the different situations in which mankind are placed, partly by the diversity of their physical circumstances, and partly by the unequal degrees of civilization which they have attained. II. For the diversity of their speculative opinions, arising from their unequal measures of knowledge or of capacity; and, III. For the different moral import of the same action under different systems of external behaviour.[12]

In order to illustrate the first point, Stewart points out – very much in the style of Hume[13] – that whereas the specific content of the concept of property right, and consequently of what constitutes theft, varies according to what people for physical or social reasons hold as property, this does nevertheless not prove that there is any variation in the basic moral principle of not 'depriving an individual of an enjoyment which he had provided for himself by a long course of persevering industry'.[14] Similarly, the fact that in pre-commercial society money-lending on interest is considered sinful and, often, criminal, whereas in commercial society it generally is accepted as much as any other form of business, does not prove any disagreement about the moral regard for the interests and happiness of other people. The point is that in the former kind of society loans cannot have the kind of objective, market-determined value which is a reflection of mutual interests between lender and borrower, and consequently the taking of interest will tend to be the direct exploitation of a particular individual's weakness.[15]

In explanation of the second point Stewart gives the following example:

> there is a wide diversity between the moral systems of ancient and modern times on the subject of suicide. Both, however, agree in this, that it is the duty of man to obey the will of his Creator, and to consult every intimation of it that his reason can discover, as the supreme law of his conduct. They differed only in their *speculative opinions* concerning the interpretation of the will of God, as manifested by

the dispensations of his providence in the events of human life.[16]

The final point is that the same mode of behaviour can receive completely different moral appreciations in different moral systems. Thus, if pain and violence are considered criteria of an honourable and happy death, then it may be benevolent to torture. And similarly when actions are symbolic or expressive of moral ideas, or ideas of politeness, they are often completely conventional and the same idea may be expressed in widely different ways.[17]

While one cannot accuse Stewart of avoiding the issue, it is hard to be satisfied with this attempt to cope with the historical and geographical diversities of morality within his moral theory. For if we accept the arguments and illustrations, the most they show is that human morality has been constant in this, that men have always and everywhere made moral distinctions and recognised moral qualities, but they have varied extremely in the content of these distinctions and recognised qualities – and that is hardly saying much more than that mankind has always and everywhere had some sort of morality. The problem is that for an objectivism of Stewart's strong brand it is not enough to show that actions which are prima facie different are yet perceived to be of the same moral value. He has to show that the actions have a real intrinsic quality in common which exists independently of perception. Presumably such an argument would take the form of showing that whatever the perceptual qualities of an action, apart from being perceived to be right, nothing follows about whether the action is right. None of Stewart's arguments goes anywhere towards showing this, and in general he simply assumes – falsely – that because the rightness of an action is independent of the judgment that the action is right, its rightness has no relation to perception or feeling. But the subjectivists distinguished the judgment that an action causes a certain perception or feeling from the perception or feeling itself, which makes an action right, and would properly reject his assumption.

Stewart's inability to accommodate the facts of history within his moral theory does, of course, not provide an argument against the possibility of moral objectivism, but it highlights the fact that in such a doctrine the history of moral phenomena plays no other role than that of providing possible obstacles in the form of counter-examples. Right moral judgment is a matter of understanding certain natural attributes of human action, and there is nothing to show that such attributes could have an historical aspect and need an historical understanding. It is, therefore, not surprising that Stewart never sees it as part of his moral-philosophical task to put forward a *theory* of the development of moral phenomena. In this he is very far from David Hume and Adam Smith. Hume had begun and Smith continued the speculation that the only basis in human nature for moral judgements is provided by a set of simple emotional responses to the behaviour of other people, and an ability to perceive such responses in others through the 'principle of communication'[18] called sympathy. This parsimony with respect to 'natural' principles in each individual then forces them to account for all other aspects of moral judgement by reference to the circumstances in which the individuals concerned find themselves. Rejecting what they take to be Montesquieu's idea that the physical circumstances will suffice, they come to the general conclusion that men's moral judgements can only be fully understood if we understand the society in which they live. Now, a group of individuals are made into a society by the collective effect of their moral judgements (i.e. judgements concerning human behaviour), some of these judgements being institutionalised, pre-eminently in the form of law; some of them being pseudo-institutionalised, such as the received code of general behaviour; and some of them standing as the more or less influential verdicts of individuals. Moral judgements are therefore to be understood as formed under the influence of a vast complexity of previous moral judgements, either directly or as they are internalised by the individual, and normally both. And at the same time the present judgement may of course well contribute to, and maybe change, this social store of moral knowledge. In this way the theory of the development of moral phenomena becomes a necessary element in the theory of morality, and this theory of development is turned into history once we add the particular circumstances of the society in question – its relationship to other societies, its physical circumstances, its exposure to accidental factors of all sorts.

For Smith the search for the moral standpoint is the search for impartiality, in a complicated sense which we need not go further into here[19] and the conditions of impartiality are in each case set by the historically given social situation. Whether the history is one of wisdom or of ignorance (e.g. of just or unjust law), it is equally necessary for an understanding of the moral judgement and the behaviour to which it may lead. For Stewart on the contrary the moral standpoint is a matter of the recognition of natural moral qualities in actions and, while such recognition may be obscured by historically given prejudices or enlightened by illustrious examples from the past, this is by no means inherent in the judgement as such but a mere circumstantial factor which can be disregarded when the minds of moral agents can be enlightened by direct education.

These reflections should make it intelligible why Stewart not only does not, but cannot take over Smith's complicated idea of the role of history in moral theory. The situation has the appearance of a pleasant paradox, for while Smith has stacked the cards so thoroughly in favour of subjectivism that he has to produce a sophisticated socio-historical theory in order to cope with the facts of social morality – and in the end also with the ideal morality of the impartial spectator – Stewart's optimistic objectivism in morals leads him to put the full explanatory burden on the moral powers of the subject.

4. Jurisprudence and Political Economy

In contrast to Adam Smith, Dugald Stewart never put forward a separate theory of natural jurisprudence; he in fact suggested that it would be a mistake to do so[20] and our over-all task here could be said to be to account for this very significant difference from Smith. But though the difference is significant, it is at the same time strangely elusive and hard to formulate clearly, not only because there are a number of things in common between the two, but also because Stewart often uses language which tends to suggest that the common ground is more extensive than is in fact the case.

At a very basic level Stewart is, of course, able to speak the language of any natural law theory, namely that there is a notion of justice amongst humankind which has certain natural and permanent features and thus provides the basis for critical assessment of all positive law.[21] And along with the Continental natural lawyers, with Hume and with Smith he takes this to be the foundation for criticism of the Hobbesian idea that we can ascribe 'moral distinctions . . . to the positive institutions of the civil magistrate'.[22] But just like (the older) Hume and Smith he of course rejects the natural lawyer's attempt to combine the idea of natural justice with the unhistorical, 'unscientific' idea of a state of nature.[23]

From the doctrine of natural justice it does, however, not follow that there is an independent discipline of natural jurisprudence; and the philosophical justification for such a doctrine can furthermore vary extremely, being in Stewart's case the common sense moral theory outlined above. But in his discussion of justice, Stewart explicitly says that what 'properly forms the subject of that part of ethics which is called Natural Jurisprudence' is justice in the sense explained by Hume and Smith, namely the negative virtue which is distinct from all the other virtues in two respects:

> in the first place its rules may be laid down with a degree of accuracy of which moral precepts do not in any other instance admit. Secondly, its rules may be enforced, inasmuch as every breach of them violates the rights of some other person, and entitles him to employ force for his defence or security.[24]

He then goes on to say that it is the accuracy of justice which led natural lawyers to attempt to formulate it in fixed rules.[25] Further evidence of natural-law thinking in Stewart is also to be found. Thus he tries to show that the right to individual property has a natural foundation in our recognition of the value of labour expended on the acquisition of property.[26] Similarly he maintains that there is a foundation in natural justice for testamentary succession[27] and he at least indicates a natural-justice element in his criticism of the laws of entail and primogeniture in the same context.[28] Finally, when Stewart is dealing directly with Smith, we find him adopting Smithian principles with much firmness:

> It is evident . . . that the most important branch of political science is that which has for its object to ascertain the philosophical principles of jurisprudence; or (as Mr Smith expresses it) to ascertain 'the general principles which ought to run through and be the foundation of the laws of all nations.[29]

It is therefore by no means clear that Stewart rejects the idea of natural jurisprudence in every sense of the word, despite his suggestion that it should not be dealt with as an independent discipline. What is clear is that he rejects what he takes to be the Continental lawyers' idea of a natural or universal code of law.[30] Montesquieu and the Scottish school of social thinkers – and especially Smith – had sufficiently taught him that law in the strict sense is an historical phenomenon and has to be understood as such.[31] Stewart's standpoint is perhaps best approached through a significant encounter with Bentham – and we are thus also hearing the voice of the future, so to speak:

> Mr Bentham's 'expressions . . . are somewhat unguarded, when he calls the *Law of Nature* "an obscure phantom, which, in the imaginations of those who go in chase of it, points sometimes to *manners,* sometimes to *laws,* sometimes to what law *is,* sometimes to what it *ought to be.*" Nothing, indeed, can be more exact and judicious than this description, when restricted to the *Law of Nature,* as com-

monly treated of by writers on Jurisprudence; but if extended to the *Law of Nature*, as originally understood
among ethical writers, it is impossible to assent to it, without
abandoning all the principles on which the science of morals
ultimately rests. With these obvious, but, in my opinion,
very essential limitations, I perfectly agree with Mr
Bentham, in considering an abstract code of laws as a thing
equally unphilosophical in the design, and useless in the
execution.'[32]

In other words, there are basic moral principles which are natural
to humankind and which ought to run through all systems of law,
but which are not in themselves law; and the sound point in
talking of natural jurisprudence is to draw attention to this. Put
in such broad and general terms Smith would certainly agree with
Stewart's standpoint, but Smith's background for this was a
distinctive theory of justice based on his idea of the impartial
spectator, and the question is whether Stewart had anything
similar to fill his general principle.

For a start it cannot escape our notice that although Stewart
mentions Hume's and Smith's distinction between the negative
virtue of justice and all the positive virtues and refers to precision
and enforcibility as the two distinguishing characteristics of justice, he never furnishes any theoretical explanation of this. Nor
does he refer to Smith's explanation, in terms of the 'moral
primacy of the negative', that is to say, that injury and harm are
universally recognised with greater certainty and reacted to with
greater force than their opposites, and that consequently the
virtue which protects against the former is on a much more
secure and permanent footing than the ones which endorse the
latter. This mere omission on Stewart's part may not in itself
seem very significant – although omissions generally may be
more significant in an author who repeats his central doctrines in
work after work – but it does lead us to speculate how he *could*
have accounted for the distinction within his own moral philosophy. And it is far from evident that he could, for in his theory
the virtues consist in doing actions which have certain natural
qualities of one moral colour or another, and presumably justice
and all the other moral qualities must be equally natural to or
inherent in their respective actions. They may of course not be
equally easy to *know*; but if we assumed that to be Stewart's
intention in distinguishing between the negative virtue of justice
and the positive virtues, then we would be looking for some
indication as to whether it is an epistemological point or simply a
report on the actual state of our knowledge. If it were to be taken

as the former, we would be looking for a theory to the effect that it is somehow inherent in our moral knowledge that we know more about, or know with more certainty about, the negative virtue – which is Smith's point. But not only does Stewart not give us any such theory; all indications are in the opposite direction. If on the other hand Stewart's point in adopting the distinction is to report that humankind at the moment in fact know more – or with more certainty – about justice than about the other virtues and thus to imply that this may well be very different in the future as moral enlightenment spreads, then he has drastically altered Smith's distinction and it is difficult to see that justice in particular should distinguish a special sub-division of moral philosophy called natural jurisprudence.

Stewart is anything but lucid in these matters, and it is quite likely that he is simply confused about the very different implications of Smith's spectator-based moral philosophy and his own common-sense theory. It is, however, clear that the latter of the proposed readings of his adopted distinction fits in with his often repeated message about the great progress which knowledge has begun and will continue to make in the world. At the same time it finds general confirmation in his tendency to speak as if all our moral duties are equally immediately derived from human nature. And it is also of interest to notice that Stewart's overture to accepting Hume's and Smith's distinction between justice and the positive virtues is to emphasise that this only applies to one very special meaning of 'justice' and that the concept also has a positive side (which can be identified with 'candour').[33] Much more important is, however, his criticism of Hume's well-known thesis that justice is an artificial virtue in the sense that it does not have direct reference to motives which form an inherent or natural part of the human frame, but depends for its reality on the interaction of individuals in social groups.[34] Smith's spectator theory had entirely by-passed this issue: for him all the virtues were equally 'artificial' (or equally 'natural') in the sense that they all arose from inter-personal, 'social', i.e. spectator-induced modifications of natural motives and passions, and they reached their perfection from the modification induced by the ideal impartial spectator. For Smith the special character of justice thus only centred around its negativity and all that was involved in that. Smith's way of arguing is, however, lost on Stewart who goes directly back to Hume's argument, maintaining that justice and benevolence – the archetypal positive virtue – are equally natural to humankind because they both depend on a direct understanding of two natural qualities. 'So far . . . as benevolence is a virtue, it is precisely on the same footing with justice; that is, we approve of it, not because it is agreeable to us, but because we feel it to be a duty'.[35]

It seems difficult to find any *raison d'être* for Smith's distinction between justice and all the other virtues – and thus for his original idea of a new natural jurisprudence of sorts – in Stewart's moral philosophy, and this is entirely borne out by a consideration of what he had to say about law – and by what he did not have to say. It is a significant fact that Stewart never in any way indicates that he wants to distinguish between laws of justice and laws with some other moral foundation; this is not to say that Stewart did not recognise the usual divisions of the law; only that he did not present any philosophical rationale for this. Smith, on the other hand, had an elaborate theory of the division of law into laws of justice on the one hand, and on the other such laws as those of 'police, revenue, and arms' which were based on considerations of public utility.[36] This is very clearly illustrated with the case of the law relating to marriage – the enforcement of monogamy and prohibition of polygamy. While Smith and Stewart were in agreement that it was necessary to have such law, Smith was quite explicit that this was not at all a matter of justice, but purely a matter of public utility.[37] Stewart on the other hand not only does not make any such distinction, but explicitly argues that the moral values protected by the marriage laws are as much part of the arrangement of nature as the justice which is protected by the laws of several property:

> marriage . . . is the result (in the first instance) of that order of things which nature herself has established; and the proper business of the legislator is here, as in other cases, limited to the task of seconding and enforcing her recommendations, by checking the deviations from her plan which are occasioned by the vices and follies of individuals. The fact is precisely similar with respect to *Property*. The idea of property is not created by municipal laws. On the contrary, one of the principal circumstances which suggested the necessity of laws and magistrates, was to guard against those violations to which the property of the weak was found to be exposed amidst the turbulence of barbarous times. It is with great propriety, therefore, that Horace classes these two *objects* of law together, the preservation of property and the protection of the marriage bed; – objects, however, which so far from being the *creatures* of municipal institutions, may be justly considered as the chief *sources* from which municipal institutions have taken rise . . . They are indeed the

two great pillars of the political fabric, and whatever tends to weaken them, threatens, we may be assured, the existence of every establishment essential to human happiness.[38]

Despite all that Stewart had learnt from Hume and Smith about social evolution, he is here operating with a rather simplistic dichotomy between the natural and the positively instituted which is clearly reminiscent of – and perhaps referring to – the early Mandeville[39] and which hardly does justice to his implied opponent and thereby to the argument. Thus Smith would certainly agree with Stewart that marriage is not a deliberate institution but has a foundation in moral values which people come to subscribe to for natural reasons. But this does not mean that these reasons, unaided by positive law, will have the same degree of uniformity in any given society or historical period as will the reasons for protecting individual rights; nor does it mean that people will react with the same natural certainty to deviations from the moral values embedded in marriage as they do to infringements of the individual rights protected by rules of justice. And part of Smith's point here is, of course, that the latter cases concern the rights of other people, whereas the former cases are about the agents' *own* moral values – assuming that all the parties to whatever deviation we are talking about (e.g. polygamy) are acting voluntarily.[40] Without implying that marriage as such is entirely factitious, Smith can therefore argue that the reasons for settling a particular form of marriage by law must derive from considerations of public utility (or 'expediency'), and they are therefore quite different from the reasons behind laws of justice, such as those protecting private property. But this line of argument is closed to Stewart by the Common-Sense moral philosophy which saw all moral attributes as equally natural qualities in human actions.

While Stewart thus, as we would expect, preserves the general idea that law is founded on a morality which is natural to humankind, he abolishes Smith's idea of a distinctive discipline of natural jurisprudence based on the peculiar features of the negative virtue of justice. This lack of distinction is of course behind his idea of one all-encompassing socio-political science for which he, as mentioned earlier, wants to adopt the label political economy, despite its traditionally narrow reference to wealth and population:

I think that the same title may be extended with much advantage to all those speculations which have for their object the happiness and improvement of Political Society,

or, in other words, which have for their object the great and
ultimate *ends* from which political regulations derive all
their value; and to which *Wealth and Population* themselves
are to be regarded as only subordinate and instrumental.
Such are the speculations which aim at ascertaining those
fundamental Principles of Policy, which Lord Bacon has so
significantly and so happily described, as 'Leges Legum, ex
quibus informatio peti possit, quid in singulis Legibus bene
aut perperam positum aut constitutum sit.'[41]

The contrast between Smith's jurisprudence-based science of a
legislator and Stewart's reconstituted 'political economy' can,
however, be even further explained, if we consider Stewart's
handling of the Smithian theme of justice and 'expediency' – or
'public utility', since expedient measures seem to be those which
promote public utility. Stewart is also here more prone to be
sanguine and often uses 'public happiness'. In Smith's work as a
whole – not just *The Wealth of Nations* – public utility is a
complex notion which is never clearly analysed, but it can be said
that the publicly useful is the aggregate of everything which will
tend to safeguard the maximum pursuit of private interest by
each individual citizen in the long run. It is therefore in a sense a
means to private interest or utility, which is the *end* – but an end
the content or character of which is never specified, as it was by
later hedonistic utilitarianism: it is for Smith a strictly individual
or private matter. This very nature of individual happiness does,
however, mean that a utilitarian approach to politics is impossible; according to Smith we simply cannot know enough to
make a simple aggregation of happiness the criterion for policy.
All we can do is to try to secure the individual in the pursuit of his
own happiness as he sees it, and that means protecting his individual rights – which is exactly what the moral primacy of justice
points out as our duty anyway. In this loose sense public utility
and justice can therefore well be said to coincide, but it should be
quite obvious that this does not mean that measures of justice
will always be of public use in all respects in all societies, nor that
the publicly useful will be in all respects just or of direct relevance
for questions of justice. To take the former first, it is certainly
just and – as it is Smith's particular pride to show – at the same
time overwhelmingly useful to enforce the strict system of law
which makes possible a market economy in commercial society;
but as it is also his concern to show, this does sometimes in some
societies lead to disutility in certain areas, such as defence and
the intellectual development of the poor.[42] And accordingly
special policies motivated by public utility may have to be

adopted in these and other areas. As to the reverse situation, Smith maintains for instance that it is a necessity for the social fabric of modern Europe that monogamous marriage be legally enforced, but he yet makes it clear that this is not according to natural justice, as we saw earlier. Further, public works, like harbours and bridges, may well be of great public utility by facilitating modes of behaviour which would otherwise not have been possible, but their relevance to issues of justice is rather indirect – as long as they are not paid for out of taxes, of course.[43]

The relationship between justice and utility in Smith is thus inherently complex. In the narrowly economic field he is confident that he can show that they could have a very close coincidence at that time and in that type of society. But it is exactly the pursuit of this kind of policy which leads to problems in other areas. And while Smith is fairly optimistic that these problems might be solved without infringement of the basic rules of justice, he is certainly not issuing any guarantee on behalf of God, History, or Nature – whether severally or as a trinity. The history of human society is open-ended for Smith, not in the sense that we can do anything with it we like – all his work was concerned to show the nature of the forces within which we have to act – but in the sense that it has openings for a diversity of developments, and human wisdom and folly will play their roles alongside other factors in determining which course is taken.

Turning to Stewart, we again find a good deal of the language and of the concerns to be those of Smith, so much so that the first impression may well be that of a Smithian turned over-optimistic. The point is, however, that there are philosophical reasons for Stewart's optimism and that these in effect amount to a thorough break with Smith. For a start it should of course be noticed that Stewart operates with the two notions of justice and expediency (or utility) as the possible bases for policies and laws. Thus:

> It was preserved for modern times to investigate those universal principles of justice and of expediency, which ought under every form of government, to regulate the social order.[44]

But the ease with which Stewart mentions the two together in the same breath, and the surprising idea of 'universal principles', not only of justice, but also of expediency, arrest the attention and make one wonder about the significance of the distinction for him. Since measures of expediency by their very nature must be aimed at taking care of particular exigencies of particular societies at particular times, it is questionable how much sense it makes to talk of universal principles behind them, but it may well make more sense in a situation where we have a 'universal' social order. This combined with the normative mode which Stewart applies give us our clue; he is talking of the great social order that can be in the future, the natural system which will gradually unfold with the growth and spread of knowledge. Stewart is undoubtedly well aware that in society as it is, the relationship between justice and utility is complicated, but it is at the very heart of the social progress which he envisages that the two will increasingly coincide. And this natural system will become a more and more universal social order, for not only will it unite existing societies internally by breaking down – although ever so slowly – such divisions as hereditary orders;[45] it will also unite different societies into one big international social order.[46] This optimism of Stewart's sets him apart from Smith simply by its supreme confidence, a confidence which is never obscured by all his warnings against precipitate actions to speed up the natural course of events, his encouragement to gradualism, to merely 'clearing the way', etc. The real difference from Smith is, however, Stewart's doctrine that we now *know* that society can develop into the natural system – and, indeed, that it *will* so develop, since human folly can only delay it.

> What else is wanting, at this moment, to the repose and prosperity of Europe, but the extension to the oppressed and benighted nations around us, of the same intellectual and moral liberty which are enjoyed in this island? Is it possible, in the nature of things, that this extension should not, sooner or later, be effected? Nay, is it possible, (*now* when all the regions of the globe are united together by commercial relations,) that it should not gradually reach to the most remote and obscure hordes of barbarians? The prospect may be distant, but nothing *can* prevent it from being one day realized, but some physical convulsion which shall renovate or destroy the surface of our planet.[47]

He arrives at this theory by superimposing the central element of his own Common-Sense moral philosophy upon the methodological doctrines which he takes over from Hume:

> in proportion as these prospects, with respect to the progress of reason, the diffusion of knowledge, and the consequent improvement of mankind, shall be realized, the political history of the world will be regulated by steady and uniform causes, and the philosopher will be enabled to form probable conjectures with respect to the future course of human affairs. It is justly remarked by Mr Hume, that 'what

depends on a few persons, is, in a great measure, to be ascribed to chance, or secret and unknown causes: what arises from a great number, may often be accounted for by determinate and known causes.'

. . . From these principles, it would seem to be a necessary consequence, that, in proportion as the circumstances shall operate which I have been endeavouring to illustrate, the whole system of human affairs, including both the domestic order of society in particular states, and the relations which exist among different communities, in consequence of war and negotiation, will be subjected to the influence of causes which are 'known and determinate'. Those domestic affairs, which, according to Mr Hume, are already proper subjects of reasoning and observation, in consequence of their dependence on general interests and passions, will become so more and more daily, as prejudices shall decline, and knowledge shall be diffused among the lower orders: while the relations among different states which have depended hitherto, in a great measure, on the 'whim, folly, and caprice' of single persons, will be gradually more and more regulated by the general interest of the individuals who compose them, and by the popular opinions of more enlightened times.[48]

For Hume and for Smith the causes which were found to be 'determinate and known' from their recurrence in the generality of humankind were on the whole basic needs, wants, and interests; and this was of course the foundation for a scientific explanation of the economic and some of the more elementary political features of human society. But to these causes Stewart can foreshadow the addition of knowledge. Now, normally we would tend to think that knowledge and ideas bring diversity rather than uniformity to human behaviour and thus make it more difficult to understand. But the kind of knowledge Stewart has in mind is naturally the moral knowledge we dealt with above, i.e. knowledge of the true moral qualities of actions, including their coincidence with private and public happiness. His point is, therefore, that moral knowledge makes human behaviour regular and thus subject to general explanation because it is knowledge of The Truth. For, as he says – ironically with a quotation from Hume – 'Truth . . . is *one thing*, but errors are numberless, and every man has a different one'.[49]

On this background it is hardly surprising to find Stewart declaring that it 'is *easy* for the statesman to form to himself a distinct and steady idea of the ultimate objects at which a wise legislator ought to aim, and to foresee that modification of the social order to which human affairs have, of themselves, a tendency to approach' (my emphasis).[50]

While Smith certainly thought it most important for the statesman and legislator to seek a systematic understanding of the social order and its possible development, he had no foundation for this kind of confident claim to knowledge, and his taciturnity on the subject of the future does indeed seem nearly demonstrative. For him men's moral judgement, and hence their behaviour, had an inherently historical and thus contingent element. But that point had to escape Stewart, partly because of the nature of his moral philosophy, and partly because he tended to see any reference to history in moral matters as nothing but prescriptive traditionalism in the style of vulgar whiggism and Edmund Burke. This is particularly evident in his repeated insistence that the 'natural' or permanent foundation for law is to be found directly in the principles of human nature, and not in the historical record.[51] It is true that he often in these contexts talks of human nature and 'its circumstances', but he never clarifies what that means or how it influences the operation of man's moral judgement, and he certainly never takes Smith's point that amongst 'the circumstances' are inescapable historical elements.

Stewart has turned Smith's science of a legislator into a science of the possible – and more than possible – future, but in doing this he has at the same time shifted the focus from the individual moral agent to the moral system of which the former is a part, and he has transformed the normative issue involved from the justice of individual human action to the goodness of the over-all system. This may not be immediately evident, for from one point of view Stewart is of course the complete individualist: it is the morally well-informed behaviour of individual members of society which will make up the natural order of society, and it would therefore seem obvious that it is the moral rightness of such behaviour which justifies the over-all system. But while this is quite true, the perspective changes rather drastically once we realise that the morally right action coincides with the publicly useful, the action which contributes to the over-all system, and that it is part of the moral enlightenment of people to make them see this. This makes it intelligible why Stewart is never very clear about where the ultimate ground of justification lies, for it raises the possibility that it is not the moral rightness of individual actions which justifies the natural system, but that the latter provides some sort of justification for the former, and consequently we are faced with the question of what could provide some independent justification of the natural system.

This is where Stewart's religious views come to play a significant role. He always makes it clear that he sees not only the physical, but also the moral world in teleological terms. There is a benevolent design of divine origin which is slowly unfolding as humankind progresses, and this design provides the directive ideal which informs and justifies our individual actions.[52] The natural order of society which is described by political economy thus carries a divine imprint which makes it prescriptive for statesmen and legislators – but of course it is one of the most important aspects of the design, and thus of the prescription, that it will unfold itself spontaneously and not by the deliberate planning and construction of men.

Stewart obviously held his teleological views very strongly, and he gave lengthy teleological arguments for the existence of God.[53] He did, however, distinguish between final and efficient causation, and he quotes Smith's criticism of the confusion between the two to support this.[54] But instead of drawing the conclusion which Smith drew, namely that explanation by means of final causes is vacuous, Stewart maintains that the two kinds of causes are equally valid explanatory principles as long as they are not confused – although he himself is prone to speak of efficient causes in teleological terms, as means or tools in the over-all design of the universe. He blames Smith for inconsistently using teleological language despite his criticism of teleological explanations,[55] thus showing that he misses Smith's point, namely that although there is a natural tendency in the human mind to view things teleologically, this cannot be sustained by rational explanatory principles. It is therefore hardly surprising that when Smith speaks of 'the natural course of things' in society, Stewart takes this to mean that we have to understand it as a divinely instituted *design* of things, and quotes it as identical with the view of Quesnai: 'Ces lois forment ensemble ce qu'on appelle *la loi naturelle*. Tous les hommes et tout les puissances humaines doivent être soumis à ces lois souveraines, instituées par l'Etre Suprème : Elles sont immuables et irréfragables, et les meilleures lois possibles'.[56] But of course Smith's whole concern was to explain social order without having recourse to design; and whether or not we should take order as evidence of design was a question the answer to which he left obscured by a haze of conventional and ambiguous modes of speaking nearly as impenetrable as those of Hume.[57]

The idea that the natural order with its divine backing has

some sort of moral primacy over the behaviour of individuals, constitutes a very significant change of perspective from that of Smith and sheds a good deal of light over the fate of his science of a legislator and, particularly, of the natural jurisprudence around which it centred. For Smith the central moral problem of social significance was that of the justice of individual actions, and the discipline which dealt with this problem, namely natural jurisprudence, was therefore both the connecting link between the fundamental moral philosophy and all social and political studies, and also the organising principle for the latter. But once the central moral problem in society becomes that of the relationship between individual actions and an over-all order, the moral goodness of which is divinely assured, the organising principle for all study naturally becomes this order, and Stewart saw his 'political economy' as the all-encompassing discipline which would study the natural order as a whole.

> Although the obligations of Justice are by no means resolvable into considerations of Utility, yet in every political association they are so blended together in the institutions of men, that it is impossible for us to separate them completely in our reasonings. . . . It seems, therefore, to be proper, instead of treating of jurisprudence merely as a system of natural justice, to unite it with Politics, and to illustrate the general principles of justice and of expediency, as they are actually combined in the constitution of society. This view of the subject (which properly belongs to the consideration of man as the member of a political body) will show, at the same time, how happily these principles coincide in their application.[58]

The consequence is thus that the study of justice and of its institutionalisation in the legal establishments becomes a subordinate part of this new total study of public and private happiness and their coincidence. The study of law will remain the most important part for the immediate future[59] because law will remain important (although it will be dwindling), but it will nevertheless be subordinate to the wider vistas of 'political economy'.

See the bibliography for Stewart for references to *Pol.Econ.*, *Diss.*, *Powers*, *Outlines*, *Elements* and *Life of Smith*.

1 Smith, 1978.
2 See Haakonssen, 1978, 1981, 1982.
3 *Pol.Econ.*, 1, 9–29; *Diss.*, 22; Winch, 1983.

4 *Pol.Econ.*, I, 20–29; II, 413 and 419–21; *Diss.*, 93–4.
5 *Powers*, II, 364–6; *Diss.*, 171, 178–9, 192–3.
6 See Grave, 1960; Raphael, 1947.
7 *Powers*, I, 264–74.
8 See Haakonssen, 1981.
9 *Outlines*, II, § 181–210; *Powers*, I, 219–32; 280–301.
10 *Outlines*, II, § 159–70; *Powers*, I, 205–18.
11 *Powers*, I., 279–80.
12 *Ibid.*, II, 237.
13 Hume, 1978, II.II.3.
14 *Powers*, II, 237.
15 *Ibid.*, 239–43.
16 *Ibid.*, 246.
17 *Ibid.*, 247–50.
18 Hume, 1978, 427; see Árdal, 1966, ch.3.
19 See Haakonssen, 1981, ch.3, esp.54–62.
20 *Powers*, II, 259.
21 *Diss.*, 181–2, 183–4, 187. See also panegyric on Bacon, *Diss.*, 71–3.
22 *Diss.*, 173–4.
23 *Ibid.*
24 *Powers*, II, 255.
25 *Ibid.*, 256–7; *Outlines*, II, § 370.
26 *Powers*, II, 260–73.
27 *Pol.Econ.*, II, 204–10.
28 *Ibid.*, 197–204.
29 *Life of Smith*, 55.
30 See *Diss.*, 107–87; see Medick, 1973.
31 *Diss.*, 69–70, 188–93.
32 *Ibid.*, 187.
33 *Outlines*, II, § 358–62; *Powers*, II, 243–4, 248–54.
34 Hume, 1975, E.P.M., III and App.III; 1978, III.II.II.; See Haakonssen, 1981, 21–26; *Outlines*, II, § 365–7; *Powers*, II, 255.
35 *Powers*, II, 255.
36 Smith, 1978, A, I, 1–26; B, 1–11; see Haakonssen, 1981, 99–105.
37 Smith, 1978, A, III, 23–48; B, III–17; HAAKONSSEN, 1981, 124–5.
38 *Pol.Econ.*, I, 79–80.
39 *Powers*, I, 264–73.
40 See Smith, 1978, A, III, 23–5; B, III–12; Haakonssen, 1981, 124–5.
41 *Pol.Econ.*, I, 10.
42 SMITH, 1976C, v,i,f; HAAKONSSEN, 1981, 92–6.
43 Smith, 1976 c, v, i, c-e.
44 *Life of Smith*, 54; cf. *Diss.*, 71–3.
45 *Elements*, I, 239.
46 *Ibid.*, 250–1.
47 *Diss.*, 490.
48 *Elements*, I, 249–50.
49 *Powers*, II, 212; cf. *Diss.*, 524.
50 *Elements*, I, 230–1.

51 See e.g. *Pol.Econ.*, I, 69–72, 86, 91–2; *Powers*, II, 260–73.

52 *Diss.*, 489–92; *Elements*, I, 247; *Powers*, II, 120–60.

53 *Powers*, II, 12–160; *Outlines*, II § 252–315; cf. *Elements*, II, 335–7.

54 *Powers*, II, 102–3.

55 *Ibid.*, 103–4.

56 *Ibid.*, 106–7.

57 See Haakonssen, 1981, 74–7.

58 *Powers*, II, 259.

59 See *Diss.*, 191–2.

NEIL MACCORMICK

The Idea of Liberty: Some Reflections on Lorimer's Institutes

1. Introduction

FOR THOSE who were students in the Scottish Universities at the time of first publication of George Davie's *Democratic Intellect*, that publication was a momentous event. It enabled us to see the intellectual roots out of which our curriculum of studies had grown, and to appreciate in an informed way the remaining if emasculated virtues of the tradition and intellectual heritage to which we belonged. To participate in the present volume of essays is to repay only a little of one's debt of gratitude to the author of *The Democratic Intellect*. It seems particularly fitting to participate through the medium of some reflections on a work by one of the heroes of George Davie's book, namely James Lorimer, author *inter alia* of *Scottish Universities Past, Present and Possible,* the 'memorial volume' (in Davie's words) for the last serious attempt to enable the Scottish Universities 'to evolve their own distinctive kind of modern education'.[1]

My task here will not be to celebrate Lorimer's work as propagandist for a revival and re-development of the old Scots educational system, but to examine some of the ideas he developed in the work he published during his tenure (1862–89) of the Regius Chair of Public Law and the Law of Nature and Nations in the University of Edinburgh. In particular I shall focus upon *The Institutes of Law : a Treatise on the Principles of Jurisprudence as determined by Nature* (cited hereafter as *Inst.*), in which by his exposition of a philosophy of law Lorimer (a former pupil of Sir William Hamilton) established his position as one of the last exponents of the Scottish common sense philosophy and as the only one to make the philosophy of law his primary concern. Faithful equally to my own inclination and to the methodological principles expounded by Lorimer as an inheritance from Hamilton and Reid, I shall treat philosophically rather than historically of certain themes from the *Institutes*, the question being not from whom Lorimer derived his theses and how they stand in relation to others' theses, but what instruction we should derive from them and how we should stand in relation to them; not why Lorimer came to think what he thought, but whether, in thinking it, he was right; or whether, if in error, he yet offers us the instruction of instructive error in matters of present concern.

Despite being in full vigour a proponent of the 'Democratic Intellect', Lorimer was by strong and explicit profession intellectually hostile to democracy, of which he delivered the following judgment:

> [D]emocracy identifies itself with that condition of lawlessness or disorganization, that non-political condition, which is known as anarchy; and we shall approach to it more and more nearly only as the State approaches its dissolution. Democracy, or equality realized, is the antithesis of political life – it is political death . . .[2]

To the prejudices and even the considered judgments of our times, these words might of themselves suffice to exclude Lorimer's thought from the category of instructive, as against that of crass, error. Yet we should hasten slowly if at all so to dismiss him. Universal suffrage, though he did not favour its immediate implementation in 1872, was for him a desired and hoped-for development, but not the same thing as democracy.[3] By his definition democracy (as distinct, e.g. from representative government) means 'the reign of absolute equality realized';[4] and, taken in that sense, it may well imply a death or withering away of law and state – certainly Friedrich Engels also thought so,[5] the difference between him and Lorimer lying in their different evaluations of that prospect.

For Lorimer, certainly, the prospect of an absolute equalisation of all persons in the distribution of resources and in the organisation of government, e.g. by submitting every question for public decision to a public plebiscite, was absolutely 'forbidden by nature, and excluded from the objects of jurisprudence'.[6] With some prescience, he argued that attempts to achieve this would inevitably lead to extremes of despotism. So far from facilitating an expression of the rational will of a community, such systems would guarantee its repression. The proper object of jurisprudence in his view was the securing of Liberty through Order, and a central part of his case was to deny the commonly stated contrast as between Liberty and Order. Indeed he represented perfect liberty and perfect order not as opposites but as equivalents – the same condition of things viewed in different aspects.[7] While a régime of liberty in turn requires recognition of the demands of equality in one of its senses – equality before the law – it is necessarily hostile to all other egalitarian schemes save those allowing of proportional equality, equal treatment of equals, unequal of unequals in proportion to their inequality.[8] (Here indeed we find perhaps the foundation of Lorimer's commitment to the Democratic Intellect – a system of education which secures to each the opportunity for fullest development of his or her natural gifts, and a régime of careers open to talents rather than hereditary privileges.)

The question of the proper balance between private liberty and public order, as well as of that between liberty and equality, is with us no less than in Lorimer's time a live and challenging one. My aim in this paper will be to confront some of the problems posed by Lorimer, relating them as much to present controversies as to intellectual history. I shall proceed to this in three stages: the first will treat of Lorimer's views on the methods proper to legal philosophy; the second, of Lorimer's thesis on the relations of natural and positive law; the third, of Lorimer's observations on liberty and order.

2. Epistemology and Method

If the topic of an inquiry is law, a necessary question must be that concerning the methods of inquiry. On the one hand, legal orders are orders of human behaviour, and human behaviour is open to human observation. On the other hand, they are orders of meaningful and intelligible conduct of human beings as social beings. In their former aspect, they invite some sort of behavioural study – what do those who purport to carry forward the business of the law actually do? In their latter aspect, they invite what may be considered a form of hermeneutic study (for an explanation and justification of the use of this term in this context, see MacCormick, 1981.) – How are we to understand and explicate those elements in our consciousness which transform *mere* behaviour into meaningful and intelligible social conduct? Subject to what categories of thought do our actions acquire the character of legal or illegal acts, rightful or wrongful?

To remark upon this duality of modes of inquiry about law is, of course to state something of a truism. We might cite a host of witnesses to it. To mention but two, Max Weber[9] propounds the thesis that a sociology of law, albeit concerned with describing probable regularities of legal behaviour, yet must acknowledge that it is the conscious orientation of human agents towards norms which constitutes such behaviour as belonging at all within the realms of the legal; and H. L. A. Hart's contribution to legal theory has at its core the insistence that there is an 'internal' as well as an 'external' aspect of the study of all forms of social rules and standards, the legal included; hence any attempt to reduce discussion of law to the level of pure 'external' observation will necessarily fail to capture the essence of its subject matter.[10]

The method of inquiry which Lorimer commended to the student of jurisprudence belongs, I think, in the same broad camp as that of Weber or of Hart. In rejecting the view that one could derive a complete and adequate understanding of law from theology and divine revelation, Lorimer sees himself as compelled towards what he calls an 'inductive' method:

> . . . all that we know either of the law of nature, or of anything else, must be learned by the ordinary processes of conscious observation and reasoning; and consequently all the actual, or indeed possible, schools of jurisprudence, except the theological, belong, strictly speaking, to a single class, viz. the inductive or observational.[11]

But what he is careful to insist upon is that his observation is and has to be two-sided, both 'subjective' and 'objective' as Lorimer expresses it. We have to attend both to the data of our own subjective consciousness and to 'objective' evidence, whether statistical or historical, as to the conduct and opinion of others.[12] The great flaw of utilitarianism, in Lorimer's view of it, was that it left out of account the 'subjective' element in philosophising and purported to rest entirely on objective or external observations; yet, as he rightly points out, such evidence is unintelligible save as interpreted through categories capable of being understood only by the 'subjective' method.[13] To that extent he must be at one with Thomas Reid in the view that 'the chief and proper source of this branch of knowledge is accurate reflection upon the operations of our own minds'.[14] I confess that this quotation is taken a little out of context, since discussions of law belong with Reid to discussion of the 'Active Powers'; but his appeal to 'reflection' is in substance an appeal followed faithfully by Lorimer in the *Institutes*.

At least at the most general and abstract level of epistemological or methodological discussion, Lorimer seems to me to be entirely correct. In all the human or social studies a complete view must seek to hold in balance – indeed in reflective equilibrium[15] – both the subjective and the objective, the subjective enjoying primacy. A concern with, for example, the 'rule of law' cannot be satisfied simply by a recording of all that is done in the name of law anywhere or even somewhere, for what we are concerned with is an ideal standard for human ordering, not only the actual manifestations of attempts to achieve that standard, all of them at least in part unsuccessful. But neither would it be sufficient simply to seek some aggregation or averaging of all or some that others have said as to what constitutes the relevant ideal standard. For that simply ascribes authority to what others have thought regarding the ideal and passes over the question whether those others' reflections merit any such authority. In any event, even to understand and appreciate what somebody else has said upon such a topic calls for an effort of imagination aimed at discovering in what way one's conduct would be guided and affected if one adopted as one's own the proposed standard of judgment and of action.

That said, I must not go too far in assimilating Lorimer's views on method with those of Weber or of Hart; at least, I must acknowledge a difference in the purpose to which he applied his methodological precepts. Whereas they define their tasks in terms of a positivistic conception of law and aim on the one hand to give a descriptive sociological account of the causes and consequences of adherence to particular conceptions of law or on the other hand to explain central features of the concept of law as an actual social institution, Lorimer's ambitions are pitched at the grander level of capturing the ideal essence of law and the lawful. Lorimer is, in short and without apology, a natural lawyer. His aim is to establish what are the fundamental principles for the right ordering of human communities, positive law being in its ideal sense whatever compulsory ordering of a community is in accordance with these fundamental principles, making all proper adjustment to allow for special circumstances of time and place. (See *Institutes*, Book III, Chapter 3, where it is insisted that positive law is an expression of the 'rational will' of a community; and pp.427–9 for the necessary elements of relativism even in ideal 'positive law'.) Actual codes or systems of municipal law may or may not realise the essence of (ideal) positive law so understood. But in ascribing them to the genus of the legal, we in effect assume that they partake of the character of genuine if misguided attempts to realise that essence.

That to which Lorimer urges us to direct ourselves from the internal point of view or, rather, through subjective observation of our nature as conscious beings is therefore by no means the simple Hartian question about the nature of our activity in following or applying given common rules of social groups. It is, rather, the question of what we find ourselves aware of as the fundamental ground of our own and others' rights. The search is for the rights of human beings, if any, which we find to be grounded in human nature.[16] (Since, for Lorimer, 'human nature' is not a matter of 'objectively' observed fact, but one

involving a subjective apprehension of value, there is here no
illegitimate inference of 'ought' from 'is'.) Whether this is a
possible enterprise at all is a profounder question than I can
broach here if at all, being none other than the question whether
there is moral knowledge as distinct from knowledge about
morals or *mores*. Yet at least it seems that if there is moral
knowledge, it is unlikely that there is a better way of investigating
its content than that proposed by Lorimer as by others of the
Common Sense school.

3. Natural Law and Positive Law

One standard and obvious objection to any such inquiry after
natural right and natural law as that which Lorimer proposes is
the objectively obvious fact of legal and cultural relativism. The
claim that there is a set of known or knowable principles of right
seems defeated *ab initio* by the manifest pluralism of human legal
endeavour and moral opinion. Conversely, most attempts to
state general and necessary principles of natural law appear to
the candid reader to be so closely related to actual systems of
municipal law as to assume the guise of ideological legitimations
of far from timeless principles generalised out of one or several
legal systems, rather than exhibiting the character of universal
truths.

   To this objection at least Lorimer's jusnaturalism is immune.
For indeed he takes it himself as against traditional systems of
natural law:

> [We] find that, whenever it has been attempted to develop a
> detailed system of natural law, it has invariably run into the
> municipal law of some particular country, or has borrowed
> accidental provision from the municipal laws of several
> countries. . . . In place of being a system universally appli-
> cable to mankind in all times and places, it was a system for
> which the most that could be said was that, if it had gone a
> little more into detail, it might have been applicable, for the
> time being, to England or to Holland . . . I entirely agree
> with Dugald Stewart when he says that 'an abstract code of
> laws is a thing equally unphilosophical in design and useless
> in execution'.[17]

On that very ground, he professes to have restricted himself to
treating in the most general terms of the objects of natural law
unencumbered by a view of the more concrete principles which
they generate in particular and variable social relations and
circumstances. To put it differently, we might say that Lorimer's
is not a conception of natural laws as an ideal rule-book to be

replicated through the human institutions of positive law. Rather, it is a conception of natural law as prescribing the *point* or *aim* of systems of positive law under the recognition that the practical achievement of this point or aim must admit of many variances according to the variation of human circumstances. It comes, then, to much the same thing as Stammler's subsequent and more widely celebrated if far from pellucid theory about 'natural law with a variable content'.[18]

Still, any such argument is open to the objection that law itself has no single standing point, aim, or purpose.[19] It is on the contrary the case that human beings have a multiplicity of aims and purposes which aims and purposes they manifest in the variety of laws they from time to time lay down. Yet even the most austere proponents of such scepticism as to the universal purposiveness of law have admitted at least some constraints upon their scepticism. Hans Kelsen, for example, allows that at least in a minimal sense all legal orders are orders of peace ;[20] and H. L. A. Hart follows David Hume in working out the implications of the truism that legal systems concern societies with some aim of individual and communal survival rather than being rules for suicide clubs.[21] Hart, moreover, when posing the question whether there are any natural rights (as distinct from any universal elements of positive law), has found himself concluding that if there are any natural rights, there must at least be acknowledged an equal right of all human beings to freedom.[22] Since what Lorimer takes to be the fundamental object prescribed by natural law is the securing of life and liberty through order, it may after all be concluded that at least this modest ascription of purposiveness to law as such could be confuted only by a positivism more radical than that of Hart or Kelsen or, at least, that represented by some fusion of their two positions.

In any event, these styles of positivistic legal thought have of late years been thrown somewhat on the defensive by the critique offered by Ronald Dworkin.[23] This critique aims to subvert the positivistic assertion of a clean conceptual divide between the legal and the moral, by exhibiting legal order as a special case of moral order. Dworkin's thesis appears to be that legal orders are essentially orders for the institutional establishment and protection of rights. As such, they do not directly embody either the whole of ideal morality or even that special part of ideal moral theory which establishes the rights properly to be enjoyed by human beings. But from that special part of ideal moral theory we can derive a more particular moral theory adapted to justifying and making sense of given legal and political institutions.

And the 'institutional rights' declared by such a theory are properly a part of the law even if the actual decisions of courts and legislatures mistakenly fail to fulfil them or purport to override them.

It deserves to be recognised that what Lorimer has to say about natural law and positive law and their relation to each other and to the municipal law as currently enforced and enacted constitutes at least in its broad outline an analogy or prefiguring of this Dworkinian view. The following points of resemblance are worthy to be stressed: for Lorimer the object of ethics in general is human perfection, while the special object of natural law is liberty (the fundamental 'background right' of all law, one might say);[24] although this does not constitute a detailed blueprint for any system of positive law, positive law is envisaged as the ideal system of social order which for given social, political and economic circumstances is best adapted to securing that object;[25] and hence even 'positive law' in this relativised sense remains a partly ideal system for the guidance alike of judges and legislators, rather than being identical with the actual moment by moment content of the municipal legal system as enforced and enacted through their decisions.[26] The terms used and the style of arguing may be different as between Lorimer and Dworkin (nor is it in the least likely that the latter was influenced by the former); but the structures of their theories have substantial points of resemblance. Ideas which in our contemporaries we do the compliment of taking seriously even without full acceptance deserve no less a compliment in our predecessors; and perhaps rather the more for their having got there first, even when they did so in that full fine cloudiness of style and utterance which (be it confessed) Lorimer made all his own. At the bare minimum, it must remain open to supposition that there is a case in Lorimer worth answering; and that whatever there is of error in it, it may so far be ascribed unhesitatingly to the category of the instructive.

We have now reached the point of conceding to Lorimer at least the soundness of his intellectual method and the strength of his version of natural law theory, evading as it does the obvious and standard objections to such theories. Allowing that there may possibly be moral knowledge, we must allow that Lorimer's way of connecting moral truths with legal systems is of the form least exposed to knock-down refutation. We are now therefore in a position to turn finally to the content of the claimed knowledge, to the assertion about liberty as the object of natural law. And here, if we have above noticed an analogy with Dworkin as to structure, we find a head-on disagreement as to content. For

Dworkin, there is no fundamental right to liberty as such, but rather a right to equality (equality of concern and respect, grounding a claim to equality in the distribution of resources); rights to liberty are consequential upon the more basic right to equality, and extend only so far as authorised by it.[27] For Lorimer, it is liberty which is the fundamental right, while to equality there are only such rights as are compatible with or authorised by the more basic right of liberty.[28] Let us see how he makes out his case, and what we are to make out of it.

4. Liberty and Order

It is an obvious if an unhappy truth that in present common usage 'law and order' as a political slogan is rarely conceived as announcing a libertarian programme. Some at least of recent and of proposed extensions of police powers of detention and questioning of suspects may be argued to help the cause of order but do not seem friendly to that of liberty. If Lorimer was right, this is a standing problem:

> . . . the realization of order, and not the attainment of liberty, came very generally to be regarded as the final and exclusive object of jurisprudence. The error, like most errors, was a half-truth . . . but the practical results of the error have not been on this account less fatal; for it has been by considering order as an end in itself, and by forgetting that its value ceases the moment that it fails to fulfil the function of a means towards the attainment of liberty, that authority has hardened into despotism . . . till humanity itself has groaned under the burden which was bound on its back by honest and upright, but ignorant hands.[29]

His point is clear enough. It may indeed be definitive of a legal system that it comprises a compulsory not an optional code of conduct. But it does not follow that mere order can be conceived as an end in itself. What is desirable is not order for order's sake, but order as a means to or element in some larger end. Yet even if we allow him for the moment the assumption that liberty is the justifying end of order, it may yet seem too violent a paradox to claim, as Lorimer does, that 'the highest liberty involves the most perfect order, and, reciprocally, the highest order, the most perfect liberty'.[30]

Let us investigate why such a claim seems paradoxical. The answer is not far to seek. In the aspect in which legal systems constitute an order of behaviour, they set compulsory or obligatory requirements upon people as to their conduct. But if one is legally required to do a, one is then not legally at liberty to refrain

from *a*-ing. The more numerous and stringent the law's requirements the smaller is the range of purely autonomous choice left
to the subjects to *a* or not *a* as they think best in given cases.
One's liberty under law covers the ranges of choice left open
once all legal requirements are satisfied. Law-as-order sets and
defines duties; legal liberty is the opposite, or, it might be better
to say, the absence of legal duty.[31]

Widely held though such a definition of 'liberty' no doubt is, it
is not free from objections. Some might say (Lorimer and Dworkin to name but two) that the proper term for absence of duty is
not 'liberty' but 'licence'.[32] And, it may be said, it is not liberty
but licence which is the antithesis of order. It is not the free but
the licentious who acknowledge no calls upon themselves in the
name of duty.

The temptation to which this line of thought draws us is that of
favouring 'positive liberty' over 'negative liberty'.[33] Liberty is not
merely being free from externally imposed constraints, it is also
being internally in command of one's life, a player in the game
rather than a pawn being played with, a person whose life has the
structure and meaning bestowed upon it by autonomous choices
and freely entered projects and commitments. Such 'liberty as
independence' is worth having, in contrast with mere 'liberty as
licence' (Dworkin's terms).

Even if we succumb awhile to this temptation, we cannot but
note that at least some measure of liberty as licence seems
necessarily built into liberty as independence; one can admire
the stoic his capacity for inner liberty while in chains, but cannot
on that account equate a condition so unhappy with the desirable
condition of being a free person. To be a genuinely free and
independent person requires some genuine and considerable
range of merely negative liberty, or 'licence', if so we should call
it.

In any event, we ought not to over-stress the Dworkinian point
of 'independence', for indeed as Lorimer forcefully remarks, no
human being is in fact or could possibly be entirely independent
of all others.[34] The human condition is one of interdependence.
The projects which it befits humans to pursue, the goods which
they can seek to realise in their lives, must inevitably and invariably depend upon the support and co-operation of others in
most cases and at least on the forbearance or non-interference of
others in all cases. If others acknowledged no positive obligations towards me from the cradle to the grave, the latter would
supervene all too swiftly upon the former; and if they acknowledged no restraints upon their intervention in my affairs, I

should have but little chance of pursuing them with any satisfaction of continuity. This thought receives characteristic expression with Lorimer in terms of a need to keep 'subject' and 'object' in proper balance:

> Liberty is something more than the mere negation of restraint. It is only by the help, the active aid and co-operation, of the object, that the subject can be free; and were I to succeed, not only in robbing you of your liberty, but in annihilating the whole objective world, I should be more limited by my own impotence, more enslaved by myself, than I could possibly be by its encroachments.[35]

Here Lorimer both makes and yet goes beyond the rather banal point of observing that there is no real possibility of a subject's being free unless others owe him or her some duties. For if a subject's freedom requires the *active* co-operation of others, then it requires that they too be free. This, he argues, is the key to what is sound in 'fraternity' as an ideal. 'It is then the maximum, and not the minimum of objective, which is the condition of the attainment of the highest subjective liberty'. This requires us to define the legitimate bounds of each. 'But the arrangement by which their respective borders are defined, as it were, by an ideal line, which robs neither of its territory, is the arrangement to which I give the name of *order*.' Thence follows his conclusion that liberty and order are not, after all, antitheses but equivalents, or mutual conditions of each other.[36]

The claim then is that I, as subject, can only be really free if I am under some restraints in your favour which leave you – as 'object' to me – free, and thus able if you choose actively to co-operate and collaborate with me; and the same goes for you as 'subject' and so on for all possible subjects. Crusoes do not lose, but gain, in liberty when Fridays arrive, provided each acknowledges the potential for free agency in the other and assists in making it actual. And by contrast, we can figure the example of Solzhenitsyn's Stalin as portrayed in *The First Circle*. As a creature above the law and in command of all but absolute means of coercion of all his subjects, he is hardly to be viewed as a paradigm of human liberty.

All such reflections as these must prompt us, surely, to acknowledge considerable force in Lorimer's line of argument about liberty, and other like ways of making a case for 'positive liberty'. When we postulate 'liberty' or 'freedom' as an ideal state for human beings we do seem to be envisaging the same sort of desirable condition of things as Lorimer sets before us. And in that light it does not after all seem paradoxical to treat liberty and order as mutual conditions, nor to join Lorimer in endorsing Cicero's epigrammatic remark (Pro Cluentio, v, 3) that we are 'slaves of the law in order that we may be free'.[37]

It nevertheless appears to me unsatisfactory to leave the matter there. For the whole discussion seems to me to have been shot through with a confusion as between the *meaning* and the *value* of 'liberty'.[38] This seems to me to be a general deficiency of all varieties of 'positive libertarianism'. It is indeed not desirable to be, or that anyone be, a *princeps legibus solutus* such as Solzhenitsyn's Stalin. Yet it is perfectly intelligible to say that such a being is indeed free from the legal restraints to which most humans are subject. Sometimes we all wish we were free of friendly and well-meant attentions of neighbours, and it is conceivable that someone could wish always to be free of every such attention from any and every other human being. You or I might think this a pretty hateful sort of liberty, but a kind of liberty (liberty from ties of humanity) is what it would be. Like every form of liberty or freedom, it amounts to the absence of a constraint undesired by the subject in question.[39]

There is in fact a great range of modes or types of constraint or restraint under which humans can be placed. There are constraints of legal or of moral or social duty; there are constraints of actual or threatened coercive human interference; there are constraints of purely psychological pressure; there are economic constraints; there are constraints of natural forces, like strong-running tides; and so on and so forth. Avoidance or cancellation of any such mode of constraint is a condition of being free *from that constraint.* One can be legally or morally or socially or psychologically or physically or whatever at liberty to do things which, in other circumstances, one would be constrained or prevented from doing. Analytically, to be free or to be at liberty is to be unconstrained within some mode of possible constraint. That is a matter of the mere *meaning* of 'freedom' or 'liberty' in the most general usage of the terms.

Why then is it ever of value to be free or at liberty in any respect or respects? The answer is obvious: only given a substantial and more or less constant sphere of non-constraint can humans pursue their projects or their life-plans, or however we shall express the idea of a life structured by an agent's conscious forethought and choices. (On the concept of a 'life plan', see J. Rawls, 1972, 407–16; the term seems to me an unhappy one, suggesting, as it does, life according to some 'blueprint'. But the idea is sound.) If it is of value to lead such a life, then to have a secure sphere of non-constraint is of value. For the reasons

Lorimer states it is a part of this value that there be others in like case. But it must also be noted that different modes of constraint can be in conflict with each other. One present legal constraint upon me is my duty not to use violence upon other persons. Although this is a legal limit on my freedom, the presence of that constraint is some control on my actually using physical violence or coercion or threats thereof against others. It is of value to those others that I am legally constrained from so constraining them; and of value to me that they lie under like constraint in my favour. Not all of the constraints of various kinds to which humans may be subject are constraints freedom from which are essential to the shaping and pursuit of a *reasonable* way of life. For indeed a reasonable way of life must, as Lorimer rightly says, allow of human interdependence and the need of active and willing mutual support, co-operation and assistance as between 'subject' and 'object', as he (perhaps misleadingly) expresses the point. Hence, if one could be a sort of Faust who procures a release from all moral obligation, or if one were a psychopath for whom moral demands in favour of other humans had no psychological grip at all, one would indeed be at liberty from constraints to which human life is normally subject. There is no need to deny that this would be a kind of liberty or liberation. But there is every reason to deny that a wish to be so liberated is a *reasonable* wish; and for those of us who confine ourselves to wishing reasonable wishes, there is every reason to deny the least value to any such liberty or liberation in any possible manifestation.

In short, it may always be true that there is no constraint of any sort whose presence may not be in some circumstances irksome, yet it does not follow that it is an object of reasonable desire to have a life free of all constraints of every sort. The kind of liberty which it is of value to have is liberty within a working legal moral and political order such that for each of its members there is a genuine opportunity to shape and pursue some reasonable way of life alongside of others enjoying like opportunities. Thus when we allow for the contextual implications of summing that up in the presentation of 'human liberty' or 'a free society' as morally desirable political ends, we must acknowledge a degree of solid sense in (at least some) theories of 'positive liberty'. Such theories presuppose some prior evaluation of the ways in which essentially 'negative' freedoms come to be desirable, and of the forms of life which appropriate congeries of particular such freedoms make possible. Since these are debatable evaluations, it is not surprising that 'human liberty' and 'free society' belong so obviously within the category of W. B. Gallie's well-named 'essentially contested concepts'.[40] But I venture to suggest that the essential contests would be best conducted through a discussion which constraints can and should be lifted from human lives, and to what end; not by beating our head against 'liberty' as a concept, as though it had secrets here to unfold for us.

'To what end?' Lorimer's answer to that question has been a leitmotif in the foregoing. The whole argument has rested on the assumption that the realisation of human potential through human choice and action is a good end in itself. Such indeed was Lorimer's theory of value – not a particularly original one for a later 19th century philosopher. Somewhat more original, perhaps, was Lorimer's argument that in the light of such a value theory, the alleged conceptual distinction between justice and charity was based on a mistake. The derivation of that argument runs roughly as follows: implicit in anyone's consciousness of existence is an apprehension of the rightfulness of one's existence – 'the fact of being involves the right to be';[41] but the right to be is a right to realise one's powers and potentials, as distinct from merely sustaining a minimum of animal vitality – 'the right to be implies a right to develop our being, and to the conditions of its Development'.[42] Hence, if I have a right to the conditions of my development, it is no work of supererogation on your part to supply me with such of these conditions as are in your power. All such provision is a matter of justice, and so-called 'charity' cannot add anything to the duties of justice; at best, it will denote a special and worthy motive for acting as it is in all events incumbent on one to act.[43]

At a time of growth in scepticism about the justification of a welfare state, these are fortifying reminders to those who challenge the sceptics. Yet the argument unfolded in brief above has other more troubling implications, all the more troubling to the extent that self-realisation is back on the current agenda of discussion as an ultimate moral value. For it raises the very problem about equality or 'democracy' with which this paper commenced. Take it for granted that human beings ought always to be respected as ends-in-themselves, never treated merely as means; assume that this is a matter of equally respecting all human beings as equally bearing distinctively human potentialities; we still face the difficulty that different persons appear to be bearers of different human potentialities. That we all equally have human potentialities does not mean that we all have equal human potentialities, nor indeed is this so.

Just as we saw that the proposition that all men are equally men did not involve the proposition that all men are equal men, so now we see that the proposition that all citizens are equally citizens does not involve the proposition that all citizens are equal citizens, or that because all citizens ought to be voters, all voters ought to be equal voters.[44]

My brother or sister the nuclear physicist is in the way of realising potentialities which I never had in the same measure and which in any event my own not less reasonable path of life has now irrevocably closed off to me. The resources consumed in his or her pursuit of this instance of a higher human excellence vastly outweigh those for which I make any demands on my fellows; both of us are expensive compared with, and work at the expense of, the butcher, the baker and the candlestick maker. Are all our rights to be measured, as Lorimer thought, by the single metric of our natural powers and potentialities? What if this results in very substantial inequalities in the use and consumption of available resources? Does it not in fact do so?

For my part, for reasons I have adumbrated elsewhere[45], the inegalitarianism to which an argument like Lorimer's leads is unacceptable. There are other requirements of respect for persons than those which tell in favour of universal self-realisation even at costs of great inequality. By this judgment, Lorimer is indeed in error (and sometimes nasty error, as in the case of his argument for a right to aggression[46], or in his enthusiastic adoption of contemporary ideas about racial superiority and inferiority).[47] Surely, however, the error is of the instructive class, nowhere more so than in the problems raised by his theory of liberty. Certainly, reflection on those problems may help us to clarify the ostensible rivalry between 'licence' and 'liberty', between 'negative' and 'positive' aspects of human freedom; and to perceive the sense in which legal order is indeed a condition of human liberty.

1 Davie, 1961, 47; see ch.3, *passim*, for discussion of Lorimer's pamphlet on the universities.
2 *Inst.*, 443; cf. bk.ii, ch.3.
3 *Ibid.*, 349.
4 *Ibid.*, 443.
5 Oakeshott, 1941, 130–1.
6 *Inst.*, 443.
7 *Ibid.*, 295–6.
8 *Ibid.*, 321–32.
9 See Weber, 1949, 138–52 and cf. Kronman, 4–5, 34–6.
10 See Hart, 1961, 44–6 and MacCormick, 1981.
11 *Inst.*, 31.

12 *Ibid.*, 32–4.
13 *Ibid.*, 34–8.
14 Reid, 1895, 238; I.P., I.V.
15 Rawls, 1972, 20f, 48–51.
16 See in particular *Inst.*, I, chs 7 and 8.
17 *Inst.*, 428.
18 Stammler, 1925.
19 See Hart, 1957; cf. Fuller, 1957–8.
20 Kelsen, 1960, 38–41.
21 Hart, 1961.
22 Hart, 1967.
23 Dworkin, 1978.
24 *Inst.*, 219–91; cf. Dworkin, 101–5.
25 *Inst.*, 422–35; cf. Dworkin loc.cit.
26 *Inst.*, 342–58; cf. Dworkin, 118–23.
27 Dworkin, 1978, 268–78.
28 *Inst.*, 291–332.
29 *Ibid.*, 292.
30 *Ibid.*, 295–6.
31 Cf. Hohfeld, 1919 and Glanville Williams, 1968.
32 Dworkin, 1978, 262 and *Inst.*, 293.
33 See Berlin, 1969, ch.3 and Gray, 1980.
34 *Inst.*, 294–5.
35 *Ibid.*, 294.
36 *Ibid.*, 295–6.
37 *Ibid.*,292.
38 From Hart, 1967; cf. Rawls, 1972, 204–6.
39 See MacCormick, 1982, 39–40.
40 Gallie, 169.
41 *Inst.*, 167–9.
42 *Ibid.*, 173–6.
43 *Ibid.*, 248–76.
44 *Ibid.*, 350.
45 MacCormick, 1982, chs 1 and 2.
46 *Inst.*, 332–7.
47 See *Inst.*, 369–70 on the inferiority of Celtic peoples.

BIBLIOGRAPHY

ANSCOMBE, G.E.M. (1963) *Intention*. Oxford.
(1978) 'Rules, Rights and Promises,' *Midwest Studies in Philosophy*. Minnesota.

ÁRDAL, P.S. (1966) *Passion and Value in Hume's Treatise*. Edinburgh.
(1968) 'And that's a promise,' *Philosophical Quarterly*, 18, 225–37.

AUNE, B. (1975) *Reason and Action*. Dordrecht.

AUSTIN, J. (1861–3) *Lectures in Jurisprudence*. London.

BAILEY, E.B. (1967) *James Hutton – the Founder of Modern Geology*. London.

BAILLIE, R. (1841) *The Letters and Journals of Robert Baillie, A. M., Principal of the University of Glasgow* (Ed. D. Laing) Edinburgh, Bannantyne Club.

BAIRD, R.M. (and DUNCAN, EEH.) (1977) 'Thomas Reid's criticisms of Adam Smith's *The Theory of Moral Sentiments*,' *Journal of the History of Ideas*, 38, 509–22.

BAMBROUGH, R. (1979) *Moral Scepticism and Moral Knowledge*. London.

BAYLE, P. *Pensées Diverses*. (Denoted in refs. by 'P. D.'.)

BECKER, G.S. (1976) *The Economic Approach to Human Behaviour*. Chicago.

BENNETT, J. (1971) *Locke, Berkeley, Hume*. Oxford.

BENTHAM, J. (1843) *Works* (ed. J. Bowring) Edinburgh.
(1970) *An Introduction to the Principles of Morals and Legislation*, eds. J. H. Burns and H. L. A. Hart. London.

BERLIN, I. (1969) *Four Essays on Liberty*. London.
(1977) 'Hume and the sources of German Anti-Rationalism' in *David Hume, Bicentenary Papers*, ed. G. P. Morice. Edinburgh 93–116.

BEROFSKY, B. (1966) *Free Will and Determinism*. New York.

BOWLES, R. (1978) 'Creeping Economism: A Counter-View,' *British Journal of Law and Society*, 5, 96–100.

BRADLEY, F. H. (1927) *Ethical Studies*. Oxford.

BRICKE, J. (1974) 'Emotion and Thought in Hume's *Treatise*,' *Canadian Journal of Philosophy*, Supp. vol. 1, 53–71.
(1980) *Hume's Philosophy of Mind*. Edinburgh.

BUCHANAN, J.M. (1976) 'The Justice of Natural Liberty,' *Journal of Legal Studies*, 10.

CALABRESI, G. (1970) *The Costs of Accidents*. New Haven.
(1975) 'Optimal Deterrence of Accidents,' *Yale Law Journal*, 84.

CAMPBELL, A.H. (1954) 'The Structure of Stair's Institutions,'
Glasgow University Publication XCVIII.

CAMPBELL, R.H (and A.H. SKINNER, eds) (1982) *The Origins and Nature of the Scottish Enlightenment.* Edinburgh.

CAMPBELL, T.D. (1971) *Adam Smith's Science of Morals.* London.
(1975) 'Scientific Explanation and Ethical Justification in the *Moral Sentiments*,' in Skinner, 1975.
(1977) 'Adam Smith and Natural Liberty,' *Political Studies*, 25, 523-34.

(and ROSS, I.S.) (1981) 'The Utilitarianism of Adam Smith's Policy Advice,' *Journal of the History of Ideas*, 42, 73-92.

CARMICHAEL, G. (1699) *Theses philosophicae Praesidio Gerschomi Carmichael.* Glasgow.
(1722) *Breviuscula Introductio ad Logicam.* Edinburgh.

COASE, R.H. (1960) 'The Problem of Social Cost,' *The Journal of Law and Economics*, 3.
(1976) 'Adam Smith's View of Man,' *Journal of Law and Economics*, 5

COOTER, R. (1982) 'The Cost of Coase,' *Journal of Legal Studies*, II, 1-34.

CRAIG, G.Y. (ed.) (1978) *James Hutton's Theory of the Earth: The Lost Drawings.* Edinburgh.

DALGARNO, M. (1975) 'Anarchical Fallacies,' *Archiv für Rechts-und Sozialphilosophie*, LXI.

DAVIDSON, D. (1980) Essays on Action and Events. Oxford

DAVIE, G.E. (1961) *The Democratic Intellect.* Edinburgh.
(1965) 'Berkeley's Impact on Scottish Philosophers,' *Philosophy*, 40, 222-234.
(1973) 'The Social Significance of the Scottish Philosophy of Common Sense,' the Dow Lecture of 1972 delivered before the University of Dundee.
(1977) 'Edmund Husserl and "the as yet, in its most important respect, unrecognised greatness of David Hume," in *David Hume. Bicentenary Papers* ed. G. P. Morice. Edinburgh.
(1981) *The Scottish Enlightenment*, a monograph for the Historical Association. London.

DEAN, D.R. (1975) 'James Hutton on Religion and Geology: the Unpublished Preface to his Theory of the Earth (1788),' *Annals of Science*, 32.

DONOVAN, A. (1975) *Philosophical Chemistry in the Scottish Enlightenment.* Edinburgh.
(and PRENTISS, J. eds.) (1980) *James Hutton's Medical Dissertation*, Trans. Amer. Phil. Soc., 70.

DOWNS, A.(1957) *An Economic Theory of Democracy.* New York.

DUGGAN, T. (with B. GERT) (1979) 'Free Will as the Ability to Will,' *Nous*, 13, 197-217.

DWORKIN, R. (1978) *Taking rights seriously.* London.

ELLENBERGER, F. (1972) 'La Metaphysique de James Hutton,' *Revue de Synthe*̀*se.*

EMERSON, R.L. (1977) 'Scottish Universities in the Eighteenth Century, 1690-1800,' *Studies in Voltaire and the Eighteenth Century*, 158.
(1982) (with G. GIRARD and R. RUNTE, eds.) *Man and Nature.* London, Ontario.

EYLES, V. (1972) 'James Hutton,' *Dictionary of Scientific Biography*, 6. New York.

FIRTH, R. (1951) 'Ethical Absolutism and the Ideal Observer,' *Philosophy and Phenomenological Research*, XII, 317–45.

FORBES, D. (1975) *Hume's Philosophical Politics*. Cambridge.

FRIED, C. (1978) *Right and Wrong*. Cambridge, Mass.

FULLER, L.L. (1957–8) 'Positivism and Fidelity to Law – A Reply to Professor Hart,' *Harvard Law Review*, 71, 630–72.

GALBRAITH, W.H. (1974) *James Hutton: An Analytic and Historical Study*, Ph.D. thesis, University of Pittsburgh, (University Microfilms International, London.)

GALLIE, W.B. (1955) 'Essentially contested concepts,' *Proceedings of the Aristotelian Society*, 1955–6, LVI, 167–98.

GERT, B. See Duggan (1979)

GERSTNER, P.A. (1968) 'James Hutton's Theory of the Earth and His Theory of Matter,' *Isis*, 59.

GINET, C. (1962) 'Can the will be caused?', *Philosophical Review*, LXXI, 49–55.

GIRARD, G. (with R. L. EMERSON and R. RUNTE, eds.) (1982) *Man and Nature*. London, Ontario. (Faculty of Education Publications.)

GRAY, J.N. (1980) 'On Negative and Positive Liberty,' *Political Studies*, 28, 507–26.

GRAVE, S.A. (1960) *The Scottish Philosophy of Common Sense*. Oxford.

GREEN, T.H. (and T.H. GROSE, eds.) (1874–5) *David Hume: Philosophical Works*. London.

GREGORY, J. (1792) *Philosophical and Literary Essays*

GROTIUS, H. (1738) *The Rights of Peace and War*. London.

HAAKONSSEN, K. (1978) *Natural Justice. The Development of a Critical Philosophy of Law from David Hume and Adam Smith to John Millar and John Craig*, Ph.D. thesis for Edinburgh University.
(1981) *The Science of a Legislator: the Natural Jurisprudence of David Hume and Adam Smith*. Cambridge.
(1982) 'What might properly be called natural jurisprudence?' in *The Origins and Nature of the Scottish Enlightenment*, ed. R. H. Campbell and A. S. Skinner. Edinburgh.

HAMPSHIRE, S. (and H.L.A. HART) (1958) 'Decision, Intention and Certainty,' *Mind*, LXVII, 1–12.

HARMAN, G. (1975) 'Practical Reasoning', *The Review of Metaphysics*, 29, 431–63.

HARRE, R. (1980) 'Knowledge', in Porter (1980).

HARRISON, J. (1976) *Hume's Moral Epistemology*. Oxford.

HART, H.L.A. (1957) 'Positivism and the Separation of Law from Morals,' *Harvard Law Rev.* 71, 593–629. Hampshire (1958)
(1961) *The Concept of Law*. Oxford.
(1967) 'Are there any natural rights?', *Political Philosophy*, ed. Anthony Quinton, London.

HEIMANN, P.M. (and MCGUIRE, J.E.) (1971) 'Newtonian Forces and Lockean Powers,' in *Historical Studies in the Physical Sciences*, 3, ed. R. McCormmach. Philadelphia.

HENDEL, C.W. (Jun) (1925) *Studies in the Philosophy of David Hume*. Princeton.

HOBBES, T. (1946) *Leviathan*, ed. M. J. Oakeshott. Oxford.
(1949) *De Cive*, ed. S. P. Lamprecht. New York.
(1969) *The Elements of Law*, ed. F. Tönnies. London.
HOHFELD, W.N. (1919) *Fundamental Legal Conceptions*. New Haven.
HONT, I. (with M. IGNATIEFF) (1983) *Wealth and Virtue: the Shaping of Scottish Political Economy*. Cambridge.
HORN, J.C. (1980) 'Zwei anthropologische Angeln in Hegels Phaenomenologie.' *Sinn und Geschichtlichkeit. Werk und Wirkingen Theodor Litts*. Stuttgart. (Ed. J. Derbolav and others.)
HUME, DAVID (1875) *Essays Moral, Political and Literary*, edited by T. H. Green and T. H. Grose, 2 vols. London.
(1932) *The Letters of David Hume*, edited by J. Y. T. Greig, 2 vols. Oxford.
(1938) *An Abstract of A Treatise of Human Nature*, ed. J. M. Keynes and P. Sraffa. Cambridge.
(1963) *Hume on Religion*, edited by R. Wollheim. London.
(1970) *The History of Great Britain: The Reigns of James I and Charles I*, edited by D. Forbes. London.
(1972) *A Treatise of Human Nature*, ed. with intro. by P. S. Ardal. London.
(1975) *Enquiries Concerning Human Understanding and Concerning the Principles of Morals*, ed. L. A. Selby-Bigge, Oxford, 1902, third edition revised with notes by P. H. Nidditch, Oxford.
(1978) *A Treatise of Human Nature*, ed. L. A. Selby-Bigge, Oxford, 1888, 2nd edition with text revised by P. H. Nidditch. Oxford.
(1980) *Dialogues concerning Natural Religion*, ed. N. Kemp-Smith. Indianapolis.
HUTCHESON, F. (1724) Letters to the *London Journal* (Nov. 14 and 21).
(1725) Letters to the *Dublin Journal* (June 5, 12, 19).
(1726) Letters to the *Dublin Journal* (Feb. 4, 11, 18); reprinted London 1729 and as *Reflections on Laughter and Remarks upon the Fable of the Bees*. Glasgow, 1750.
(1730) *De Naturali Hominum Socialitate*. Glasgow.
(1747) *A Short Introduction To Moral Philosophy, in Three Books; Containing the Elements of Ethicks and the Law of Nature*. Glasgow.
HUTTON, J. (1788) 'Theory of the Earth,' *Transactions of the Royal Society of Edinburgh*, I.
(1792) *Dissertations on Different Subjects in Natural Philosophy*. Edinburgh.
(1794a) 'Observations on Granite,' *Trans. R. S. E.*, III.
(1794b) *An Investigation of the Principles of Knowledge, and of the Progress of Reason, from Sense to Science and Philosophy*. Edinburgh.
(1795) *Theory of the Earth*. Edinburgh. (Facsimile reprint, New York, 1959.) III, LONDON, 1899.
IGNATIEFF, M. See Hont (1983).
JONES, J. (1982) 'James Hutton and the Forth and Clyde Canal,' *Annals of Science*, 39.
(1983) 'James Hutton: Exploration and Oceanography,' *Annals of Science*, 40.

JONES, P. (1982) *Hume's Sentiments*. Edinburgh.

KEENAN, D. (1981) 'Value Maximisation and Welfare Theory,' *Journal of Legal Studies*, 10, 109–19.

KELSEN, H. (1960) *Reine Rechtslehre*, 2nd edition. Vienna.

KEMP-SMITH, N. (1941) *The Philosophy of David Hume*. London.

KENNY, P. (1982) 'Economic Analysis and Efficiency in the Common Law,' in *Law and Economics*, ed. Ross Cranston and Anne Schick. Canberra.

KING, C. (see SHEPHERD) *Philosophy and Science in the Arts Curriculum of the Scottish Universities in the Seventeenth Century*, Ph.D. thesis, University of Edinburgh.
(1982) 'Newtonianism in Scottish Universities in the Seventeenth Century' in Campbell, R.H. (1982).

KRONMAN, A.T. (1983) *Max Weber*. London.

LAUDAN, L.L. (1970) 'Thomas Reid and the Newtonian Turn in British Methodological Thought' in *The Methodological Heritage of Newton*, eds. R.E. Butts and J.W. Davis. Toronto.

LEFF, A.A. (1974) 'Economic Analysis of Law: Some Realism about Nominalism,' *Virginia Law Review*, vol. 60, 451–92.

LEHRER, K., ed. (1966) *Freedom and Determinism*. New York.

LEIBNIZ, G.W. (1972) *The Political Writings of Leibniz*, translated and edited by Patrick Riley. Cambridge.

LINDGREN, J.R. (1973) *The Social Philosophy of Adam Smith*. The Hague.

LOCKE, J. (1975) *An Essay Concerning Human Understanding*, ed. P.H. Nidditch. Oxford.
(1982) *The Correspondence of John Locke*, VII, ed. E.S. de Beer. Oxford and New York.

LORIMER, J. (1872) *Institutes of Law*. Edinburgh.

MACCORMICK, D.N. (1978) *Legal Reasoning and Legal Theory*. Oxford.
(1981) *H.L.A. Hart*. London.
(1982a) *Legal Right and Social Democracy*. Oxford.
(1982b) 'Law and Enlightenment' in Campbell, R.H. (1982).

MACFIE, A.L. (1967) *The Individual in Society*. London.

MACHAN, T.R. (1980) 'Some Recent Work in Human Rights Theory,' *American Philosophical Quarterly*, vol. 17, 103–15.
(1982) 'A Reconsideration of Natural Rights Theory,' *Ibid.* 19, 61–72.

MACPHERSON, C.B. (1967) 'Natural Rights in Hobbes and Locke,' in *Political Theory and the Rights of Man*, ed. D.D. Raphael. London.

MCNEILLY, F.S. (1972) 'Promises De-Moralized,' *Philosophical Review*, 81, 63–81.

MEDICK, H. (1973) *Naturzustand und Naturgeschichte der bürgerlichen Gesellschaft*. Göttingen.

MELDEN, A.I. (1956) 'On Promising,' *Mind*, 65, 49–66.

MILL, J.S. (1967) *Utilitarianism*, ed. M. Warnock. London.
(1973) 'Use and Abuse of Political Power' in *Collected Works*, ed. J.M. Robson, XVIII, *Essays in politics and society*. Toronto.

MOORE, J. (and M. SILVERTHORNE) (1980) 'Gerschom Carmichael and the Natural Jurisprudence Tradition in Eighteenth-Century Scotland', a paper prepared for the Political Economy and Society Seminar at King's College Research Centre, 4 Dec., 1980.

BIBLIOGRAPHY   254

(1982) 'Gerschom Carmichael and the Natural Jurisprudence
  Tradition in Eighteenth Century Scotland' in Emerson. Reprinted
  in Hont (1983).
MOSSNER, E.C. (1936) 'The Enigma of Hume,' *Mind*, n.s. 45, 334–49.
NIETZSCHE, F. (1969) 'Jenseits von Gut und Bose,' *Werke Bd.* II, ed.
  K. Schlechta. Muenchen.
NORTON, D.F. (with STEWART-ROBERTSON, J.C.) (1980) 'Thomas
  Reid on Adam Smith's Theory of Morals,' *Journal of the History
  of Ideas*, XLI, 381–98.
OAKESHOTT, M.J. (1941) *Social and Political Doctrines of
  Contemporary Europe*. (2nd edition) Cambridge.
O'ROURKE, J.E. (1978) 'A Comparison of James Hutton's *Principles
  of Knowledge* and *Theory of the Earth*,' *Isis*, 69.
PLAYFAIR, J. (1805) 'Biographical Account of the late Dr James
  Hutton,' *Trans. Royal Society of Edinburgh*, v.
PARTLETT, D. (1982) 'Economic Analysis in the Law of Torts,' in *Law
  and Economics*, eds. Ross Cranston and Anne Schick. Canberra.
PASSMORE, J.A. (1952) *Hume's Intentions*. Cambridge.
PENELHUM, T. (1975) *Hume*. London.
PIGOU, A.C. (1932) *The Economics of Welfare* (4th edition). London.
POPPER, K.R. (1975) 'Conjectural Knowledge : My solution of the
  Problem of Induction,' in *Objective Knowledge. An Evolutionary
  Approach*. Oxford.
POSNER, R.A. (1972) *The Economic Analysis of Law*. Boston.
  (1975) 'The Economic Approach to Law,' *Texas Law Review*, 53.
  (1979) 'Utilitarianism, Economics and Legal Theory', *Journal of
  Legal Studies*, 8.
PRICHARD, H.A. (1957) 'The Obligation to Keep a Promise,' in *Moral
  Obligation*. Oxford.
PRIEST, G.L. (1977) 'The Common Law Process and the Section of
  Efficiency Rules,' *Journal of Legal Studies*, 6.
PRIOR, A.N. (1949) *Logic and the Basis of Ethics*. Oxford.
PUFENDORF, S. (1724) *De Officio Hominis et Civis Juxta Legem
  Naturalem, Libri duo. Supplementis et Observationibus in
  Academicae Juventutis usum auxit et illustravit Gerschomus
  Carmichael*. Edinburgh.
  (1729) *Of the Law of Nature and Nations*. London.
  (1820) *Les Devoirs de l'Homme et du Citoyen*, trad. Jean
  Barbeyrac. Paris.
  (1927) *De Officio Hominis et Civis Juxta Legem Naturalem*, Libri
  duo. New York.
RAPHAEL, D.D. (1947) *The Moral Sense*. Oxford.
  (1967) (editor) *Political Theory and the Rights of Man*. London.
  (1975) 'The Impartial Spectator,' in *Essays on Adam Smith*, eds.
  A.S. Skinner and T. Wilson. Oxford.
  (1976) (editor with A.L. Macfie) *The Theory of the Moral
  Sentiments*. Oxford.
RAWLS, J. (1972) *A Theory of Justice*. Oxford.
REID, T. (1765) MS 2131/8/IV/1, Aberdeen University Library
  (1766) MS 2131/8/IV/4, Aberdeen University Library
  (1767) MS 2131/8/VII, Aberdeen University Library
  (1770) MS 2131/7/VII/1–26, Aberdeen University Library
  (1791) MS 2131/3/III/8, Aberdeen University Library
  (1796) 'Sketch of the career of the late Thomas Reid, D.D., with

Observations on the Danger of Political Innovation,' from a
Discourse delivered on Nov. 29, 1794, by Dr Reid before the
Literary Society of Glasgow College. Glasgow.
(1895) *Works*, edited by Sir Wm Hamilton, including *Essays on
the Intellectual Powers of Man*, denoted in references by 'I. P.' and
Essays on the Active Powers of Man, denoted by 'A.P.'

ROBINS, M.H. (1976) 'The Primacy of Promising,' *Mind*, LXXXV,
321–40.

ROBISON, W. (1976) 'David Hume, Naturalist and Meta-sceptic' in
Hume. A Re-evaluation, eds. D. W. Livingston and J. T. King.
New York. 23–49.

ROSS, I.S. Campbell (1981).

ROXBEE COX, J.W. (1963) 'Can I know Beforehand what I am going to
decide?,' *Philosophical Review*, LXXII, 88–92.

RUBIN, P.H. (1977) 'Why is Common Law Efficient?', *Journal of
Legal Studies*, 6.

RUNTE, R. Emerson (1982).

RUSSELL, B. (1946) *A History of Western Philosophy*. London.

SARTRE, J. P. (1957) *Being and Nothingness*. (Translated by
H. E. Barnes) London.

SEARLE, J. R. (1969) *Speech Acts*, Cambridge.
(1979) 'What is an Intentional State?,' *Mind*, 88, 74–92.

SELBY-BIGGE, L.A. (1897) *British Moralists*, Oxford.
(1975) *Hume's Treatise of Human Nature*. Oxford.
(Revised by P. H. Nidditch)
(1975) *Hume's Enquiries Concerning Human Understanding and
Concerning the Principles of Morals*. Oxford. (Revised by
P. H. Nidditch)

SHEPHERD, C. See KING.

SELLERS, W. (1966) 'Thought and Action' in *Freedom and
Determinism*, ed. K. Lehrer. New York.

SIDGWICK, H. (1907) *Methods of Ethics*. 7th edition, London.

SILVERTHORNE, M. See Moore.

SKINNER, A. S. (with T. WILSON, eds) (1975) *Essays on Adam
Smith*, Oxford.

SMITH, A. (1963) *Lectures on Rhetoric and Belles Lettres*, ed.
J. M. Lothian. London. Reprinted by Carbondale and
Edwardsville.
(1976a) *The Theory of Moral Sentiments*, eds. D. D. Raphael and
A. L. Macfie. Oxford.
(1976b) 'Anderson Notes', from *John Anderson's Commonplace
Book*, vol. I, in the Andersonian Library, University of
Strathclyde, printed in R. L. Meek, 'New Light on Adam Smith's
Glasgow Lectures on Jurisprudence', *History of Political
Economy*, vol. VIII, 439–77.
(1976c) *An Inquiry into the Nature and Causes of the Wealth of
Nations*, edited by R. H. Campbell and A. S. Skinner. Oxford.
(1978) *Lectures on Jurisprudence*, edited by R. L. Meek,
D. D. Raphael and P. G. Stein. Oxford.

STAIR, JAMES, VISCOUNT (1981) *Institutions of the Law of Scotland*,
edited by D. M. Walker. Edinburgh.

STAMMLER, R. (1925) *A Theory of Justice*. New York.

STEIN, P. (1963) 'The Influence of Roman Law on the Law of
Scotland,' *The Juridical Review*, N. S., 8, 205–45.

STEWART, D. (1854) *The Collected Works,* ed. Sir Wm Hamilton, Edinburgh.

> *Diss.* = *Dissertation Exhibiting the Progress of Metaphysical, Ethical and Political Philosophy since the Revival of Letters in Europe: Works,* I.
> *Elements* = *Elements of the Philosophy of the Human Mind,* 3 vols: *Works,* II–IV.
> *Life of Smith* = *Account of the Life and Writings of Adam Smith, Ll.D.: Works,* X.
> *Outlines* = *Outlines of Moral Philosophy* I: *Works,* II; II, *Works:* VI.
> *Pol. Econ.* = *Lectures on Political Economy,* 2 vols: *Works,* VIII–IX.
> *Powers* = *The Philosophy of the Active and Moral Powers of Man,* 2 vols: *Works,* VI–VII.

STEWART-ROBERTSON, J.C. See Norton (1980).

STRAUSS, L. (1951) *Natural Rights and History.* Chicago.

TAYLOR, R. (1963) *Metaphysics.* Englewood Cliffs.

> (1964) 'Deliberation and Foreknowledge,' *American Philosophical Quarterly,* 1, 73–80.
> (1966) 'Foreknowledge and Freewill,' in Berofsky (1966).

TERREBONE, R.P. (1981) 'A Strictly Evolutionary Model of Common Law,' *Journal of Legal Studies,* 10, 397–408.

VESEY, G.N.A. (1964) 'Volition,' in *Essays in Philosophical Psychology,* ed. Donald F. Gustafson. New York.

WEBER, M. (1949) *Methodology of the Social Sciences,* translated by E. A. Shils and H. A. Finch, Glencoe, Ill.

WHITE, G.W. (ed.) (1973) *Contributions to the History of Geology.* New York.

WILLIAMS, GLANVILLE (1968) 'The Concept of a Legal Liberty,' in *Essays in Legal Philosophy,* ed. R. S. Summers. Oxford.

WILSON, T. Skinner (1974).

WINCH, D. (1983) 'The System of the North: Dugald Stewart and His Pupils,' in *That Noble Science of Politics. A Study in 19th Century Intellectual History* by Stefan Collini, Donald Winch and John Burrow. Cambridge.

WINCH, P. (1980–81) 'Eine Einstelling zur Seele,' *Proceedings of the Aristotelian Society.*

WITTGENSTEIN, L. (1958) *Philosophical Investigations,* translated by G. E. M. Anscombe. Oxford.

INDEX